A Taste of Torah

For permission to reprint, please contact:

URJ Press
633 Third Avenue
New York, NY 10017–6778

(212) 650–4124
press@urj.org

Library of Congress Cataloging-in-Publication Data

Isaacs, Ronald H.
    A Taste of Torah : an introduction to thirteen challenging Bible stories/by Ronald Isaacs.
        p. cm.
    Bible text in Hebrew with English translation; commentary in English.
    Includes bibliographical references.
    ISBN 0-8074-0813-1 (pk. : alk. paper)
        1. Bible stories, English–O.T. Pentateuch. 2. Bible stories, English–O.T.
    Pentateuch–History and criticism. 3. Bible. O.T. Pentateuch–Criticism, interpretation,
    etc., Jewish. I. Bible. O.T. Pentateuch. Hebrew. Selections. 2005. II. Bible. O.T.
    Pentateuch. English. Selections. 2005. III. Title.

BS550.3.I83 2006
222'.1077–dc22'

                                                                        2005046741

Designer: Shaul Akri
Typesetting: El Ot Ltd., Tel Aviv
This book is printed on acid-free paper.
Text copyright © 2006 by Ronald H. Isaacs
Manufactured in the United States of America
10 9 8 7 6 5 4 3 2 1

A Taste of Torah

An Introduction to Thirteen Challenging Bible Stories

Ronald H. Isaacs

URJ PRESS

FOR A LIFETIME OF JEWISH LEARNING

New York, New York

Permissions

Every attempt has been made to obtain permission to reprint previously published material. The authors gratefully acknowledge the following for permission to reprint previously published material:

JASON ARONSON: Excerpt from *Biblical Images* by Adin Steinsaltz. Copyright © 1994 by Jason Aronson, an imprint of Rowman & Littlefield Publishing, Inc. Reprinted by permission of Jason Aronson.

THE JEWISH AGENCY: Excerpts from *Studies in Bereshit (Genesis) In the Context of Ancient and Modern Jewish Bible Commentary*, *Studies in Shemot (Exodus) Part I* and *Part II*, and *Studies in Bamidbar (Numbers)* by Nehama Leibowitz, translated by Aryeh Newman. Copyright © The Jewish Agency, Eliner Library, Jerusalem, Israel. Reprinted by permission of the The Jewish Agency.

JEWISH LIGHTS: Excerpts are from *The Women's Torah Commentary: New Insights From Women Rabbis on the 54 Weekly Torah Portions* © 2000 Elyse Goldstein (Woodstock, VT: Jewish Lights Publishing). $34.95+$3.95s/h; Excerpt from *Self, Struggle & Change: Family Conflict Stories in Genesis and Their Healing Insights for Our Lives* © 1995 Norman J. Cohen (Woodstock, VT: Jewish Lights Publishing). $18.99+$3.95s/h. Order by mail or call 800-962-4544 or on-line at www.jewishlights.com. Permission granted by Jewish Lights Publishing, P.O. Box 237, Woodstock, VT 05091

JEWISH PUBLICATION SOCIETY: JPS Torah translation, copyright 1962, 1985, 1999. Used and adapted with permission from The Jewish Publication Society; Reprinted from *Etz Hayim: Torah and Commentary*, © 2001, by The Rabbinical Assembly, published by The Jewish Publication Society with the permission of the publisher.

JEFFREY TIGAY: Printed by permission of Jeffrey Tigay and Hadassah Magazine.

RANDOM HOUSE: Excerpts from *Messengers of God: Biblical Portraits and Legends* by Elie Wiesel, translated from the French by Marion Wiesel. Copyright © 1976, by Random House.

YAVNEH PUBLISHING HOUSE: Excerpts from *Torah Gems*, edited by Aharon Yaakov Greenberg, translated by Shmuel Himelstein. Copyright © 1998 by Yavneh Publishing House. Reprinted with permission of Yavneh Publishing House.

A Taste of Torah:
An Introduction to Thirteen Challenging Bible Stories

Contents

Preface

The Bible is the oldest and most widely read book in our civilization. It has been in continuous circulation for almost two thousand years and has been the source of religious ideals and values for millions of people. Ever since Sinai, the moral imperatives of the Torah and the books of the Prophets have provided great inspiration to social reformers and religious idealists. The Hebrew Bible, known as the *Tanach* in Hebrew, comprises the Torah (also known as the Five Books of Moses), the Prophets, and the Writings.

Throughout the English-speaking world, many well-known writers, poets, and dramatists have studied the Bible for its profound issues and values. Political ideas and institutions have been shaped by biblical teachings. For example, the statement in the Declaration of Independence "We hold these truths to be self-evident, that all men are created equal..." was surely influenced by the prophet Malachi, who said, "Have we not all one Father? Has not one God created us?" (Malachi 2:10).

The first five books of the Bible—Genesis, Exodus, Leviticus, Numbers, and Deuteronomy—comprise the Torah, regarded as Judaism's central document. Along with the stories about the Patriarchs Abraham, Isaac, and Jacob; the Matriarchs Sarah, Rebekah, Rachel, and Leah; and Moses and Aaron as leaders of the Exodus of the Israelites out of Egypt, the Torah contains the 613 commandments, the backbone of all later Jewish law. Our values in almost every area of life are suffused with images and concepts from the Torah.

A Taste of Torah is intended both to introduce students to selected stories in the Torah and to teach how to study Torah using the often conflicting opinions of generations of Jewish interpreters. These stories have been chosen because they are interesting to read but at the same time frequently leave readers with many unanswered questions. Often the language is confusing and elusive, which makes understanding them even more difficult. The goal of this book is to provide students with an entry into the study of Torah that will help them explore and think about important contemporary issues and problems that are inherent in the stories. In addition, students will be presented with both traditional and modern interpretations of the Torah text that they can refer to when answering the questions.

Each chapter uses an identical paradigm. First, the Bible story is presented, followed by a section titled "Understanding the Story." This section provides background information to help edify and make the text more understandable. It also presents an entry point to several of the problems and questions that are raised by the story. The next section, "From the Commentators," presents commentaries culled from both Rabbinic and modern sources. The commentaries that have been selected provide an excellent cross section of interpretative techniques. Most of the commentaries are responses to a particular biblical phrase. For instance, when Rebekah is told by God that two nations are in her womb and that the older shall serve the younger (Genesis 25:23), the modern Bible scholar Nahum Sarna suggests in his commentary that the Torah is not condoning what has been obtained by trickery (i.e., when the younger Jacob wrests the birthright from Esau by dressing up as his brother). Rather Sarna suggests that the way the biblical narrative is handled makes clear that Jacob has a claim on the birthright wholly and solely by virtue of God's predetermination. In other words, the presence of the oracle in the story constitutes, a moral judgment upon Jacob's behavior.

Both important classical and modern commentators are included, representing all of the branches of Judaism. Some are Bible scholars, while others are rabbis and Jewish educators. The "Who's Who of Commentators" section at the back of this volume will familiarize readers with each of the commentators appearing in this book.

The last section of each chapter, titled "Questions for Discussion," provides students with questions to answer and issues to ponder or debate. To answer the questions, it is recommended that students further review and reread sections of the chapter, as well as do additional research.

This book is intended as a "first taste" of Torah texts and the use of biblical commentary. The stories have been selected because they are among the author's favorites and because of the variety of issues that they raise. They are stimulating, challenging, and intriguing tales that are certain to delight the curious reader.

The love of learning has always dominated our faith. I hope that you will enjoy reading and studying these Bible stories. I would be especially grateful to learn that your study has led you to a love of learning Torah that will continue to flourish and blossom throughout your life.

Introduction

The Bible and Our Culture

The Bible appears today in hundreds of different languages and dialects, and it heads the best-seller list each year, with millions of copies sold annually. Over the years, our language, literature, art, and various other phases of our culture have been greatly affected by the writings in the Bible.

For Jews, study is a religious obligation. Listening to the reading of the Torah each week enables us to understand precisely what our religion demands of us. The siddur, our prayer book, is made up of numerous Torah passages, as in the case of the *Sh'ma* and *V'ahavta*, both of which are taken from Deuteronomy 6:4–9.

But we must also remember that whatever was introduced into Judaism after the completion of the Bible entered mainly through the process of reinterpreting its meaning. During the period beginning around the turn of the Common Era and continuing on through the fifth century, Rabbis living in Palestine and Babylon ardently engaged in studying and interpreting the Bible. From these discussions came first the Mishnah and then the Talmud, still the most important collection of postbiblical Jewish law.

Interpretation of the Bible has never ceased, and today new biblical commentaries continue to be written in all of the major branches of Judaism. As in the past, the Bible still stands at the very center of the Jewish faith. Without sound knowledge of it, the proper understanding and practice of our religion are inconceivable.

Today, Jews continue to study the Bible in many different ways. Studying in groups is popular, with *chavurot* getting together to study the Torah portion of the week. Lunchtime has become a popular time for people to convene and study as they dine. These so-called "Lunch and Learns," often led by local rabbis, have provided an ideal opportunity for people to come together and immerse in Bible learning. Often called *chevruta* learning, people are encouraged to choose a partner with whom to study, answering questions that are posed by the facilitator of the biblical lesson.

You are invited to read and study the challenging stories in this volume, all of which are taken from the five books of the Torah. Even though many of you may have likely seen and to some degree examined these stories before, be reminded of something one of the Sages of the Mishnah once said. Speaking of the Torah, he urged:

> Turn it and keep turning it, for everything is in it. Grow
> gray and old over it, and do not turn away from it, for there
> is no better rule for living than this. (*Pirkei Avot* 5:25)

The Sage was simply reminding us that the Torah, and the Bible as a whole, is well worth studying because it is an ever-living book.

The Art of Torah Interpretation

Traditionalist Approach

What we think the Torah is helps determine the way in which we read it. Commentators who hold the traditionalist view believe literally that the words of the Torah were revealed by God to Moses. Therefore, when there seems to be a contradiction in the text, the commentators will attempt to harmonize the inconsistencies into what they see as one true and consistent Torah text. They will also try to explain any discrepancies between biblical concepts and the ideas and beliefs of their own time. Traditional methods of interpretation interpret the biblical text using the following approach, known as PaRDeS, an acronym for these four methodologies:

P'shat: This is the plain, literal sense of the verse in its context, that is, what the text meant at the time in which it was written. For example, the plain sense of "eye for eye" (Exodus 21:24) is that the punishment must be commensurate with the deed and never exceed it.

Remez (hint or symbol): This is the allegorical meaning of the verse. Each character or place in the text has a symbolic meaning. For example, in Genesis 28, after Jacob leaves Beersheba, he lays down for the night. The text reads, "Coming upon a [certain] place" (Genesis 28:11). The word in this verse for "place," *makom*, is also used as a name for God in postbiblical Hebrew. Therefore, using the *remez* methodology, this "place" is not just any place, but is understood allegorically to mean God. The verse would thus be read as "Coming upon God."

D'rash: This refers to the homiletical or sermonic meaning of the verse as viewed outside of its original context. Specific ideas and values are derived from the text, whether the text, in its literal meaning, could support this meaning or not. Rabbis enjoy homiletical interpretations of the text and often use them in their sermons. For example, when the Torah says that "thick darkness descended upon all the land of Egypt" (Exodus 10:22), the literal interpretation would be a darkness due to a sandstorm or possibly even an eclipse. But in the *d'rash* interpretation, this could be understood as "darkness of the mind" of the Egyptians. In this reading, the Egyptians were people who experienced the worst kind of darkness, unable to "see" their neighbors, note their distress, or help them. In a sense, they lost their sense of humanity. This point then becomes a rabbinic teaching opportunity.

Sod: This is the secret, mystical interpretation of the verse. For instance, in the story of Jacob's ladder in Genesis, the Torah states that "[Jacob] dreamed, and lo—a ladder was set on the ground, with its top reaching to heaven, and lo—angels of God going up and coming down on it" (Genesis 28:12). Using the *sod* method of interpretation, commentators have noted that the ladder (*sulam* in Hebrew) was a symbol of Sinai (*sinai*), since both Hebrew words have the same numerical value of 130.

Modern Approach

Modern critical scholarship reads the Bible as a document of religious faith expressed within a specific culture and tied to a specific time. Because the Torah is a collection of documents written in human language by human authors, it is subject to the same methods of historical and literary investigation as all other books and documents. Modern biblical scholarship employs many methods of interpretation, the most important of which are textual criticism, source criticism, and literary criticism.

Textual criticism attempts to understand the words. This type of criticism is the basis for the translation of the Bible from its original

Hebrew and Aramaic into the languages of the modern reader. For example, the commentator Rashi stated that the river that went out of Eden (Genesis 2:11) was named Pishon because it makes flax (*pishtan* in Hebrew) grow.

Source criticism is based on the theory that the Torah is a compilation from several sources, different streams of literary traditions, that were composed and collected over the course of the biblical period (1200–400 B.C.E.). This theory is known as the Documentary Hypothesis. Because the Torah, from this perspective, is a combination of the works of different authors or schools, it contains many factual inconsistencies, differences in style and vocabulary, and different theology. For example, in one accounting Noah sends out a raven (Genesis 8:7), and in the other Noah sends out a dove (Genesis 8:8). Similarly, in one accounting Noah is told to take pairs of animals into the ark (Genesis 6:19), while in another Noah is commanded to take seven pairs of certain animals into the ark (Genesis 7:2). These inconsistencies are thus explained as the result of differing details from two stories being interwoven into one.

Literary criticism examines the literary characteristics of the text, including narrative technique, tone, theme, structure, imagery, and repetition of words and phrases. For example, in the story of the Binding of Isaac (Genesis 22), there is repetition of phrases depicting Abraham and Isaac walking together: "And the two of them went on together" (Genesis 22:6); "And the two of them went on together" (Genesis 22:8); "they...traveled together to Beersheba" (Genesis 22:19). Literary critics might conclude that the repetition of the togetherness theme is intended to teach that this story must be read as a paradigm of a father-son relationship. The fact that Abraham and Isaac stay together (both physically and mentally), even under such difficult circumstances, is an indication of the strong bond that has been established between father and son.

1. The Garden of Eden: Eating the Forbidden Fruit

The Bible Story: From Genesis 2–3

Genesis 2:9] Then, out of the soil, God Eternal grew trees alluring to the eye and good for fruit; and in the middle of the garden, the Tree of Life and the Tree of All Knowledge. . . .

16] God Eternal then commanded the man, saying, "You may eat all you like of every tree in the garden— **17]** but of the Tree of All Knowledge you may not eat, for the moment you eat of it you shall be doomed to die." . . .

25] Now the two of them were naked, the man and his wife, and they were not ashamed.

3:1] Of all the wild animals that God Eternal made, the serpent was the most cunning. It said to the woman, "Did God really say, 'You many not eat of any tree in the Garden'?" **2]** The woman said to the serpent, "Of any tree in the Garden we may eat the fruit; **3]** but God said, 'Of the fruit of the tree in the middle of it do not eat, and do not [even] touch it, or you will die." **4]** But the serpent said to the woman, "You most certainly will not die! **5]** On the contrary: God knows that when

ב 9 וַיַּצְמַ֞ח יְהֹוָ֤ה אֱלֹהִים֙ מִן־הָ֣אֲדָמָ֔ה
כָּל־עֵ֛ץ נֶחְמָ֥ד לְמַרְאֶ֖ה וְט֣וֹב לְמַאֲכָ֑ל וְעֵ֤ץ
הַֽחַיִּים֙ בְּת֣וֹךְ הַגָּ֔ן וְעֵ֕ץ הַדַּ֖עַת ט֥וֹב וָרָֽע׃

16 וַיְצַו֙ יְהֹוָ֣ה אֱלֹהִ֔ים עַל־הָֽאָדָ֖ם לֵאמֹ֑ר
מִכֹּ֥ל עֵֽץ־הַגָּ֖ן אָכֹ֥ל תֹּאכֵֽל׃ 17 וּמֵעֵ֗ץ
הַדַּ֙עַת֙ ט֣וֹב וָרָ֔ע לֹ֥א תֹאכַ֖ל מִמֶּ֑נּוּ כִּ֗י
בְּי֛וֹם אֲכָלְךָ֥ מִמֶּ֖נּוּ מ֥וֹת תָּמֽוּת׃

25 וַיִּֽהְי֤וּ שְׁנֵיהֶם֙ עֲרוּמִּ֔ים הָֽאָדָ֖ם וְאִשְׁתּ֑וֹ
וְלֹ֖א יִתְבֹּשָֽׁשׁוּ׃

ג 1 וְהַנָּחָשׁ֙ הָיָ֣ה עָר֔וּם מִכֹּל֙ חַיַּ֣ת הַשָּׂדֶ֔ה
אֲשֶׁ֥ר עָשָׂ֖ה יְהֹוָ֣ה אֱלֹהִ֑ים וַיֹּ֙אמֶר֙ אֶל־
הָ֣אִשָּׁ֔ה אַ֚ף כִּֽי־אָמַ֣ר אֱלֹהִ֔ים לֹ֣א תֹֽאכְל֔וּ
מִכֹּ֖ל עֵ֥ץ הַגָּֽן׃ 2 וַתֹּ֥אמֶר הָֽאִשָּׁ֖ה אֶל־
הַנָּחָ֑שׁ מִפְּרִ֥י עֵֽץ־הַגָּ֖ן נֹאכֵֽל׃ 3 וּמִפְּרִ֣י
הָעֵץ֮ אֲשֶׁ֣ר בְּתוֹךְ־הַגָּן֒ אָמַ֣ר אֱלֹהִ֗ים לֹ֤א
תֹֽאכְלוּ֙ מִמֶּ֔נּוּ וְלֹ֥א תִגְּע֖וּ בּ֑וֹ פֶּן־תְּמֻתֽוּן׃
4 וַיֹּ֥אמֶר הַנָּחָ֖שׁ אֶל־הָֽאִשָּׁ֑ה לֹֽא־מ֖וֹת
תְּמֻתֽוּן׃ 5 כִּ֚י יֹדֵ֣עַ אֱלֹהִ֔ים כִּ֗י בְּיוֹם֙

you do eat of it, your eyes will be opened and you will be like gods, knowing all things." 6] So when the woman saw how good to eat the tree's fruit would be, and how alluring to the eyes it was, and how desirable the insight was that the tree would bring, she took some of its fruit and ate; and then she gave some to her man who was with her, and he ate. 7] Then the eyes of both of them were opened, and, realizing that they were naked, they sewed fig leaves together and made themselves skirts....

9] But God Eternal called out to the man, saying, "Where are you?" 10] He said, "I heard the sound of You in the Garden; I was afraid because I was naked, so I hid myself." 11] Then [God] said, "Who told you that you were naked? Did you eat the fruit of the tree that I forbade you to eat?" 12] The man said, "The woman whom You gave me, she gave me the fruit of the tree, so I ate." 13] God Eternal then said to the woman, "What is this that you have done?" And the woman said, "The serpent tricked me into eating it."...

22] God Eternal then said, "Look, the humans are like us, knowing all things. Now they may even reach out to take fruit from the Tree of Life and eat, and live forever." 23] So the Eternal God drove them out of the Garden of Eden to work the soil from which they had been taken.

אֲכָלְכֶם מִמֶּנּוּ וְנִפְקְחוּ עֵינֵיכֶם וִהְיִיתֶם כֵּאלֹהִים יֹדְעֵי טוֹב וָרָע : 6 וַתֵּרֶא הָאִשָּׁה כִּי טוֹב הָעֵץ לְמַאֲכָל וְכִי תַאֲוָה־הוּא לָעֵינַיִם וְנֶחְמָד הָעֵץ לְהַשְׂכִּיל וַתִּקַּח מִפִּרְיוֹ וַתֹּאכַל וַתִּתֵּן גַּם־לְאִישָׁהּ עִמָּהּ וַיֹּאכַל : 7 וַתִּפָּקַחְנָה עֵינֵי שְׁנֵיהֶם וַיֵּדְעוּ כִּי עֵירֻמִּם הֵם וַיִּתְפְּרוּ עֲלֵה תְאֵנָה וַיַּעֲשׂוּ לָהֶם חֲגֹרֹת :

9 וַיִּקְרָא יְהֹוָה אֱלֹהִים אֶל־הָאָדָם וַיֹּאמֶר לוֹ אַיֶּכָּה : 10 וַיֹּאמֶר אֶת־קֹלְךָ שָׁמַעְתִּי בַּגָּן וָאִירָא כִּי־עֵירֹם אָנֹכִי וָאֵחָבֵא : 11 וַיֹּאמֶר מִי הִגִּיד לְךָ כִּי עֵירֹם אָתָּה הֲמִן־הָעֵץ אֲשֶׁר צִוִּיתִיךָ לְבִלְתִּי אֲכָל־מִמֶּנּוּ אָכָלְתָּ : 12 וַיֹּאמֶר הָאָדָם הָאִשָּׁה אֲשֶׁר נָתַתָּה עִמָּדִי הִוא נָתְנָה־לִי מִן־הָעֵץ וָאֹכֵל : 13 וַיֹּאמֶר יְהֹוָה אֱלֹהִים לָאִשָּׁה מַה־זֹּאת עָשִׂית וַתֹּאמֶר הָאִשָּׁה הַנָּחָשׁ הִשִּׁיאַנִי וָאֹכֵל :

22 וַיֹּאמֶר | יְהֹוָה אֱלֹהִים הֵן הָאָדָם הָיָה כְּאַחַד מִמֶּנּוּ לָדַעַת טוֹב וָרָע וְעַתָּה | פֶּן־יִשְׁלַח יָדוֹ וְלָקַח גַּם מֵעֵץ הַחַיִּים וְאָכַל וָחַי לְעֹלָם : 23 וַיְשַׁלְּחֵהוּ יְהֹוָה אֱלֹהִים מִגַּן־עֵדֶן לַעֲבֹד אֶת־הָאֲדָמָה אֲשֶׁר לֻקַּח מִשָּׁם :

Understanding the Story

In the Garden of Eden, Adam and Eve live in a beautiful environment that is free of pain, worry, and toil. Their only responsibility is to tend to the garden. In Genesis 2 we learn that God allows man and woman to eat from any tree in the garden, with the exception of the Tree of All Knowledge. They are told that if they eat of that tree, they will die. The Tree of Life mentioned earlier in the story appears only one additional time in the story.

Later, in Genesis 3, the serpent asks Eve whether she is allowed to eat of any tree in the garden. This time Eve answers by saying that the tree in the middle of the garden is forbidden, adding that if it is eaten from, or even touched, death will be the result. There is nothing concerning "touching" in the original prohibition in Genesis 2:17. Interestingly too, the tree in the middle of the garden is not identified in Eve's version.

There are a number of problems inherent in the story. For one, the Tree of Life appears only two times in the story. What is the purpose of mentioning it, since nobody ever eats from its fruit? Secondly, if God did not want Adam and Eve to eat of the Tree of All Knowledge in the middle of the garden, why does God provide such easy access to it? And why does God create the tree in the first place, if eating from it is forbidden?

It also seems odd that Adam is given one version of the commandment in Genesis 2:16–17 and that Eve reports another to the serpent in Genesis 3:2–3. Adam is told that if they eat from the Tree of All Knowledge, they will die. Eve reports that if they either eat from the tree in the middle of the garden *or touch it*, they will die. She not only fails to report the name of the tree, but adds a new condition of touching to God's original statement. This addition is left un-explained.

Finally, God tells Adam and Eve that if they eat of the forbidden fruit, they will be doomed to die. But they do not die! Why does God seem to go back on God's word? And what are God's real intentions in putting these forbidden trees in the garden in the first place? The ultimate question is thus, what does God want man and woman ultimately to be, moral automatons or free spirits?

From the Commentators

Another important element in the Eden story is the role of Eve as arch-temptress and hence the one responsible for the expulsion from the Garden. The description of Eve's seduction by the serpent and her seduction of Adam raises many questions that have troubled students in every age—among them the question why this particular sequence of events and why it was Eve who tempted Adam.

One of the significant explanations turns upon a peculiarity of this first human generation that was afterward rectified. Adam, it seems, had been commanded directly by God, while Eve received the commandment only through Adam. From this circumstance, a far-reaching conclusion can be drawn: obedience to the divine imperative, whether negative or positive, must be based upon a direct personal relationship. When, in the absence of such a relationship, obligation is mediated through some third party, failure is invited.

Adin Steinsaltz, *Biblical Images*, trans. Yehuda Hanegbi and Yehudit Keshet (Northvale, NJ: Jason Aronson, 1994), pp. 6–7.

[A variant translation] *the tree of knowledge of good and bad* [Genesis 2:9] Ibn Ezra, followed by many modern scholars, explained "knowledge of good and bad" as referring to carnal knowledge, because the first human experience after eating the forbidden fruit is the consciousness of nudity accompanied by shame. Most likely, "good and bad" is a phrase that means "everything," implying a mature perception of reality. Thus "knowledge of good and bad" is to be understood as the capacity to make independent judgments concerning human welfare.

David L. Lieber and Jules Harlow, eds., *Etz Hayim: Torah and Commentary* (New York and Philadelphia: Rabbinical Assembly and Jewish Publication Society, 2001), p. 14.

thou shalt not eat [Genesis 2:17]. Man's most sacred privilege is freedom of will, the ability to obey or disobey his Maker. This sharp limitation of self-gratification, this "dietary law," was to test the use that he would make of his freedom; and it thus begins the moral discipline of man. . . .
thou shalt surely die [Genesis 2:17]. *i.e.* thou must inevitably become mortal (Symmachus). While this explanation removes the difficulty that Adam and Eve lived a long time after they had eaten of the forbidden fruit, it assumes that man was created to be a deathless being.

J. H. Hertz, ed., *Pentateuch and Haftorahs* (London: Soncino Press, 1960), p. 8.

Hezekiah said: How do we know that he who adds [to the word of God] subtracts [from it]?—From the verse, God has said, You shall not eat of it neither shall you touch it. [Eve added to God's words by telling the serpent that she was not even permitted to touch the tree. The serpent then pushed her into contact with the tree and told her: See, just as death did not ensue from the touch, so it will not follow from eating of it.]

Babylonian Talmud, Sanhedrin 29a.

In the Torah, we are told that God planted the Garden of Eden and placed the tree of life in the middle of the garden [Genesis 2:9]. Why in the middle and not at the side? So that everyone can reach the tree of life—every person in accordance with his ability and the possibilities available to him.

> Chafetz Chayim, in *Torah Gems*, vol. 1, ed. Aharon Yaakov Greenberg, trans. Shmuel Himelstein (Tel Aviv: Yavneh Publishing House, 1998), p. 30.

Torah Gems

Compiled by Aharon Yaakov Greenberg, *Itturei Torah* (Torah Gems) is a collection of various Torah commentaries taken from Jewish literature throughout the ages, especially from Chasidic literature. The passages are known for their novelty and brevity, and are culled from a variety of sources. In 1992 the passages were translated into English by Rabbi Shmuel Himelstein and are now available in a three-volume set published by the Yavneh Publishing House in Tel Aviv, Israel.

The quest for immortality seems to have been an obsessive factor in ancient Near Eastern religion and literature. . . . By relegating the "tree of life" to an insignificant, subordinate role in the Garden of Eden story, the Bible dissociates itself completely from this pre-occupation. Its concern is with the issues of living rather than with the question of death, with morality rather than mortality.

> Nahum M. Sarna, *Understanding Genesis*
> (New York: Schocken Books, 1966), pp. 26–27.

The special characteristic that the Bible attributes to the serpent is *cunning*, and since it does not ascribe any other quality to him, it intends, apparently, to convey that the evil flowing from the serpent emanated only from his *cunning*. In the ultimate analysis, we have here an allegorical allusion to the craftiness to be found in *man himself*. The man and his wife were, it is true, still devoid of comprehensive knowledge, like children who know neither good nor bad; but even those who lack wisdom sometimes possess slyness. The duologue [*sic*] between the serpent and the woman is actually, in a manner of speaking, a duologue [*sic*] that took place in the woman's mind, between her wiliness and her innocence, clothed in the garb of a parable.

Umberto Cassuto, *A Commentary on the Book of Genesis*, trans. Israel Abrahams (Jerusalem: Magnes Press, 1961), p. 142.

Rashi

No commentator is more widely studied and respected than French rabbinical scholar Rabbi Solomon [Shlomo] Yitzchaki (1040–1105), better known by the acronym Rashi. Throughout his lifetime many Jewish legal questions were addressed to him, and his decisions have been preserved in the works of his students. Rashi's chief contribution was his lucid commentaries on both the Bible and the Babylonian Talmud. Rashi's style is simple and concise, and his objective in most cases is to present the direct rational meaning of the text (*p'shat*). He frequently quotes the French equivalent (*laaz*) in Hebrew transliteration for rare words. Rashi's commentaries served as the basis for later scholars such as Nachmanides and ibn Ezra in their interpretations of the Torah. Rashi's brilliant mind developed so many ideas that he had difficulty writing them down fast enough. So he used a shorthand Hebrew script (known as "Rashi script") that helped him to write faster, which is often used in printed versions of his commentaries.

The serpent took advantage of Eve's misrepresentation of God's commandment to Adam (i.e., she added the words "do not [even] touch it"). When Eve told the serpent that God had warned her, "Do not eat of it and do not [even] touch it, or you will die" (Genesis 3:3), the serpent pushed her until she actually touched the tree. Then the serpent said to her, "You see, you have not died after touching it. And you will not die after you eat from its fruit."

Rashi on Genesis 3:4.

Just as in the children's game Telephone, the more people who transmit a message, the more distorted and garbled that message becomes. God-to-Adam-to-Eve-to-the-snake seems to have been one layer too many. That is why Eve may have added the words "you shall not touch it" (Genesis 3:3) when speaking to the serpent, even though they were not part of God's original prohibition.

Brad Artson, *The Bedside Torah: Wisdom, Visions, and Dreams* (New York: Contemporary Books, 2001), p. 6.

Perhaps the greatest sin of man was not so much his deviation from God's command instructing him to refrain from partaking of certain fruit, but rather the sin of accusing his wife, "She gave me of the tree and I ate it" [Genesis 3:12]. He was not concerned about what would happen to her as long as he saved himself. This might have been his greatest failing, which caused the expulsion from the Garden of Eden.

Ephraim Shimoff, "The Well of Living Waters: Thoughts on the
Weekly Bible Portion, Bereshit," self-published, n.d.

At the center of the story, as in the middle of the garden, stands the Tree of Knowledge. The tree is unique to biblical tradition, and three major interpretations have been offered to explain it.

Ethical Interpretation. Eating from the Tree of All Knowledge (or "Good and Evil" as most older translations render it) provided humanity with moral discrimination and thereby made human beings capable of committing sin....

Intellectual Interpretation. In the Bible, the expression *tov vara* (טוֹב וָרָע), literally "good and evil," means "everything."...The tale may therefore be understood to say that primal humans ate of the Tree of Omniscience. Having tasted of it, they forever after will attempt to know everything; they will, in other words, play the part of God....

Sexual Interpretation. The Eden story may also be read as the discovery...of our sexuality. This is suggested by the Hebrew word for "knowledge" (דַעַת), which has the meaning of "experience," including sexual experience....Reading the Eden tale in this light we see a link between the Tree of (Sexual) Knowledge and the Tree of Life. The latter, whose fruit would have bestowed earthly immortality, is no longer accessible. We must now perpetuate our species through procreation, in the same way as other creatures do....All humans repeat the journey from Eden into the world. As infants they live in a garden of innocence; when they discover their sexual impulse and grow up, they must leave the garden forever.

W. Gunther Plaut, ed., *The Torah: A Modern Commentary*, rev. ed.
(New York: URJ Press, 2005), pp. 37–38.

The verse "the moment you eat of it, you shall be doomed to die" (Genesis 2:17) does not mean that Adam will die the moment he eats the fruit; rather, it means that he will be doomed to die eventually. In other words, had Adam not sinned, God would have allowed him to live forever.

Ramban (Nachmanides) on Genesis 2:17.

[Then the eyes of both of them were opened (Genesis 3:7)]...The Torah should simply have stated "their eyes"—*eineihem* in Hebrew—rather than "the eyes of them both"—*einei sheneihem*. This teaches us that after [Adam and Eve] had eaten of the tree of knowledge, their eyes were opened for them to realize that they were two people, separate from one another.

R. Bunim of Pshischa, in *Torah Gems*, vol. 1, p. 35.

AND, REALIZING THAT THEY WERE NAKED, etc. Even of the one precept which they had possessed they had stripped themselves (They were naked of obedience).

B'reishit Rabbah 19:6.

Rather than focusing on Eve's disobedience, I am drawn to her dynamic life force and the initiative she takes in exercising her God-given free will. Rather than a temptress, Eve acts as Adam's equal "helper," reaching out to him with the nourishing fruit of wisdom. She realizes that the sheltered greenhouse of Eden will never be conducive to intellectual or spiritual growth. I see Eve as a trailblazer who leads humanity from childlike innocence toward an adult life of challenge and responsibility.

Naomi H. Rosenblatt, *Wrestling with Angels: What Genesis Teaches Us about Our Spiritual Identity, Sexuality, and Personal Relationships*, with Joshua Horwitz (New York: Dell Publishing, 1996), p. 45.

[N]owhere in chapter 3 does Eve use any means of seduction to tempt Adam into eating. There are no pleas, no tantrums, none of the feminine wiles that the verbs "seduce" and "tempt" suggest. . . . Eve is neither a seductress nor a temptress. These are male fears projected onto this story. Rather, Eve acts out of her own sense of adventure and curiosity.

Lori Forman, "The Untold Story of Eve," in *The Women's Torah Commentary: New Insights from Women Rabbis on the 54 Weekly Torah Portions*, ed. Elyse Goldstein (Woodstock, VT: Jewish Lights Publishing, 2000), p. 54.

Questions for Discussion

1. Why do you think that God put the Tree of All Knowledge in the middle of the Garden of Eden?

2. Do you think that the expulsion of Adam and Eve from the Garden of Eden fits their crime? Why or why not?

3. What is the purpose of the Tree of Life in the story? Why don't Adam and Eve try to eat from that fruit first?

4. Why do you think God says to Adam and Eve that if they eat of the forbidden fruit, they will be doomed to die? Why does God not fulfill this warning?

5. The Hebrew word for "garden" is *gan*. The ancient Greek version of the Bible, called the Septuagint, translates the word as *paradeisos*, from which the English word "paradise" derives. Do you see a connection between the Garden of Eden and paradise? Is paradise a good or bad place to want to live?

6. The poet Milton, in *Paradise Lost*, blames Eve for her disobedience but perversely admires Adam for his loyalty to Eve, not wanting to survive while she perishes. Who do you think is to blame in the story? Who is the story's hero?

7. From a literary perspective, who is the serpent, and what is its role in the biblical story? Is the serpent God's agent?

8. The Hebrew word used to describe the serpent as "cunning" is *arum*. The Hebrew word for "naked" also happens to be *arum*. Do you see a connection here between the serpent's cunningness and man's nakedness?

9. Nowhere in this Torah story is there mention that the eating of the forbidden fruit is a sin. If this is not a sin, why does God expel Adam and Eve from the Garden of Eden?

10. The account of Adam and Eve disobeying God's command in the Garden of Eden is a strange and elusive story. If they gained a knowledge of good and evil by eating the forbidden fruit, does that mean that they did not know good from evil before that? If so, how could they be held accountable for doing wrong?

2. Cain and Abel: Whose Sacrifice Will God Accept?

The Bible Story: Genesis 4:1–16

Genesis 4:1] The man now was intimate with his wife; she became pregnant and gave birth to Cain, saying, "Both I and the Eternal have made a man." 2] She then continued, giving birth to his brother Abel. Abel became a shepherd, while Cain tilled the soil.

3] [One day,] in the course of time, Cain brought some of his harvest as an offering to the Eternal, 4] and Abel, too, brought [an offering] from among the choice lambs of his flock and their fattest parts. The Eternal approved Abel and his offering, 5] but did not approve Cain and his offering. Cain was filled with rage; his face fell. 6] The Eternal One then said to Cain, "Why are you so angry? / Why your fallen face? / 7] Would you not do well to lift it? / For if you do not do well— / sin is a demon at the door; / you are the one it craves, / and yet you can govern it."

8] Cain now thought about his brother Abel. . . . Then, when they were in the field, Cain turned on his brother Abel and killed him. 9] Then the Eternal One said to Cain, "Where is your brother Abel?" And he replied, "How should I know; am I my

ד 1 וְהָאָדָם יָדַע אֶת־חַוָּה אִשְׁתּוֹ וַתַּהַר וַתֵּלֶד אֶת־קַיִן וַתֹּאמֶר קָנִיתִי אִישׁ אֶת־יְהֹוָה: 2 וַתֹּסֶף לָלֶדֶת אֶת־אָחִיו אֶת־הָבֶל וַיְהִי־הֶבֶל רֹעֵה צֹאן וְקַיִן הָיָה עֹבֵד אֲדָמָה:

3 וַיְהִי מִקֵּץ יָמִים וַיָּבֵא קַיִן מִפְּרִי הָאֲדָמָה מִנְחָה לַיהֹוָה: 4 וְהֶבֶל הֵבִיא גַם־הוּא מִבְּכֹרוֹת צֹאנוֹ וּמֵחֶלְבֵהֶן וַיִּשַׁע יְהֹוָה אֶל־הֶבֶל וְאֶל־מִנְחָתוֹ: 5 וְאֶל־קַיִן וְאֶל־מִנְחָתוֹ לֹא שָׁעָה וַיִּחַר לְקַיִן מְאֹד וַיִּפְּלוּ פָּנָיו: 6 וַיֹּאמֶר יְהֹוָה אֶל־קַיִן לָמָּה חָרָה לָךְ וְלָמָּה נָפְלוּ פָנֶיךָ: 7 הֲלוֹא אִם־תֵּיטִיב שְׂאֵת וְאִם לֹא תֵיטִיב לַפֶּתַח חַטָּאת רֹבֵץ וְאֵלֶיךָ תְּשׁוּקָתוֹ וְאַתָּה תִּמְשָׁל־בּוֹ:

8 וַיֹּאמֶר קַיִן אֶל־הֶבֶל אָחִיו וַיְהִי בִּהְיוֹתָם בַּשָּׂדֶה וַיָּקָם קַיִן אֶל־הֶבֶל אָחִיו וַיַּהַרְגֵהוּ: 9 וַיֹּאמֶר יְהֹוָה אֶל־קַיִן אֵי הֶבֶל אָחִיךָ וַיֹּאמֶר לֹא יָדַעְתִּי הֲשֹׁמֵר

brother's keeper?" 10] And [God] said, "What have you done? Your brother's blood is shrieking to Me from the ground! 11] Now you are cursed by this very soil, which has opened its mouth to receive your brother's blood from your hands. 12] When you till the soil, no longer shall it give you its yield. You shall become a rootless wanderer on the earth." 13] Cain then said to the Eternal One, "My punishment is too heavy to bear! 14] Seeing as now You have expelled me from the face of the soil and I must hide from Your face, I am become a rootless wanderer on the earth, and anyone who finds me might kill me!" 15] "Not so," said the Eternal One. "Should anyone kill Cain, he would be avenged sevenfold." And the Eternal gave Cain a sign, that none who came upon him would kill him. 16] Cain then went away from before the Eternal, and settled in the Land of Nomads, east of Eden.

אָחִי אָנֹכִי: 10 וַיֹּאמֶר מֶה עָשִׂיתָ קוֹל דְּמֵי אָחִיךָ צֹעֲקִים אֵלַי מִן־הָאֲדָמָה: 11 וְעַתָּה אָרוּר אָתָּה מִן־הָאֲדָמָה אֲשֶׁר פָּצְתָה אֶת־פִּיהָ לָקַחַת אֶת־דְּמֵי אָחִיךָ מִיָּדֶךָ: 12 כִּי תַעֲבֹד אֶת־הָאֲדָמָה לֹא־תֹסֵף תֵּת־כֹּחָהּ לָךְ נָע וָנָד תִּהְיֶה בָאָרֶץ: 13 וַיֹּאמֶר קַיִן אֶל־יְהֹוָה גָּדוֹל עֲוֹנִי מִנְּשׂוֹא: 14 הֵן גֵּרַשְׁתָּ אֹתִי הַיּוֹם מֵעַל פְּנֵי הָאֲדָמָה וּמִפָּנֶיךָ אֶסָּתֵר וְהָיִיתִי נָע וָנָד בָּאָרֶץ וְהָיָה כָל־מֹצְאִי יַהַרְגֵנִי: 15 וַיֹּאמֶר לוֹ יְהֹוָה לָכֵן כָּל־הֹרֵג קַיִן שִׁבְעָתַיִם יֻקָּם וַיָּשֶׂם יְהֹוָה לְקַיִן אוֹת לְבִלְתִּי הַכּוֹת־אֹתוֹ כָּל־מֹצְאוֹ: 16 וַיֵּצֵא קַיִן מִלִּפְנֵי יְהֹוָה וַיֵּשֶׁב בְּאֶרֶץ־נוֹד קִדְמַת־עֵדֶן:

Understanding the Story

The human aspect of evil is stressed in the story of Cain and Abel, the Torah's first naturally born human beings. Cain is a tiller of the soil, Abel a shepherd. Both bring offerings to God from the products with which each deals. Abel's animal sacrifice is acceptable, but God does not approve Cain's gift of fruit. But why? Some scholars see the story of Cain and Abel as representing an ancient conflict between shepherds, who wanted their flocks to roam freely, and the farmers who tried to fence off a piece of land and prevent the sheep from grazing there. The wandering shepherds thought that farmers were wicked people for trying to claim some of God's earth as their private domain and then violating Mother Earth with their plows and tools instead of waiting for it to yield its bounty as shepherds did. However, a *p'shat* reading of the story does not present even the slightest suggestion of a comparative evaluation of the vocations of the two brothers, only of the offerings they bring.

As a story, it is tantalizingly incomplete. The narrative of events is sketchy, and no reason is explicitly given as to why Cain's offering is not approved, nor is it related how the brothers become aware of God's response. To what, or to whom, could Cain be referring when he expresses the fear that anyone who meets him might kill him (Genesis 4:14)? Yet God takes his remarks seriously enough to utter a curse upon a would-be avenger and give Cain a protective sign so that "none who came upon him would kill him" (Genesis 4:15). Where is the mysterious "Land of Nomads" in which Cain settles (Genesis 4:16), and how does he find a wife (Genesis 4:17)?

What does Cain think or say to Abel when they go out into the field (Genesis 4:8)? The Torah never tells us, and we can only use our imaginations. And furthermore, given the Torah's repeated insistence on capital punishment for premeditated murders, why is Cain condemned to eternal exile—"You shall become a rootless wanderer on the earth" (Genesis 4:12)? There is much in this story that is left unexplained.

Finally, few biblical phrases have been quoted more often than the bold counter-question that Cain flings back to God, "Am I my brother's keeper?" (Genesis 4:9). But the meaning is far from clear, and God does not reply to Cain's question. Thus the question "Am I my brother's keeper?" remains unanswered and has remained so despite the questions of succeeding generations. Why is God silent when men kill each other? Where does God's power begin, and where does it end?

From the Commentators

It is important to notice that in the biblical story, God warns Cain of the danger of sin *before* he murders his brother. Before Cain is guilty of murder, he is guilty of the sin of hatred and resentment. The story of Cain and Abel is not about the conflict between farmers and shepherds. It is about the pain and anger we all feel when we suspect that someone else is loved more than we are.

Harold S. Kushner, *How Good Do We Have to Be? A New Understanding of Guilt and Forgiveness* (New York: Little, Brown and Company, 1996), p. 122.

Some commentators maintain that the key to God's preference [for Abel's offering over that of Cain] may be found in the intent of the two worshipers. While Cain merely brings "an offering," Abel brings "the choicest" of his flock. One performs outward motions, the other offers the service of his heart.

A better interpretation, however, is that God's rejection of Cain's offering is inexplicable in human terms. God acts in accordance with divine wisdom: "I will be gracious to whom I will be gracious" (Exodus 33:19). His reasons are unknown to us.

> W. Gunther Plaut, ed., *The Torah: A Modern Commentary,* rev. ed.
> (New York: URJ Press, 2005), p. 40.

The text says of sin that "its urge is toward you" (Genesis 4:7). This implies that sin wants to be conquered by us, but if we fail to conquer it, sin returns to God and accuses us. [This interpretation suggests that Cain was tested by God and that the temptation was instituted for Cain's benefit.— W. Gunther Plaut]

> Samson Raphael Hirsch, in *The Torah:*
> *A Modern Commentary,* rev. ed., p. 49.

Samson Raphael Hirsch
Nineteenth-century German Jewish scholar Samson Raphael Hirsch (1808–1888) is regarded as the progenitor of neo-Orthodoxy in Western countries. Believing that the modern generation should be raised to the Torah and not the Torah lowered to the generation, his commentary on the Torah seeks to derive the explanation of the text from the words themselves. He makes use of early rabbinic views along with those of other commentators to underscore his belief that Jewish tradition offers the highest form of human life. He also asserts that the Torah was revealed directly by God at Mount Sinai, and therefore nothing in it can be changed.

According to the rabbis, the phrase *"bloods cry out"* [Genesis 4:10] is an indication that Cain murdered more than just Abel. He also destroyed Abel's future generations. They tell us that God said to Cain: "Not only are you responsible for murdering your brother, but you have also murdered his unborn offspring. The voice of your brother's blood, and of all his would-be descendants whom you prevented from coming into the world, cries out to Me."

> Harvey J. Fields, citing *Midrash Aggadah* 4, 9, in *A Torah Commentary*
> *for Our Times,* vol. 1 (New York: UAHC Press, 1998), p. 26.

sin coucheth ["sin couches at the door" (Genesis 4:7)]. Sin is compared to a ravenous beast lying in wait for its prey. It crouches at the entrance of the house, to spring up upon its victim as soon as the door is opened. By harboring feelings of vexation, Cain opened the door of his heart to the evil passions of envy, anger, violence, which eventually ended in murder.

> J. H. Hertz, ed., *Pentateuch and Haftorahs* (London: Soncino Press, 1960), p. 14.

The words translated as ["too"] (*gam hu*) can be understood literally as "he too," implying that Abel brought "himself" to God along with his offerings.

S'fat Emet on Genesis 4:4,
as cited in *Etz Hayim*, p. 25.

Cain came to worship God "in the process of time" ["in the course of time," Genesis 4:3], when he was old, after he had lost all of his vigor. Abel, though, brought of "the firstlings" of his flock—he served God even when he was young. And that was why God accepted Abel's sacrifice.

R. Bunim of Pshischa (Simchah Bunim), in *Torah Gems*, vol. 1,
ed. Aharon Yaakov Greenberg, trans. Shmuel Himelstein
(Tel Aviv: Yavneh Publishing House, 1998), p. 47.

God asking, "Where is your brother Abel?" (Genesis 4:9) was God's attempt to soften Cain with gentle words so that he would repent.

Rashi on Genesis 4:9.

CAIN NOW THOUGHT ABOUT [SPOKE TO] HIS BROTHER ABEL, etc. (IV, 8). What did they speak about? "Come," said they, "let us divide the world." One took the land and the other the movables. The former said, "The land you stand on is mine." One said: "Strip"; the other responded: "Fly [off the ground]." Out of this quarrel, CAIN TURNED ON HIS BROTHER ABEL.

B'reishit Rabbah 22:7.

[Cain] spoke to Abel soothingly, always referring to him as "my brother," so as to get him off his guard. Thus what Cain said to Abel was "his brother"—he spoke to him with brotherly love. That is what is meant by the continuation of the verse, "Cain rose up against Abel *his brother* and slew him." That is why God asked Cain: "Where is Abel your brother?"—where is the brotherly affection that you always showed Abel?

The Gaon of Vilna, in *Torah Gems*, vol. 1, p. 50.

R. Simeon b. Yohai said: It is difficult to say this thing, and the mouth cannot utter it plainly. Think of two athletes wrestling before the king; had the king wished, he could have separated them. But he did not wish to do so, and one overcame the other and killed him, he [the victim] crying out [before he died], "Let my cause be pleaded before the king!" Even so, YOUR BROTHER'S BLOOD IS SHRIEKING TO ME FROM THE GROUND!

B'reishit Rabbah 22:9.

Cain's real sin is his inability to recognize his responsibility toward his brother and for his own actions, and to admit his guilt. Cain does respond, but he does not acknowledge that he bears any guilt at all for the death of his brother, his other side.

Norman J. Cohen, *Self, Struggle and Change: Family Conflict Stories in Genesis and Their Healing Insights for Our Lives* (Woodstock, VT: Jewish Lights Publishing, 1995), p. 53.

Questions for Discussion

1. Why do you think God approves Abel's offering over that of Cain?

2. If God is infinite in wisdom, why does God ask Cain (after he has killed Abel), "Where is your brother Abel?" (Genesis 4:9)?

3. Several midrashim note that Cain is not condemned to death because death had not yet been experienced in the Bible, and he had no way of knowing that his blow would extinguish his brother's life. Is he thus guilty of homicide, and not murder? Do you agree or disagree, and why?

4. What do you think Cain means when he says to God, "I must hide from Your face" (Genesis 4:14)?

5. Abel's name in Hebrew is *hevel,* which literally means "breath." What is the connection between his name and his destiny?

6. Why is Cain so distraught to receive the punishment of wandering? After all, his punishment for the murder of his brother is not of a physical nature. He does not receive capital punishment, nor is he whipped or imprisoned.

7. Count the number of times in the Bible story that it says that Cain is Abel's brother. How might this repetition be interpreted? What might be the reason for stressing the fact?

8. In commenting on this story, Bible scholar Nahum Sarna says that the story teaches that "a crime against man is a sin against God." What verse or verses in the biblical story support his thesis?

9. To what, or to whom, could Cain be referring when he expresses the fear that anyone who meets him might kill him?

3. Sodom and Gomorrah: Abraham's Plea for Justice

The Bible Story: Genesis 18:20–33

Genesis 18:20] The Eternal One then said, "The outcry in Sodom and Gomorrah—how great it is; and their crime—how grave it is! **21]** Let Me go down and determine whether they are wreaking havoc in equal measure to the shrieking that is coming to Me. If not, I will know."

22] The men now turned away and went toward Sodom, while Abraham remained standing before the Eternal. **23]** Abraham then came forward and said, "Will You indeed sweep away the innocent along with the wicked? **24]** Suppose there are fifty innocent in the city—will You indeed sweep away the place, and not spare it for the sake of the fifty innocent who are in its midst? **25]** Far be it from You to do such a thing, killing innocent and wicked alike, so that the innocent and the wicked suffer the same fate. Far be it from You! Must not the Judge of all the earth do justly?" **26]** The Eternal One said, "If I find fifty innocent people in Sodom, I will pardon the whole place for their sake."

27] Again Abraham spoke: "Look now—let me undertake to speak up to my lord, though I am but dust and ashes: **28]** What if the fifty innocent are five short; will you

יח 20 וַיֹּ֣אמֶר יְהֹוָ֔ה זַעֲקַ֛ת סְדֹ֥ם וַעֲמֹרָ֖ה כִּי־רָ֑בָּה וְחַטָּאתָ֕ם כִּ֥י כָבְדָ֖ה מְאֹֽד: 21 אֵֽרְדָה־נָּ֣א וְאֶרְאֶ֔ה הַכְּצַעֲקָתָ֛הּ הַבָּ֥אָה אֵלַ֖י עָשׂ֣וּ ׀ כָּלָ֑ה וְאִם־לֹ֖א אֵדָֽעָה:

22 וַיִּפְנ֤וּ מִשָּׁם֙ הָֽאֲנָשִׁ֔ים וַיֵּֽלְכ֖וּ סְדֹ֑מָה וְאַ֨בְרָהָ֔ם עוֹדֶ֥נּוּ עֹמֵ֖ד לִפְנֵ֥י יְהֹוָֽה: 23 וַיִּגַּ֥שׁ אַבְרָהָ֖ם וַיֹּאמַ֑ר הַאַ֣ף תִּסְפֶּ֔ה צַדִּ֖יק עִם־רָשָֽׁע: 24 אוּלַ֥י יֵ֛שׁ חֲמִשִּׁ֥ים צַדִּיקִ֖ם בְּת֣וֹךְ הָעִ֑יר הַאַ֤ף תִּסְפֶּה֙ וְלֹֽא־תִשָּׂ֣א לַמָּק֔וֹם לְמַ֛עַן חֲמִשִּׁ֥ים הַצַּדִּיקִ֖ם אֲשֶׁ֥ר בְּקִרְבָּֽהּ: 25 חָלִ֨לָה לְּךָ֜ מֵעֲשֹׂ֣ת ׀ כַּדָּבָ֣ר הַזֶּ֗ה לְהָמִ֤ית צַדִּיק֙ עִם־רָשָׁ֔ע וְהָיָ֥ה כַצַּדִּ֖יק כָּרָשָׁ֑ע חָלִ֣לָה לָּ֔ךְ הֲשֹׁפֵט֙ כָּל־הָאָ֔רֶץ לֹ֥א יַעֲשֶׂ֖ה מִשְׁפָּֽט: 26 וַיֹּ֣אמֶר יְהֹוָ֔ה אִם־אֶמְצָ֥א בִסְדֹ֛ם חֲמִשִּׁ֥ים צַדִּיקִ֖ם בְּת֣וֹךְ הָעִ֑יר וְנָשָׂ֥אתִי לְכָל־הַמָּק֖וֹם בַּעֲבוּרָֽם:

27 וַיַּ֥עַן אַבְרָהָ֖ם וַיֹּאמַ֑ר הִנֵּה־נָ֤א הוֹאַ֨לְתִּי֙ לְדַבֵּ֣ר אֶל־אֲדֹנָ֔י וְאָנֹכִ֖י עָפָ֥ר וָאֵֽפֶר: 28 אוּלַ֥י יַחְסְר֛וּן חֲמִשִּׁ֥ים הַצַּדִּיקִ֖ם

destroy the whole city because of five?"
[God] answered, "If I find forty-five there,
I will not destroy it."

29] Once more Abraham spoke up: "What
if forty are found there?" And [God]
answered, "For the sake of forty, I will
not do it."

30] Then he said, "Do not be angry, my
lord, and let me speak: What if thirty are
found there?" "If I find thirty there," said
[God], "I will not do it."

31] And Abraham said, "Look now—let
me undertake to speak up before my lord:
What if twenty are found there?" And
[God] said, "For the sake of the twenty,
I will not destroy it."

32] Then Abraham said, "Let not my lord
be angry, and let me speak up one last
time: What if ten are found there?" And
[God] said, "For the sake of the ten, I will
not destroy it." 33] Then, done speaking
to Abraham, the Eternal departed; and
Abraham returned to his place.

חֲמִשָּׁה הֲתַשְׁחִית בַּחֲמִשָּׁה אֶת־כָּל־
הָעִיר וַיֹּאמֶר לֹא אַשְׁחִית אִם־אֶמְצָא
שָׁם אַרְבָּעִים וַחֲמִשָּׁה:

29 וַיֹּסֶף עוֹד לְדַבֵּר אֵלָיו וַיֹּאמַר אוּלַי
יִמָּצְאוּן שָׁם אַרְבָּעִים וַיֹּאמֶר לֹא אֶעֱשֶׂה
בַּעֲבוּר הָאַרְבָּעִים:

30 וַיֹּאמֶר אַל־נָא יִחַר לַאדֹנָי וַאֲדַבֵּרָה
אוּלַי יִמָּצְאוּן שָׁם שְׁלֹשִׁים וַיֹּאמֶר לֹא
אֶעֱשֶׂה אִם־אֶמְצָא שָׁם שְׁלֹשִׁים:

31 וַיֹּאמֶר הִנֵּה־נָא הוֹאַלְתִּי לְדַבֵּר אֶל־
אֲדֹנָי אוּלַי יִמָּצְאוּן שָׁם עֶשְׂרִים וַיֹּאמֶר
לֹא אַשְׁחִית בַּעֲבוּר הָעֶשְׂרִים:

32 וַיֹּאמֶר אַל־נָא יִחַר לַאדֹנָי וַאֲדַבְּרָה
אַךְ־הַפַּעַם אוּלַי יִמָּצְאוּן שָׁם עֲשָׂרָה
וַיֹּאמֶר לֹא אַשְׁחִית בַּעֲבוּר הָעֲשָׂרָה:

33 וַיֵּלֶךְ יְהֹוָה כַּאֲשֶׁר כִּלָּה לְדַבֵּר אֶל־
אַבְרָהָם וְאַבְרָהָם שָׁב לִמְקֹמוֹ:

Understanding the Story

Just as to the modern ear Las Vegas connotes gambling, to the Jewish ear the biblical twin cities of Sodom and Gomorrah signify one thing: human wickedness. Despite both Sodom and Gomorrah's reputation for cruelty, when God's intention to destroy the cities is shared with Abraham, he tries to change God's mind. Abraham is convinced that there are undoubtedly some good people in these cities and, if so, questions how God can destroy the innocent along with the wicked. One of the problems in this story is that Abraham also seems to be arguing on behalf of the evil people, otherwise he would have requested that only the good people be spared. Instead, he appeals to God to save all the people of Sodom and Gomorrah, provided that some good people be found among them.

This is the first instance recorded in the Torah of a human being arguing with God. After Abraham's initial protest, he entreats God to save the cities if fifty righteous people can be found within them. God agrees, whereupon Abraham starts "bargaining" with God, asking that God spare the cities if forty-five, then forty, thirty, twenty, and finally, only ten righteous people can be found. God accedes to each of Abraham's appeals. Only when it becomes apparent that, with the exception of Lot's family, the entire population of the cities is evil, does God proceed to destroy them.

This exchange raises many difficult questions. What did the people of Sodom and Gomorrah do that was so wicked to warrant their complete destruction? Does Abraham really doubt the existence of God's justice? Is it permissible for any person to "bargain" and argue with God? What gives Abraham the "right" to argue with God and question God's intentions? We see in the story that Abraham's question about God's justice is not rejected outright. It is possible to argue with God, but God, it appears, always has the last word.

From the Commentators

Above all, the Bible is concerned with the problem of divine justice. Just because God is universal and omnipotent, mankind needs assurance that His mighty power is not indiscriminately employed and that His ways are not capricious. God must act according to a principle that man can try to understand, and that principle is the passion for righteousness.

Thus, when Abraham ask the questions, "Will you sweep away the innocent along with the guilty? Shall not the Judge of all the earth deal justly?" (18:23–25), it is taken for granted that the respective answers cannot possibly be other than a resounding, "Of course not!" "Indubitably!"

> Nahum M. Sarna, *Understanding Genesis*
> (New York: Schocken Books, 1966), p. 147.

The rule is that when the good predominate in the world and good deeds exceed the bad, the wicked too, are saved through the merits of the righteous. The reverse, though, that when the wicked predominate the good should be punished alongside the wicked, is not true, for that would be unjust. As to the discrepancy between the two cases, our Sages tell us that God's attribute of doing good exceeds His attribute of punishing people five hundred times over, namely that if a good deed and an evil deed are of equal rank, the reward for the good deed will be five hundred times the punishment for the evil deed.

> Be'er Mayim Hayyim, in *Torah Gems*, vol. 1, ed. Aharon Yaakov Greenberg, trans. Shmuel Himelstein (Tel Aviv: Yavneh Publishing House, 1998), p. 155.

The Torah: A Modern Commentary

Published by the Union of American Hebrew Congregations (now the Union for Reform Judaism) in 1981 and edited by Rabbi W. Gunther Plaut, an esteemed scholar in the Reform Movement, *The Torah: A Modern Commentary* proceeds from the assumption that the Torah is a book that had its origins in the hearts and minds of the Jewish people. It presents the modern reader with tools for understanding the text, using both traditional and modern commentary. It also makes use of archaeological, linguistic, and anthropological scholarship. The URJ Press published a revised edition of the commentary in 2005 that includes a gender-sensitive translation of the Torah.

Abraham does not plead merely for the innocent but for the sinners as well, through the merit of the few righteous. The story thereby introduces the concept of merit (זְכוּת), important in biblical and especially in postbiblical religion. The concept stipulates that a handful of concerned, decent, and "righteous" people could have averted Sodom's calamity by their merit.

Yet the story also suggests that there are limits to the influence of even the best. Unless they find a minimum of like-minded associates, they will be ineffective. Eventually, if they persist in such a society, they will perish with it. Thus, Abraham does not, in his pursuit of divine equity, go below the number ten.

W. Gunther Plaut, ed., *The Torah: A Modern Commentary*, rev. ed.
(New York: URJ Press, 2005), p. 139.

LET ME GO DOWN (18:21). R. Simeon b. Yohai taught: This is one of the ten descents mentioned in the Torah [If God is omnipotent, why does he have to go down?]. R. Abba b. Kahana said: This teaches that the Holy One, blessed be God, gave them the opportunity of repenting.

B'reishit Rabbah 49:6.

Because of their wealth, the people of Sodom became haughty. They said to one another: "Since gold and silver flow from our land, why should we allow strangers to visit in our borders, eat our food, use our resources, and share what is ours? They will only take what we have, and there will be less for us. Let's keep them from entering, and let's drive out those who get in as soon as possible—especially the poor or the sick ones."

Tosefta, Sotah 3, *Sanhedrin* 109a, in Harvey J. Fields, *A Torah Commentary for Our Times*, vol. 1 (New York: UAHC Press, 1998), p. 49.

Rabbi Nathaniel commented that the people of Sodom refused to give food to the stranger or traveler, and they even constructed fences above their gardens so that no bird flying by could eat from their trees.

Pirkei D'Rabbi Eliezer 25, in Harvey J. Fields, *A Torah Commentary for Our Times*, vol. 1, p. 49.

According to the Spanish Jewish interpreter Abraham Ibn Ezra (1092–1167), not one citizen of Sodom protested the cruel treatment of strangers. Instead, they remained silent. They chose the safety of "not getting involved."

Harvey J. Fields, *A Torah Commentary for Our Times*, vol. 1, p. 50.

Although it appears from the language of the narrative that Abraham is teaching God a lesson about justice, it may well be that it is really God—the great pedagogue—who is teaching Abraham a lesson about the inherent limitations on human justice, so that Abraham could instruct his descendants to do justice in a mature and balanced fashion—rejecting both extremes of acquitting everyone about whose guilt there is any doubt and convicting everyone against whom there is any suspicion. By accepting Abraham's moral principle—that a sufficient number of innocent people in a group requires the sparing of the entire group, including the guilty—God was teaching Abraham how to strike the appropriate balance.

Alan M. Dershowitz, *The Genesis of Justice*
(New York: Warner Books, 2000), p. 87.

Questions for Discussion

1. Why do you think that God does not allow the messengers or Abraham to warn the people of Sodom of the impending disaster, in the hope of arousing them to possible atonement? It could be said that the possibility of repentance is absent in this story. Why do you think the people of Sodom and Gomorrah are denied that chance?

2. If God is all-knowing, why does God say, "Let Me go down and determine whether they are wreaking havoc in equal measure to the shrieking that is coming to Me" (Genesis 18:21)?

3. Are there times that you have questioned God? What were the occasions? Is it ever appropriate to question God, or "bargain" with God, and if so, when might it be?

4. Why does Abraham stop bargaining once God agrees not to destroy the cities if ten innocent people can be found there? What is the significance of the number ten?

5. On whose behalf does Abraham attempt to intercede? Is it the righteous only, or the wicked as well? Do you think he was right or wrong to do this? Why or why not?

6. What might the text mean at the end of the story when it says, "Abraham returned to his place" (Genesis 18:33)?

7. What was the sin of the Sodomites, and what was it about their sin that made God angry enough to destroy an entire city?

8. In Genesis 13:13 the text states that the people of Sodom were "wicked, hardened sinners against the Eternal." In your opinion, what is a "sin against God"? What was the sin of the people of Sodom and Gomorrah? (Note: You may want to refer to Ezekiel 16:49–50 for an opinion regarding the sin of the people.)

9. What would you say is the moral of this Bible story? Can you identify contemporary situations where a person confronts the justice system? How are those situations the same? Different?

10. Have you ever been in a situation where someone was about to be punished, and you were able to intervene and change or lessen the punishment? How were you able to do it?

11. There is a rabbinic concept known as "merit" (z'chut), which stipulates that a handful of concerned, decent, and righteous people could have averted Sodom's calamity by their merit. How does this concept relate to this story?

12. In what ways is the story of Sodom similar to the stories of Cain and Abel? To the story of Noah?

13. Both Noah and Abraham learn that people are going to be destroyed. Compare Noah's reaction to God's announcement in Genesis 6:22 to that of Abraham. Which person is more morally sophisticated? Why?

14. Can God's justice be judged by human beings according to standards of human justice? If not, by whom and by what standards can God's justice be evaluated?

4. The Binding of Isaac: How Could Abraham Do It?

The Bible Story: Genesis 22:1–24

Genesis 22:1] After these things, God tested Abraham, saying to him, "Abraham!" And he said, "Here I am." 2] [God] said, "Take your son, your only one, the one you love, Isaac, and go forth to the land of Moriah. Offer him there as a burnt-offering, on one of the mountains that I will show you."

3] Abraham rose early, saddled his donkey, chopped wood for the burnt-offering, took Isaac his son and his two lads, and set out for the place that God had spoken of to him. 4] On the third day, Abraham lifted up his eyes and saw the place from afar. 5] Abraham said to his servant lads, "Stay here with the donkey; the lad and I will go yonder. We will worship and return to you." 6] Abraham then took the wood for the burnt-offering and laid it on Isaac his son; in his own hand he held the firestone and the knife. And the two of them went on together.

כב ¹ וַיְהִי אַחַר הַדְּבָרִים הָאֵלֶּה וְהָאֱלֹהִים נִסָּה אֶת־אַבְרָהָם וַיֹּאמֶר אֵלָיו אַבְרָהָם וַיֹּאמֶר הִנֵּנִי: ² וַיֹּאמֶר קַח־נָא אֶת־בִּנְךָ אֶת־יְחִידְךָ אֲשֶׁר־אָהַבְתָּ אֶת־יִצְחָק וְלֶךְ־לְךָ אֶל־אֶרֶץ הַמֹּרִיָּה וְהַעֲלֵהוּ שָׁם לְעֹלָה עַל אַחַד הֶהָרִים אֲשֶׁר אֹמַר אֵלֶיךָ:

³ וַיַּשְׁכֵּם אַבְרָהָם בַּבֹּקֶר וַיַּחֲבֹשׁ אֶת־חֲמֹרוֹ וַיִּקַּח אֶת־שְׁנֵי נְעָרָיו אִתּוֹ וְאֵת יִצְחָק בְּנוֹ וַיְבַקַּע עֲצֵי עֹלָה וַיָּקָם וַיֵּלֶךְ אֶל־הַמָּקוֹם אֲשֶׁר־אָמַר־לוֹ הָאֱלֹהִים: ⁴ בַּיּוֹם הַשְּׁלִישִׁי וַיִּשָּׂא אַבְרָהָם אֶת־עֵינָיו וַיַּרְא אֶת־הַמָּקוֹם מֵרָחֹק: ⁵ וַיֹּאמֶר אַבְרָהָם אֶל־נְעָרָיו שְׁבוּ־לָכֶם פֹּה עִם־הַחֲמוֹר וַאֲנִי וְהַנַּעַר נֵלְכָה עַד־כֹּה וְנִשְׁתַּחֲוֶה וְנָשׁוּבָה אֲלֵיכֶם: ⁶ וַיִּקַּח אַבְרָהָם אֶת־עֲצֵי הָעֹלָה וַיָּשֶׂם עַל־יִצְחָק בְּנוֹ וַיִּקַּח בְּיָדוֹ אֶת־הָאֵשׁ וְאֶת־הַמַּאֲכֶלֶת וַיֵּלְכוּ שְׁנֵיהֶם יַחְדָּו:

7] Isaac then said to Abraham his father, "Father!" He answered: "Here I am, my son." And Isaac said, "Here is the firestone and the wood, but where is the lamb for the burnt-offering?" 8] Abraham replied, "God will see to the lamb for the burnt-offering, my son." And the two of them went on together.

9] They came to the place that God had shown him. There Abraham built the altar and arranged the wood and bound Isaac his son and laid him on the altar, upon the wood. 10] Abraham now reached out and took the knife to slay his son, 11] but out of heaven an angel of the Eternal called to him, saying, "Abraham, Abraham!" He replied: "Here I am." 12] [The angel] then said, "Do not lay your hand on the lad; do nothing to him; for now I know that you are one who fears God, as you did not withhold your son, your only one, from Me."

13] Abraham lifted his eyes: he now could see a ram [just] after it was caught by its horns in a thicket. Abraham went and took the ram and offered it as a burnt-offering in place of his son. 14] Abraham named that place *YHVH Yir'eh*; to this day people say: "On the mount of the Eternal, [God] will be seen."

15] Then out of heaven an angel of the Eternal called to Abraham a second time, 16] saying, "By Myself I swear, says the

7 וַיֹּ֨אמֶר יִצְחָ֜ק אֶל־אַבְרָהָ֤ם אָבִיו֙ וַיֹּ֣אמֶר אָבִ֔י וַיֹּ֖אמֶר הִנֶּ֣נִּֽי בְנִ֑י וַיֹּ֗אמֶר הִנֵּ֤ה הָאֵשׁ֙ וְהָ֣עֵצִ֔ים וְאַיֵּ֥ה הַשֶּׂ֖ה לְעֹלָֽה: 8 וַיֹּ֙אמֶר֙ אַבְרָהָ֔ם אֱלֹהִ֞ים יִרְאֶה־לּ֥וֹ הַשֶּׂ֛ה לְעֹלָ֖ה בְּנִ֑י וַיֵּלְכ֥וּ שְׁנֵיהֶ֖ם יַחְדָּֽו:

9 וַיָּבֹ֗אוּ אֶֽל־הַמָּקוֹם֮ אֲשֶׁ֣ר אָֽמַר־ל֣וֹ הָאֱלֹהִים֒ וַיִּ֨בֶן שָׁ֤ם אַבְרָהָם֙ אֶת־הַמִּזְבֵּ֔חַ וַיַּעֲרֹ֖ךְ אֶת־הָעֵצִ֑ים וַֽיַּעֲקֹד֙ אֶת־יִצְחָ֣ק בְּנ֔וֹ וַיָּ֤שֶׂם אֹתוֹ֙ עַל־הַמִּזְבֵּ֔חַ מִמַּ֖עַל לָעֵצִֽים: 10 וַיִּשְׁלַ֤ח אַבְרָהָם֙ אֶת־יָד֔וֹ וַיִּקַּ֖ח אֶת־הַֽמַּאֲכֶ֑לֶת לִשְׁחֹ֖ט אֶת־בְּנֽוֹ: 11 וַיִּקְרָ֨א אֵלָ֜יו מַלְאַ֤ךְ יְהֹוָה֙ מִן־הַשָּׁמַ֔יִם וַיֹּ֖אמֶר אַבְרָהָ֣ם | אַבְרָהָ֑ם וַיֹּ֖אמֶר הִנֵּֽנִי: 12 וַיֹּ֗אמֶר אַל־תִּשְׁלַ֤ח יָֽדְךָ֙ אֶל־הַנַּ֔עַר וְאַל־תַּ֥עַשׂ ל֖וֹ מְא֑וּמָה כִּ֣י | עַתָּ֣ה יָדַ֗עְתִּי כִּֽי־יְרֵ֤א אֱלֹהִים֙ אַ֔תָּה וְלֹ֥א חָשַׂ֛כְתָּ אֶת־בִּנְךָ֥ אֶת־יְחִֽידְךָ֖ מִמֶּֽנִּי:

13 וַיִּשָּׂ֨א אַבְרָהָ֜ם אֶת־עֵינָ֗יו וַיַּרְא֙ וְהִנֵּה־אַ֔יִל אַחַ֕ר נֶאֱחַ֥ז בַּסְּבַ֖ךְ בְּקַרְנָ֑יו וַיֵּ֤לֶךְ אַבְרָהָם֙ וַיִּקַּ֣ח אֶת־הָאַ֔יִל וַיַּעֲלֵ֥הוּ לְעֹלָ֖ה תַּ֥חַת בְּנֽוֹ: 14 וַיִּקְרָ֧א אַבְרָהָ֛ם שֵֽׁם־הַמָּק֥וֹם הַה֖וּא יְהֹוָ֣ה | יִרְאֶ֑ה אֲשֶׁר֙ יֵֽאָמֵ֣ר הַיּ֔וֹם בְּהַ֥ר יְהֹוָ֖ה יֵרָאֶֽה:

15 וַיִּקְרָ֛א מַלְאַ֥ךְ יְהֹוָ֖ה אֶל־אַבְרָהָ֑ם שֵׁנִ֖ית מִן־הַשָּׁמָֽיִם: 16 וַיֹּ֕אמֶר בִּ֥י נִשְׁבַּ֖עְתִּי

Eternal One, that because you did this thing, and did not withhold your son your only one, 17] I will bless you greatly, and make your descendants as numerous as the stars of heaven and the sands of the sea-shore, and your descendants shall take possession of the gates of their foes. 18] And through your descendants the nations of the earth shall be blessed, because you hearkened to My voice." 19] Abraham then returned to his servant lads; they got up and traveled together to Beersheba, and Abraham settled in Beersheba.

20] And after all these things, Abraham was told the following: Milcah, she too has borne sons, to your brother Nahor— 21] Uz his first-born, his brother Buz, Kemuel father of Aram, 22] Kesed, Hazo, Pildash, Jidlaph, and Bethuel. 23] (Bethuel fathered Rebekah.) These eight did Milcah bear to Nahor, Abraham's brother. 24] And his concubine—her name was Reumah—she too bore: Tebah, Gaham, Tahash, and Maacah.

נְאֻם־יְהֹוָה כִּי יַעַן אֲשֶׁר עָשִׂיתָ אֶת־
הַדָּבָר הַזֶּה וְלֹא חָשַׂכְתָּ אֶת־בִּנְךָ אֶת־
יְחִידֶךָ: 17 כִּי־בָרֵךְ אֲבָרֶכְךָ וְהַרְבָּה אַרְבֶּה
אֶת־זַרְעֲךָ כְּכוֹכְבֵי הַשָּׁמַיִם וְכַחוֹל אֲשֶׁר
עַל־שְׂפַת הַיָּם וְיִרַשׁ זַרְעֲךָ אֵת שַׁעַר
אֹיְבָיו: 18 וְהִתְבָּרְכוּ בְזַרְעֲךָ כֹּל גּוֹיֵי
הָאָרֶץ עֵקֶב אֲשֶׁר שָׁמַעְתָּ בְּקֹלִי:
19 וַיָּשָׁב אַבְרָהָם אֶל־נְעָרָיו וַיָּקֻמוּ וַיֵּלְכוּ
יַחְדָּו אֶל־בְּאֵר שָׁבַע וַיֵּשֶׁב אַבְרָהָם
בִּבְאֵר שָׁבַע:

20 וַיְהִי אַחֲרֵי הַדְּבָרִים הָאֵלֶּה וַיֻּגַּד
לְאַבְרָהָם לֵאמֹר הִנֵּה יָלְדָה מִלְכָּה
גַם־הִוא בָּנִים לְנָחוֹר אָחִיךָ: 21 אֶת־
עוּץ בְּכֹרוֹ וְאֶת־בּוּז אָחִיו וְאֶת־קְמוּאֵל
אֲבִי אֲרָם: 22 וְאֶת־כֶּשֶׂד וְאֶת־חֲזוֹ וְאֶת־
פִּלְדָּשׁ וְאֶת־יִדְלָף וְאֵת בְּתוּאֵל:
23 וּבְתוּאֵל יָלַד אֶת־רִבְקָה שְׁמֹנָה אֵלֶּה
יָלְדָה מִלְכָּה לְנָחוֹר אֲחִי אַבְרָהָם:
24 וּפִילַגְשׁוֹ וּשְׁמָהּ רְאוּמָה וַתֵּלֶד גַּם־
הִוא אֶת־טֶבַח וְאֶת־גַּחַם וְאֶת־תַּחַשׁ
וְאֶת־מַעֲכָה:

Understanding the Story

No biblical narrative is more dramatic, poignant, and confusing than God's command to Abraham that he sacrifice his long-awaited son Isaac. What kind of a God would ask such a thing of a father? What kind of father would accede to such a request, even from God?

This story is considered one of the most important in the entire Torah. The Rabbis titled the story *Akeidat Yitzchak*, "The Binding of Isaac," and chose it as one of the Torah readings for Rosh HaShanah. This test of Abraham is perhaps the most difficult test of faith, trust, and loyalty to God that could ever be devised. It is the ultimate test of faith, in that it asks a father to offer his beloved son to his God as a sacrifice.

In the traditional interpretation of the story, God never actually intends Abraham to slaughter Isaac, because it is ethically wrong. The justification for this reading is found at the end of the story when Abraham is told to put down his knife. Abraham, on the other hand, out of loyalty to God, was willing to violate God's moral law against murder.

One of the central problems that readers of the Bible have with Abraham's behavior is that he so easily acquiesces to God's command to kill his son. He seems to do so without hesitation, without asking any questions, and without even consulting his wife, Sarah. Thus, we are left with several questions: How ought a person show loyalty to God? Should a person who hears God's voice saying to do something that is contrary to moral law do it without question? What kind of a God would ask any person to sacrifice his son? Is blind faith what our religion is all about? And how can Sarah's absence in this story be explained? These and other questions have been debated by Jews, Christians, and Muslims for generations.

From the Commentators

The purpose of all tests mentioned in the Torah is to teach human beings how they are to act.... Abraham is commanded to sacrifice his son.... And, because he feared God and loved to do what God commanded, he thought little of his beloved child, and set aside all his hopes concerning him, and agreed to kill him.... Therefore, the angel said to him: "For now I know that you fear God," which means that from Abraham's action ... we can learn how far we must go in the fear of God.

> **Rambam**
>
> Rabbi Moses ben Maimon, also called Maimonides (1135–1204), was one of the great medieval philosophers, codifiers, and commentators. In addition to his *Mishneh Torah*, a Jewish code of law that covers all subjects, he also completed *Guide for the Perplexed*. This book begins with a discussion of biblical expressions that are difficult to understand and goes on to discuss the nature of God and the nature of Jewish prophecy. Maimonides' goal was to prove to Jews with a secular education that Judaism was rational.

> Moses Maimonides, *Guide for the Perplexed*, in Harvey J. Fields, *A Torah Commentary for Our Times*, vol. 1 (New York: UAHC Press, 1998), p. 51.

The story of Abraham's faith is an example, a banner for all the peoples of the world to follow.

> Don Isaac Abravanel, in Harvey J. Fields, *A Torah Commentary for Our Times*, vol. 1, p. 52.

Loyalty to God does not mean "blind faith." Sometimes it means asking difficult questions about what it is that we should or should not be doing. Sometimes it means being willing to take risks for what we believe is just and right....

The *Akedah* is a story about Abraham's struggle to understand what it means to be loyal to God. He is an example of a person who tested his faith with questions and weighed his decisions carefully. He was not afraid to face doubts or to get all the facts. If necessary, he was ready to make sacrifices for what he believed, but he was also ready to rethink his convictions and commitments.

Perhaps for all those reasons this story of Abraham is considered one of the great examples of religious faith and loyalty to God.

> Harvey J. Fields, *A Torah Commentary for Our Times*, vol. 1, p. 51.

Abraham's greatness in the sacrifice was that even on the third day he was as enthusiastic as he had been on the first. Momentary fervor is not that great a test;

but on the third day, after a long, wearying journey, Abraham was still as enthusiastic as he had been at the beginning, and was able to lift up his eyes with the same intensity.

R. Menahem Mendl of Kotzk, in *Torah Gems*, vol. 1,
ed. Aharon Yaakov Greenberg, trans. Shmuel Himelstein
(Tel Aviv: Yavneh Publishing House, 1998), p. 174.

In the story of the *Akedah*, God is testing Abraham to see if he would remain loyal to God's moral law, but Abraham, who could not know this, was simultaneously testing God to see what kind of covenant and religion he (Abraham) was being asked to join. In testing God, as it were, Abraham was ultimately testing himself. Abraham wanted to see if God would stop him, so Abraham used the strategy of stalling for time. Abraham never intended to kill Isaac. Rather, by not rushing and taking his time, Abraham tried to give God time to change God's mind. Abraham never agrees to accept God's command and perform it. Instead, Abraham goes through a series of separate steps. First he gets up, then he dresses his animals, then he gets his retinue in order, then he cuts firewood, and then he sets off, and then he sees Moriah, and then he instructs his servants to wait. Next, he takes the firewood, then he takes the fire and the knife. At each step of the way Abraham is likely waiting for God to withdraw God's command. When that is not forthcoming, Abraham takes the next step and puts God to the next test—as it were—always showing obedience and always giving God the chance to make the moral statement that God does not want any person to murder in God's name.

Based on Lippman Bodoff, "The Real Test of the Akedah:
Blind Obedience versus Moral Choice," *Judaism* 42, no. 1 (1993): 71–92.

Where is Sarah while the story of her husband Abraham and son Isaac takes place? Sarah's voice is nowhere to be heard in the story! Some have suggested that Sarah is not present in the story because Abraham did not tell her of his plans. Others have suggested that Abraham did tell her and that this is precisely why she is silent: Sarah is in a state of shock over Abraham's intentions. Some see this shock as the reason for Sarah's death at the beginning of the subsequent chapter (Genesis 23:2).

The reason that Sarah is silent in this story is because the events are unfolding in a dream in a delayed reaction to Isaac's circumcision, a dream spawned perhaps by drinking too much at the drinking feast that Abraham made on the day of Isaac's weaning (Genesis 21:8). Sarah doesn't speak because in her dream she is working out her emotional reactions to the circumcision. Thus the knife in the story that Abraham takes with him is not for the sacrifice of his son, but for his circumcision.

Based on Dvora Yanow, "Sarah's Silence: A Newly Discovered Commentary on Genesis 22 by Rashi's Sister," *Judaism* 43, no. 4 (1994): 398–408.

If we want to understand the *Akeda*, we must...try to understand what God's command would have meant to a person living in Abraham's time.

Perhaps the clue to God's purpose is in the wording of His command: "Take your son, your only one, whom you love, Isaac, and go forth to the land of Moriah and offer him there as a burnt offering on one of the heights that I will point out to you." As Professor Nahum Sarna notes, the style of God's command—the words "go forth," the listing of what is being given up, the vagueness of the destination—recalls His words to Abraham years earlier: "Go forth from your land and your kindred and your father's house to the land that I will show you."

It is in this stylistic similarity that we find the meaning of the *Akeda*. When God first called Abraham to follow him, Abraham and Sarah were, respectively, 75 and 65 years old and childless. Yet God promised Abraham a nation full of descendants. Abraham followed and God gave him Ishmael and Isaac. After Ishmael was sent away, it was only through Isaac that God's promise could be fulfilled. In the *Akeda*, by subtly reminding Abraham of His original promise while asking him to forgo that promise by sacrificing the son through whom it would be realized, God tested whether Abraham's devotion was based on expected reward or was unconditional.

Jeffrey H. Tigay, "Judaism on the Cutting Edge," *Hadassah Magazine* 81, no. 1 (August/September 1999): 54.

From one perspective Abraham's fidelity to his God is an ultimate abuse of his son, from another it is the highest selflessness.

Peter Pitzele, *Our Fathers' Wells: A Personal Encounter with the Myths of Genesis* (San Francisco: HarperSanFrancisco, 1995), p. 127.

[Commenting on the verse "Take your son, your only one, the one you love, Isaac, and go forth to the land of Moriah" (Genesis 22:2), the Sages were intrigued with the structure of this verse. They imagined a dialogue between God and Abraham:]

God: "Take your son."

Abraham: "I have two sons."

God: "Your only son."

Abraham: "Each is an only son to his mother."

God: "The one you love."

Abraham: "I love them both."

Finally God is explicit: "Isaac."

Babylonian Talmud, Sanhedrin 89b.

After hundreds of readings of this enigmatic tale, I am struck by its many dreamlike elements: First, there are eerie time references in the story—*some time afterwards . . . early the next morning . . . on the third day*—which echo the passage of time in dreams. . . .

If we view this episode through the window of Abraham's unconscious fears and hopes, many of the unexplained elements take on meaning. Sarah's unnatural absence speaks to the loneliness of Abraham's situation. The young Isaac becomes a mouthpiece for Abraham's unspoken anxieties.

Naomi H. Rosenblatt, with Joshua Horowitz, Wrestling with Angels
(New York: Dell Publishing, 1996), p. 196.

Questions for Discussion

1. If you were Abraham and did not know what God truly had in mind in terms of the ultimate sacrifice of your son, would you have acted in a manner similar to Abraham? Is this the kind of loyalty that God demands of each of us?

2. Do you think that the story of the Binding of Isaac is a story of what true faith is all about? Explain why or why not.

3. Are there things that you would have expected Abraham to have done or not done in this story? If so, what are they?

4. Do you think that, had the angel not stopped him, Abraham would have followed through on the sacrifice? How does the text support your answer?

5. Why is Abraham so silent in the story? Compare this story to the previous story of Sodom and Gomorrah in Genesis 18:20–33. Why do you think Abraham does not argue with God here as he did earlier? Which Abraham do you prefer, the Abraham who questions God, or the Abraham who follows God?

6. What is the purpose of the servants of Abraham in the story? Why does Abraham first take them along, and why does he then leave them behind along the way?

7. Why do you think that God uses an angel rather than ordering Abraham directly to put down the knife? Why does God need to use two angels?

8. How old do you think Isaac is in this story? Do you think that Isaac knew what was about to happen to him? How can you use the text to prove your point?

9. Can you find any significant words that are repeated in this story? What are they, and why do you think these words are used with such great frequency?

10. Some Christians believe that this story is a paradigm of Jesus as the sacrificial lamb. How might they read this story this way? Do you think the reading can be supported by the text? Why or why not?

11. According to some rabbinic commentators, Abraham has questions and doubts about what God has commanded him to do. Look at the story carefully and see whether you can find examples of Abraham's doubts by virtue of his actions in the story. Does Abraham act recklessly and impetuously throughout the story? Or do you perceive that Abraham, because of his doubts, uses "stall" tactics in order to bide time and try to figure out what God really has in mind?

12. Why does Abraham sacrifice a ram in place of his own son?

13. Do you find anything odd about the way in which the story ends, and if so, what? How can you explain the ending?

14. Are we to follow the commandments of our faith without questioning them? Do you think it is disloyal to express doubts about what Jewish tradition says God "commands" us to do?

15. What do you think is the ultimate purpose of Abraham's test? Why? What in the text supports your argument?

16. It has been suggested that if people who lived in Abraham's time believed in child sacrifice, perhaps the true message of the story is to teach that God does not desire human sacrifice. Do you agree with this reading? Why or why not?

17. What are some ways in which modern society "sacrifices" children? How can children be better protected from being victimized by the many bad elements of the culture that surrounds us?

18. God's angel speaks for God and keeps Abraham's hand from harming Isaac with the words, "for now I know that you are one who fears God, as you did not withhold your son, your only one, from Me" (Genesis 22:12). Does this then mean that before the trial of Abraham, God did not know what Abraham might do? If yes, would you argue that an ignorant God is less cruel than an all-knowing God who could have anticipated Abraham's response?

19. What might be different about the story if God had commanded Sarah to sacrifice Isaac?

20. Do you think it will ever be possible for Isaac to forgive his father? To forgive God?

21. Do you believe that God always requires that we sacrifice (or be willing to sacrifice) what we love most?

5. Finding a Wife: Eliezer's Ultimate Test

The Bible Story: From Genesis 24

Genesis 24:1] Abraham was old, well advanced in years, and the Eternal had blessed Abraham in every way. **2]** Abraham now said to his slave, the elder of his household, who had oversight of all that was his, "Put your hand under my thigh, **3]** so that I may have you swear by the Eternal, God of heaven and God of earth, that you will not take a wife for my son from among the daughters of the Canaanites, in whose midst I dwell. **4]** Rather, you shall go to my land, my birthplace, and get a wife for my son Isaac." . . .

12] [The slave] prayed: "Eternal One, God of my master Abraham, please bring me luck today, and do a kindness for my master Abraham. **13]** Here I am standing at the water-fount, and the daughters of the townspeople are going forth to draw water; **14]** the girl to whom I say, 'Tip your pitcher and let me drink,' and who replies, 'Drink; and let me water your camels, too'—let her be the one You have designated for Your servant Isaac; that is how I shall know that You have done a kindness for my master."

15] Before he was done praying, Rebekah, who had been born to Bethuel, son of

כד ¹ וְאַבְרָהָם זָקֵן בָּא בַּיָּמִים וַיהֹוָה בֵּרַךְ אֶת־אַבְרָהָם בַּכֹּל: ² וַיֹּאמֶר אַבְרָהָם אֶל־עַבְדּוֹ זְקַן בֵּיתוֹ הַמֹּשֵׁל בְּכָל־אֲשֶׁר־לוֹ שִׂים־נָא יָדְךָ תַּחַת יְרֵכִי: ³ וְאַשְׁבִּיעֲךָ בַּיהֹוָה אֱלֹהֵי הַשָּׁמַיִם וֵאלֹהֵי הָאָרֶץ אֲשֶׁר לֹא־תִקַּח אִשָּׁה לִבְנִי מִבְּנוֹת הַכְּנַעֲנִי אֲשֶׁר אָנֹכִי יוֹשֵׁב בְּקִרְבּוֹ: ⁴ כִּי אֶל־אַרְצִי וְאֶל־מוֹלַדְתִּי תֵּלֵךְ וְלָקַחְתָּ אִשָּׁה לִבְנִי לְיִצְחָק:

¹² וַיֹּאמַר | יְהֹוָה אֱלֹהֵי אֲדֹנִי אַבְרָהָם הַקְרֵה־נָא לְפָנַי הַיּוֹם וַעֲשֵׂה־חֶסֶד עִם אֲדֹנִי אַבְרָהָם: ¹³ הִנֵּה אָנֹכִי נִצָּב עַל־עֵין הַמָּיִם וּבְנוֹת אַנְשֵׁי הָעִיר יֹצְאֹת לִשְׁאֹב מָיִם: ¹⁴ וְהָיָה הַנַּעַר הַנַּעֲרָה אֲשֶׁר אֹמַר אֵלֶיהָ הַטִּי־נָא כַדֵּךְ וְאֶשְׁתֶּה וְאָמְרָה שְׁתֵה וְגַם־גְּמַלֶּיךָ אַשְׁקֶה אֹתָהּ הֹכַחְתָּ לְעַבְדְּךָ לְיִצְחָק וּבָהּ אֵדַע כִּי־עָשִׂיתָ חֶסֶד עִם־אֲדֹנִי:

¹⁵ וַיְהִי־הוּא טֶרֶם כִּלָּה לְדַבֵּר וְהִנֵּה רִבְקָה יֹצֵאת אֲשֶׁר יֻלְּדָה לִבְתוּאֵל בֶּן־

Milcah, wife of Abraham's brother Nahor, was going forth with her pitcher on her shoulder. 16] She was an exceedingly beautiful girl, of marriageable age, whom no man had yet known. She went down to the spring, filled her pitcher, and went up.

17] The slave ran toward her and said, "Let me sip a little water from your pitcher." 18] And she replied, "Drink, sir!" Quickly she lowered her pitcher on her hand and let him drink. 19] The drinking done, she said, "I will draw some for your camels, too, till they are done drinking." 20] Quickly she emptied her pitcher in the trough and she again ran to the well to draw water, drawing water for all his camels.

21] The man stood staring at her, silent, in order to learn whether or not the Eternal had cleared the way for him. . . .

33] But when food was put in front of him, the man said, "I will not eat until I have had my say." He [Laban] said, "Speak!" 34] "I am the slave of Abraham," said he, 35] "and the Eternal has blessed my master exceedingly and made him rich, giving him sheep and cattle, silver and gold, male and female slaves, camels and donkeys. 36] Sarah, my master's wife, bore him a son in her old age, and my master has given him everything he owns. 37] My master adjured me, saying, 'You must not choose a wife for my son from among the daughters of the Canaanites, in whose land I now live. 38] Go, rather, to my father's

מִלְכָּה אֵשֶׁת נָחוֹר אֲחִי אַבְרָהָם וְכַדָּהּ עַל־שִׁכְמָהּ: 16 וְהַנַּעֲרָ֗ טֹבַ֤ת מַרְאֶה֙ מְאֹ֔ד בְּתוּלָ֕ה וְאִ֖ישׁ לֹ֣א יְדָעָ֑הּ וַתֵּ֣רֶד הָעַ֔יְנָה וַתְּמַלֵּ֥א כַדָּ֖הּ וַתָּֽעַל:

17 וַיָּ֥רָץ הָעֶ֖בֶד לִקְרָאתָ֑הּ וַיֹּ֕אמֶר הַגְמִיאִ֥ינִי נָ֛א מְעַט־מַ֖יִם מִכַּדֵּֽךְ: 18 וַתֹּ֖אמֶר שְׁתֵ֣ה אֲדֹנִ֑י וַתְּמַהֵ֗ר וַתֹּ֧רֶד כַּדָּ֛הּ עַל־יָדָ֖הּ וַתַּשְׁקֵֽהוּ: 19 וַתְּכַ֖ל לְהַשְׁקֹת֑וֹ וַתֹּ֗אמֶר גַּ֤ם לִגְמַלֶּ֙יךָ֙ אֶשְׁאָ֔ב עַ֥ד אִם־כִּלּ֖וּ לִשְׁתֹּֽת: 20 וַתְּמַהֵ֗ר וַתְּעַ֤ר כַּדָּהּ֙ אֶל־הַשֹּׁ֔קֶת וַתָּ֥רָץ ע֛וֹד אֶל־הַבְּאֵ֖ר לִשְׁאֹ֑ב וַתִּשְׁאַ֖ב לְכָל־גְּמַלָּֽיו:

21 וְהָאִ֥ישׁ מִשְׁתָּאֵ֖ה לָ֑הּ מַחֲרִ֕ישׁ לָדַ֗עַת הַֽהִצְלִ֧יחַ יְהֹוָ֛ה דַּרְכּ֖וֹ אִם־לֹֽא:

33 וַיּוּשַׂם֩ לְפָנָ֨יו לֶאֱכֹ֜ל וַיֹּ֙אמֶר֙ לֹ֣א אֹכַ֔ל עַ֥ד אִם־דִּבַּ֖רְתִּי דְּבָרָ֑י וַיֹּ֖אמֶר דַּבֵּֽר: 34 וַיֹּאמַ֑ר עֶ֥בֶד אַבְרָהָ֖ם אָנֹֽכִי: 35 וַיהֹוָ֞ה בֵּרַ֧ךְ אֶת־אֲדֹנִ֛י מְאֹ֖ד וַיִּגְדָּ֑ל וַיִּתֶּן־ל֞וֹ צֹ֣אן וּבָקָ֗ר וְכֶ֤סֶף וְזָהָב֙ וַעֲבָדִ֣ם וּשְׁפָחֹ֔ת וּגְמַלִּ֖ים וַחֲמֹרִֽים: 36 וַתֵּ֡לֶד שָׂרָה֩ אֵ֨שֶׁת אֲדֹנִ֥י בֵן֙ לַֽאדֹנִ֔י אַחֲרֵ֖י זִקְנָתָ֑הּ וַיִּתֶּן־ל֖וֹ אֶת־כָּל־אֲשֶׁר־לֽוֹ: 37 וַיַּשְׁבִּעֵ֣נִי אֲדֹנִ֖י לֵאמֹ֑ר לֹא־תִקַּ֤ח אִשָּׁה֙ לִבְנִ֔י מִבְּנוֹת֙ הַֽכְּנַעֲנִ֔י אֲשֶׁ֥ר אָנֹכִ֖י יֹשֵׁ֥ב בְּאַרְצֽוֹ: 38 אִם־לֹ֧א אֶל־בֵּית־אָבִ֛י תֵּלֵ֖ךְ וְאֶל־

people, to my relations, and take a wife for my son.' 39] I said to my master, 'What if the woman will not follow me?' 40] He answered, 'The Eternal, before whom I have walked, will send an angel with you who will clear the way for you. You will take a wife for my son from my clan, from my father's family. 41] You will be free from your obligation only if you go to my relations and they refuse you. In that case, you will be free from your obligation.'

42] "When I came to the well today, I prayed, 'Eternal One, God of my master Abraham, if You truly intend to clear the way on which I am going, 43] here I am at the water-fount. When a young woman comes out to get water, I will say to her, "Please give me a drink of water from your pitcher." 44] If she answers, "Go ahead and drink, and I will draw water for your camels, too"—let her be the one You have designated as the wife for my master's son.' 45] Before I had finished rehearsing my thought, Rebekah came with a water pitcher on her shoulder and went down to the well to get water. I said to her: 'Please give me a drink.' 46] She quickly lowered her pitcher and said, 'Drink, and I will water your camels, too.' So I drank, and she gave water to the camels, too. 47] I asked her, 'Whose daughter are you?' And she answered, 'I am the daughter of Bethuel son of Nahor and Milcah.' Then I put the ring on her nose and the bracelets on her wrists. 48] I knelt down in worship of the Eternal, and I praised the Eternal God of

מִשְׁפַּחְתִּי וְלָקַחְתָּ אִשָּׁה לִבְנִי: 39 וָאֹמַר אֶל־אֲדֹנִי אֻלַי לֹא־תֵלֵךְ הָאִשָּׁה אַחֲרָי: 40 וַיֹּאמֶר אֵלָי יְהֹוָה אֲשֶׁר־הִתְהַלַּכְתִּי לְפָנָיו יִשְׁלַח מַלְאָכוֹ אִתָּךְ וְהִצְלִיחַ דַּרְכֶּךָ וְלָקַחְתָּ אִשָּׁה לִבְנִי מִמִּשְׁפַּחְתִּי וּמִבֵּית אָבִי: 41 אָז תִּנָּקֶה מֵאָלָתִי כִּי תָבוֹא אֶל־מִשְׁפַּחְתִּי וְאִם־לֹא יִתְּנוּ לָךְ וְהָיִיתָ נָקִי מֵאָלָתִי:

42 וָאָבֹא הַיּוֹם אֶל־הָעָיִן וָאֹמַר יְהֹוָה אֱלֹהֵי אֲדֹנִי אַבְרָהָם אִם־יֶשְׁךָ־נָּא מַצְלִיחַ דַּרְכִּי אֲשֶׁר אָנֹכִי הֹלֵךְ עָלֶיהָ: 43 הִנֵּה אָנֹכִי נִצָּב עַל־עֵין הַמָּיִם וְהָיָה הָעַלְמָה הַיֹּצֵאת לִשְׁאֹב וְאָמַרְתִּי אֵלֶיהָ הַשְׁקִינִי־נָא מְעַט־מַיִם מִכַּדֵּךְ: 44 וְאָמְרָה אֵלַי גַּם־אַתָּה שְׁתֵה וְגַם לִגְמַלֶּיךָ אֶשְׁאָב הִוא הָאִשָּׁה אֲשֶׁר־הֹכִיחַ יְהֹוָה לְבֶן־ אֲדֹנִי: 45 אֲנִי טֶרֶם אֲכַלֶּה לְדַבֵּר אֶל־לִבִּי וְהִנֵּה רִבְקָה יֹצֵאת וְכַדָּהּ עַל־שִׁכְמָהּ וַתֵּרֶד הָעַיְנָה וַתִּשְׁאָב וָאֹמַר אֵלֶיהָ הַשְׁקִינִי נָא: 46 וַתְּמַהֵר וַתּוֹרֶד כַּדָּהּ מֵעָלֶיהָ וַתֹּאמֶר שְׁתֵה וְגַם־גְּמַלֶּיךָ אַשְׁקֶה וָאֵשְׁתְּ וְגַם הַגְּמַלִּים הִשְׁקָתָה: 47 וָאֶשְׁאַל אֹתָהּ וָאֹמַר בַּת־מִי אַתְּ וַתֹּאמֶר בַּת־בְּתוּאֵל בֶּן־נָחוֹר אֲשֶׁר יָלְדָה־לּוֹ מִלְכָּה וָאָשִׂם הַנֶּזֶם עַל־ אַפָּהּ וְהַצְּמִידִים עַל־יָדֶיהָ: 48 וָאֶקֹּד וָאֶשְׁתַּחֲוֶה לַיהֹוָה וָאֲבָרֵךְ אֶת־יְהֹוָה

my master Abraham, who had led me on the right path to get the daughter of my master's brother for his son. 49] And now, if you mean to treat my master with faithful kindness, tell me; if not, tell me, and I will turn in another direction."

50] Laban and Bethuel responded by saying, "This matter has emanated from the Eternal; we cannot answer you one way or another. 51] Look—Rebekah is before you; take [her] and go, and let her be your master's son's wife as the Eternal has decreed!"

52] When Abraham's slave heard their words he bowed low to the Eternal, 53] and brought out silver and gold objects, and articles of clothing, and gave them to Rebekah; and to her brother and mother he gave precious gifts. 54] So he and the men with him ate and drank and stayed overnight.

When they got up in the morning he said, "Send me off to my master." 55] Her brother and mother said, "Let the girl stay with us another few days—ten, perhaps—afterward she may go." 56] But he said to them, "Do not delay me, now that the Eternal has cleared the way for me; send me off and let me go to my master." 57] They answered, "Let us call the girl and see what she has to say." 58] So they called Rebekah and asked her, "Will you go with this man?" And she said, "I will go."

אֱלֹהֵי אֲדֹנִי אַבְרָהָם אֲשֶׁר הִנְחַנִי בְּדֶרֶךְ אֱמֶת לָקַחַת אֶת־בַּת־אֲחִי אֲדֹנִי לִבְנוֹ:

49 וְעַתָּה אִם־יֶשְׁכֶם עֹשִׂים חֶסֶד וֶאֱמֶת אֶת־אֲדֹנִי הַגִּידוּ לִי וְאִם־לֹא הַגִּידוּ לִי וְאֶפְנֶה עַל־יָמִין אוֹ עַל־שְׂמֹאל:

50 וַיַּעַן לָבָן וּבְתוּאֵל וַיֹּאמְרוּ מֵיְהֹוָה יָצָא הַדָּבָר לֹא נוּכַל דַּבֵּר אֵלֶיךָ רַע אוֹ־טוֹב: 51 הִנֵּה־רִבְקָה לְפָנֶיךָ קַח וָלֵךְ וּתְהִי אִשָּׁה לְבֶן־אֲדֹנֶיךָ כַּאֲשֶׁר דִּבֶּר יְהֹוָה:

52 וַיְהִי כַּאֲשֶׁר שָׁמַע עֶבֶד אַבְרָהָם אֶת־דִּבְרֵיהֶם וַיִּשְׁתַּחוּ אַרְצָה לַיהֹוָה: 53 וַיּוֹצֵא הָעֶבֶד כְּלֵי־כֶסֶף וּכְלֵי זָהָב וּבְגָדִים וַיִּתֵּן לְרִבְקָה וּמִגְדָּנֹת נָתַן לְאָחִיהָ וּלְאִמָּהּ: 54 וַיֹּאכְלוּ וַיִּשְׁתּוּ הוּא וְהָאֲנָשִׁים אֲשֶׁר־עִמּוֹ וַיָּלִינוּ וַיָּקוּמוּ בַבֹּקֶר וַיֹּאמֶר שַׁלְּחֻנִי לַאדֹנִי: 55 וַיֹּאמֶר אָחִיהָ וְאִמָּהּ תֵּשֵׁב הַנַּעַר הַנַּעֲרָה אִתָּנוּ יָמִים אוֹ עָשׂוֹר אַחַר תֵּלֵךְ: 56 וַיֹּאמֶר אֲלֵהֶם אַל־תְּאַחֲרוּ אֹתִי וַיהֹוָה הִצְלִיחַ דַּרְכִּי שַׁלְּחוּנִי וְאֵלְכָה לַאדֹנִי: 57 וַיֹּאמְרוּ נִקְרָא לַנַּעַר לַנַּעֲרָה וְנִשְׁאֲלָה אֶת־פִּיהָ: 58 וַיִּקְרְאוּ לְרִבְקָה וַיֹּאמְרוּ אֵלֶיהָ הֲתֵלְכִי עִם־הָאִישׁ הַזֶּה וַתֹּאמֶר אֵלֵךְ:

59] They then sent their sister Rebekah off with her nurse, with Abraham's slave, and with his men, 60] bestowing this blessing upon Rebekah: "Sister, may you become thousands of myriads; may your descendants take possession of the gates of their foes!" 61] Rebekah and her servant girls got up and mounted the camels and followed the man, as the slave took Rebekah and went off.

62] Now Isaac was coming from the approach to Be'er-lachai-ro'i, for he was living in the area of the Negev. 63] Going out toward evening to stroll in the field, Isaac looked up and saw—camels coming! 64] And Rebekah looked up: seeing Isaac, she got off the camel 65] and said to the slave: "Who is this man striding in the field coming to meet us?" "He is my master," said the slave. Taking a veil, she covered herself. 66] The slave then told Isaac all that he had done. 67] And Isaac brought her into the tent of his mother Sarah; he took Rebekah, and she became his wife and he loved her. Thus did Isaac take comfort after [the death of] his mother.

59 וַיְשַׁלְּחוּ אֶת־רִבְקָה אֲחֹתָם וְאֶת־מֵנִקְתָּהּ וְאֶת־עֶבֶד אַבְרָהָם וְאֶת־אֲנָשָׁיו: 60 וַיְבָרְכוּ אֶת־רִבְקָה וַיֹּאמְרוּ לָהּ אֲחֹתֵנוּ אַתְּ הֲיִי לְאַלְפֵי רְבָבָה וְיִירַשׁ זַרְעֵךְ אֵת שַׁעַר שֹׂנְאָיו: 61 וַתָּקָם רִבְקָה וְנַעֲרֹתֶיהָ וַתִּרְכַּבְנָה עַל־הַגְּמַלִּים וַתֵּלַכְנָה אַחֲרֵי הָאִישׁ וַיִּקַּח הָעֶבֶד אֶת־רִבְקָה וַיֵּלַךְ:

62 וְיִצְחָק בָּא מִבּוֹא בְּאֵר לַחַי רֹאִי וְהוּא יוֹשֵׁב בְּאֶרֶץ הַנֶּגֶב: 63 וַיֵּצֵא יִצְחָק לָשׂוּחַ בַּשָּׂדֶה לִפְנוֹת עָרֶב וַיִּשָּׂא עֵינָיו וַיַּרְא וְהִנֵּה גְמַלִּים בָּאִים: 64 וַתִּשָּׂא רִבְקָה אֶת־עֵינֶיהָ וַתֵּרֶא אֶת־יִצְחָק וַתִּפֹּל מֵעַל הַגָּמָל: 65 וַתֹּאמֶר אֶל־הָעֶבֶד מִי־הָאִישׁ הַלָּזֶה הַהֹלֵךְ בַּשָּׂדֶה לִקְרָאתֵנוּ וַיֹּאמֶר הָעֶבֶד הוּא אֲדֹנִי וַתִּקַּח הַצָּעִיף וַתִּתְכָּס: 66 וַיְסַפֵּר הָעֶבֶד לְיִצְחָק אֵת כָּל־הַדְּבָרִים אֲשֶׁר עָשָׂה: 67 וַיְבִאֶהָ יִצְחָק הָאֹהֱלָה שָׂרָה אִמּוֹ וַיִּקַּח אֶת־רִבְקָה וַתְּהִי־לוֹ לְאִשָּׁה וַיֶּאֱהָבֶהָ וַיִּנָּחֵם יִצְחָק אַחֲרֵי אִמּוֹ:

Understanding the Story

Many students of Torah find the procedure to procure a suitable wife for Isaac rather strange. The narrative reflects the custom of its time, in which Isaac's father Abraham initiates the marriage transaction. Being too old himself, he commissions his servant Eliezer. But he gives the servant no precise instructions as to the kind of wife to look for, only that she is to be sought in the land of Abraham's birth. Abraham seems certain that the right wife will be found because Isaac's marriage will be the inevitable fulfillment of God's purposes.

The camels are used to test the character of Isaac's bride-to-be. Before Abraham's servant begins his search, he prays for personal divine guidance. This is the first spontaneous prayer in the Bible. The only criteria the servant lays down is that the girl who will ultimately become Isaac's wife be generous and hospitable to strangers, and kind to animals. What is odd is that these criteria are apparently more important to him than the family relationship, since he gives Rebekah the costly gifts that he brought with him even before discovering her identity.

In the subsequent discussions between the servant and Rebekah's family, we are surely struck by the prominence of her brother Laban. Strangely, he plays an even more dominant role in the story than Rebekah's own father, Bethuel.

The servant brings Rebekah back with him to meet Isaac. Their meeting contains several unusual elements. Why does Rebekah cover her face with the veil? What is the significance of Isaac taking Rebekah into "the tent of his mother Sarah" (Genesis 24:67)? The Torah then relates that Isaac takes Rebekah as his wife, and he loves her. Many commentators ask why the Torah mentions Isaac's love for Rebekah after having taken her to be his wife, and not beforehand.

The Bible story leaves us with many other questions as well. Why does Abraham command his servant not to take a wife from the Canaanites? Were the inhabitants of Babylon—Aram-naharaim—any better than the Canaanites? Why does Abraham saddle his servant with such an important task? Should Abraham not find a suitable wife for his son by himself? The plea of Abraham's servant poses another problem. The literal rendering of his plea is "Please send me good chance this day" (Genesis 24:12). Surely there is a self-contradiction in praying to God to engineer a coincidence.

What is also striking is that Rebekah does not conduct herself *exactly* as Eliezer outlined in his prayer. She does not reply, "Drink; and let me water your camels, too" (Genesis 24:14). First she briefly indicates her willing fulfillment of his request with the words, "Drink, sir!" and then does everything to satisfy his thirst. Only afterwards does she proceed to fulfill the second requirement of giving the camels drink. Thus, one might ask: Does she thereby do more or less than is expected of her?

Finally, at the end of the story, when Eliezer asks to know what course next to pursue, Laban and Bethuel answer: "This matters has emanated from the Eternal" (Genesis 24:50). How does it happen that this matter comes forth from God, and how do these apparent heathens, Laban and Bethuel, come to acknowledge it?

From the Commentators

Rebeccah purposely did not add the words "I will also water your camels" immediately. Had she added the words immediately, before Eliezer had finished drinking, the latter might have cut short his own drinking knowing that Rebeccah would still have to go to the trouble of watering the camels. As long as she had not offered this, Eliezer had no reason to entertain such considerations.

Or HaChayim: Commentary on the Torah by Rabbi Chayim ben Attar, vol. 1, trans. Eliyahu Munk (Jerusalem: Eliyahu Munk, 1995), p. 196.

Rivkah was very precise, choosing her words carefully, not saving words as Eliezer had done when he said about what he expected her to say: "drink and I will also let your camels drink," all in one breath. Had she done the same, she would have drawn an unfavourable comparison between man and beast, putting them on the same level. In order to avoid giving such an impression, she waited until he had finished drinking before volunteering to also draw water for the camels.

Haketav Vehakabbalah: Torah Commentary by Rabbi Yaakov Tzevi Mecklenburg, vol. 1, trans. Eliyahu Munk (New York: Lambda Publishers, 2001), p. 305.

If Isaac had married one of them, it would no longer have been likely that Israel would dispossess the Caananites from their land, since they would be brothers, just as they were not to provoke war with Moab, Ammon, and Edom. It was also within the Torah's intention, by telling this story at length, to keep Israel away from intermarrying with the Caananites.

Shmuel David Luzzato (Shadal), *The Book of Genesis: A Commentary by Shadal*, trans. Daniel A. Klein (Northvale, NJ: Jason Aronson, 1998), p. 214.

Why did Abraham send Eliezer to find a wife for Isaac among his own family rather than among the Caananites, even though both were idolaters? The reason is that the Caananites, in addition to idolatry, were also corrupt morally and sexually, as we see in the verse (Lev. 18:3), "After the doings of the Land of Caanan, where I am bringing you, you shall not do." Now, even though Abraham's family were idolaters, they were moral people, and that was why he chose them for his son.

Nissim ben Reuben Gerondi (HaRan), in *Torah Gems*, vol. 1, ed. Aharon Yaakov Greenberg, trans. Shmuel Himelstein (Tel Aviv: Yavneh Publishing House, 1998), p. 186.

Hizzkuni says that had Isaac married a Canaanite, people might attribute his claim to the land to his wife's inheritance, not to God's promise.

David L. Lieber and Jules Harlow, eds., *Etz Hayim: Torah and Commentary* (New York and Philadelphia: Rabbinical Assembly and Jewish Publication Society, 2001), p. 130.

A single camel (and here there were 10!) requires at least 25 gallons of water to regain the weight it loses in the course of a long journey. It takes a camel about 10 minutes to drink this amount of water. [The implication, here, is that Rebekah was extremely patient and kind to the camels, as it was very tedious to give the camels all their required amount of water.]

Etz Hayim: Torah and Commentary, p. 133.

"We cannot speak to you bad or good" [Genesis 24:50]. We can understand why they cannot say anything bad in the circumstances, but why can't they say anything good either? "I have already mentioned earlier, writes

---

Etz Hayim

Published by the Rabbinical Assembly and the United Synagogue for Conservative Judaism and among the newest Torah commentaries to enter the field, *Etz Hayim* is a product of the Conservative Movement. Its senior editor is David Lieber, and the editor of the *p'shat* commentary is Chaim Potok. The book also has a unique feature in that it presents a *d'rash* commentary as well, edited by the best-selling author Rabbi Harold Kushner. *Etz Hayim* incorporates the very best of modern Bible scholarship derived from the works of internationally renowned scholars who are or have been associated with the Conservative Movement. At the end of the book there is a series of outstanding essays on a broad range of topics, including Biblical Archaeology, Women, Ecology, Israel, Reward and Punishment, and Dietary Laws.

Hatam Sofer, "that if the husband is a wastrel, the wife should be careful and limit the outlay of her house, so that the family can survive and not squander all its money. If the man is stingy, then his wife should be generous and give to worthwhile causes." By this, the husband and wife balance each other out. Now, as Bethuel and Laban did not know Isaac and what he was like, and all they knew was that this came from God, they were afraid to speak either good or bad, because based on Isaac's traits, what might otherwise appear good would in reality be bad.

Hatam Sofer, in *Torah Gems*, vol. 1, p. 194.

From among the many maidens who will gather at this time to draw water, [Eliezer] intended to select the most beautiful one—and ask her for a drink. Inasmuch, however, as in addition to selecting the one who was the most beautiful in form and appearance he will still need to test her character—that will have been accomplished when she declares: *Drink! and I will also give to your camels to drink.* He will know with certainty then that she is a good woman—of good character traits, humble, generous and compassionate—since she will have passed the following tests. (i) *I stand here by the spring*—hence the maiden would be expected to reply, instead: "Since you are standing at the spring, why don't you drink directly from the water in front of you!" (ii) *The daughters of the men of the city come out*—hence she could say, "Why do you want that I, particularly, should give you to drink when I have already placed the jar upon my shoulders? Go to another of the maidens who still has her jar in her hand—and let her give you water." Accordingly, *let the maiden*—that maiden who has found favor in my eyes because of her beauty—*to whom I say "Please, lower your jar that I may drink."* For I will purposely ask that maiden that she herself lower her jar. (iii) This involves the considerable exertion of lowering the jar from her shoulder into her hand, and she would be justified in becoming angry and declaring: "Why don't you yourself, then, take the jar from my shoulder and drink, and spare me the effort of it?" (iv) That she will say to me, *"Drink and I will also give your camels to drink"*—a mark of her wisdom and goodness of heart, since it would mean that she had concluded by then that this man probably has some pain in his hand which prevents him from drawing water from the spring or from taking down the jar by himself; and that if he lacks the strength to draw water for himself he is certainly not strong enough to draw water for his camels. She will then have been stirred by the generosity and goodness of her heart to take pity upon the suffering of these creatures and to offer water to the camels as well.

Malbim (Rabbenu Meir Leibush ben Yechiel Michel), *Commentary on the Torah,*
Book Two, trans. Zvi Faier (Jerusalem: Hillel Press, 1979), pp. 276–278.

In the Middle Assyrian law the veil is a mark of distinction and the prerogative of a free woman, but this is exceptional in the Near East, where wives generally went about unveiled. There is evidence, however, that the veiling of the bride was part of the marriage ceremony. . . . The Middle Assyrian laws make the raising of a concubine to the status of wife contingent upon her being veiled in the presence of the court. In light of all this, Rebekah's veiling herself has both symbolic and socio-legal significance. It is an unspoken signal to Isaac that she is his bride.

Nahum Sarna

Nahum Sarna (1923–2005) was professor of biblical studies at Brandeis University and translator for the Jewish Publication Society's new translation of the Bible. His Bible commentaries attempt to synthesize the rich findings of multifaceted research into the Bible and into the civilizations of the ancient Near East that have a bearing upon the biblical text.

Nahum Sarna, *The JPS Torah Commentary: Genesis*
(Philadelphia: Jewish Publication Society, 1989), p. 170.

Questions for Discussion

1. Why do you think that Abraham commands his servant Eliezer not to take a wife for his son Isaac from the Canaanite people? Of the commentators who discussed this question, with which do you agree? Why?

2. According to the biblical story, what are the criteria that make for a good and suitable wife?

3. The Torah relates with much detail every action of Abraham's servant in chapter 24 until verse 26. His experiences are then recapitulated in the form of his report to Rebekah's family in verses 33–49 of the same chapter. What are the differences in the recapitulation, and can you think of a reason why there would be these differences?

4. How did marriage in biblical times differ from modern-day marriage?

5. In verse 60, Rebekah is blessed with the blessing of thousands. Where in the modern-day marriage ceremony is this verse used? What is its purpose?

6. Does Rebekah conduct herself in exactly the same manner as the servant outlined in his original prayer (hint: compare verses 14 and 18–19)? Based on what Rebekah does when she sees the servant and his camels, is Rebekah's conduct more or less meritorious as compared to the servant's original criteria as stipulated at the beginning of chapter 24?

7. What might be the reason that Rebekah covers herself with a veil in verse 65? What is the purpose of a bride's veil in the modern wedding ceremony?

8. In verse 67, we are told that Isaac brought Rebekah "into the tent of his mother Sarah; he took Rebekah, and she became his wife and he loved her." Comment on the sequence of events in this verse. How does the sequence relate to modern-day marriage?

9. Abraham's servant devises a test by which he could determine Rebekah's values and those of her family. What are your most important values? How can you determine whether or not your partner in a possible long-term relationship shares those values? What test or questions should be considered when choosing such a partner?

10. The text (Genesis 24:16) states that Rebekah is *tovat mareh,* "fair to look upon." Why do you think that the Bible chooses not to tell us anything about the specific details of Rebekah's physical characteristics (e.g., height, skin complexion, and the like)? What do you think ultimately defines her as *tovat mareh* in the servant's eyes?

11. What do you think is the best way to find a suitable marriage partner? How can you judge whether a person will be loyal or loving?

12. Rebekah's feelings toward Isaac are not recorded in the text. What do you make of this absence? Create a midrash to fill in this blank.

6. The Blessing of Jacob and Esau: How Could Isaac Cheat?

The Bible Story: From Genesis 25 and 27

Genesis 25:22] The children pressed against each other inside [Rebekah]. She thought: "If this is so, why do I exist?" So she went to inquire of the Eternal.   **23]** The Eternal One said to her:

Two peoples are in your belly;
two nations shall branch off from each
  other [as they emerge] from your
  womb.
One people shall prevail over the other;
the elder shall serve the younger. . . .

27] When the boys grew up, Esau became a skillful hunter, a man of the outdoors; but Jacob was a homespun man, keeping to the tents.   **28]** Isaac favored Esau, because he [Esau] put game in his mouth, but Rebekah favored Jacob.

29] [One day,] when Jacob was cooking a stew, Esau came in from the [hunting] field. He was famished,   **30]** and he said to Jacob, "I'm famished; let me gulp down some of that red stuff!" (That is why he was named Edom.)   **31]** Jacob said, "Sell me your birthright here and now."   **32]** And Esau said, "Here I am going to die; what good is the birthright to me?"   **33]** But Jacob said, "Confirm it to me by oath here and now." So he swore it to him,

כה   22 וַיִּתְרֹצֲצ֤וּ הַבָּנִים֙ בְּקִרְבָּ֔הּ
וַתֹּ֣אמֶר אִם־כֵּ֔ן לָ֥מָּה זֶּ֖ה אָנֹ֑כִי וַתֵּ֖לֶךְ
לִדְרֹ֥שׁ אֶת־יְהֹוָֽה׃   23 וַיֹּ֨אמֶר יְהֹוָ֜ה לָ֗הּ
שְׁנֵ֤י גֹיִים֙ בְּבִטְנֵ֔ךְ
וּשְׁנֵ֣י לְאֻמִּ֔ים מִמֵּעַ֖יִךְ יִפָּרֵ֑דוּ
וּלְאֹם֙ מִלְאֹ֣ם יֶֽאֱמָ֔ץ
וְרַ֖ב יַעֲבֹ֥ד צָעִֽיר׃

27 וַֽיִּגְדְּלוּ֙ הַנְּעָרִ֔ים וַיְהִ֣י עֵשָׂ֗ו אִ֛ישׁ יֹדֵ֥עַ
צַ֖יִד אִ֣ישׁ שָׂדֶ֑ה וְיַעֲקֹב֙ אִ֣ישׁ תָּ֔ם יֹשֵׁ֖ב
אֹהָלִֽים׃   28 וַיֶּאֱהַ֥ב יִצְחָ֛ק אֶת־עֵשָׂ֖ו כִּי־
צַ֣יִד בְּפִ֑יו וְרִבְקָ֖ה אֹהֶ֥בֶת אֶֽת־יַעֲקֹֽב׃

29 וַיָּ֥זֶד יַעֲקֹ֖ב נָזִ֑יד וַיָּבֹ֥א עֵשָׂ֛ו מִן־הַשָּׂדֶ֖ה
וְה֥וּא עָיֵֽף׃   30 וַיֹּ֨אמֶר עֵשָׂ֜ו אֶֽל־יַעֲקֹ֗ב
הַלְעִיטֵ֤נִי נָא֙ מִן־הָֽאָדֹ֤ם הָֽאָדֹם֙ הַזֶּ֔ה כִּ֥י
עָיֵ֖ף אָנֹ֑כִי עַל־כֵּ֥ן קָרָֽא־שְׁמ֖וֹ אֱדֽוֹם׃
31 וַיֹּ֖אמֶר יַעֲקֹ֑ב מִכְרָ֥ה כַיּ֛וֹם אֶת־בְּכֹרָֽתְךָ֖
לִֽי׃   32 וַיֹּ֣אמֶר עֵשָׂ֔ו הִנֵּ֛ה אָנֹכִ֥י הוֹלֵ֖ךְ
לָמ֑וּת וְלָמָּה־זֶּ֥ה לִ֖י בְּכֹרָֽה׃   33 וַיֹּ֣אמֶר
יַעֲקֹ֗ב הִשָּׁ֤בְעָה לִּי֙ כַּיּ֔וֹם וַיִּשָּׁבַ֖ע ל֑וֹ וַיִּמְכֹּ֥ר

and sold his birthright to Jacob.   34] Jacob then gave Esau bread and lentil stew. He ate, drank, got up, and left. Thus did Esau disdain his birthright....

27:1] When Isaac had grown old and his eyesight had dimmed, he called his elder son Esau, saying to him, "My son!" "Here I am," he answered.   2] "Look now," said he. "I have grown old, [and] for all I know I may die any day.   3] So pick up your weapons—your quiver and your bow—and go out to the countryside and hunt me some game.   4] Then you can make me tasty dishes such as I like and bring [them] to me and I will eat, so that I can give you my heartfelt blessing before I die."

5] As Isaac was speaking to his son Esau, Rebekah was listening; and when Esau went to the countryside to hunt for some game to bring [him], 6] Rebekah said this to her son Jacob, "Look—I heard your father speaking to your brother Esau, saying,   7] 'Bring me game and make me tasty dishes, that I may eat—and [then] bless you before the Eternal before my death.'

8] "Now, son, listen to me, to what I am instructing you: 9] Go to the flock and bring me two tender kids, and I will make them into tasty dishes for your father, such as he likes.   10] You will bring them to your father and he will eat, so that he may bless you before his death."   11] But Jacob said to his mother Rebekah, "Look—my

אֶת־בְּכֹרָתוֹ לְיַעֲקֹב: 34 וְיַעֲקֹב נָתַן לְעֵשָׂו לֶחֶם וּנְזִיד עֲדָשִׁים וַיֹּאכַל וַיֵּשְׁתְּ וַיָּקָם וַיֵּלַךְ וַיִּבֶז עֵשָׂו אֶת־הַבְּכֹרָה:

כז 1 וַיְהִי כִּי־זָקֵן יִצְחָק וַתִּכְהֶיןָ עֵינָיו מֵרְאֹת וַיִּקְרָא אֶת־עֵשָׂו | בְּנוֹ הַגָּדֹל וַיֹּאמֶר אֵלָיו בְּנִי וַיֹּאמֶר אֵלָיו הִנֵּנִי: 2 וַיֹּאמֶר הִנֵּה־נָא זָקַנְתִּי לֹא יָדַעְתִּי יוֹם מוֹתִי: 3 וְעַתָּה שָׂא־נָא כֵלֶיךָ תֶּלְיְךָ וְקַשְׁתֶּךָ וְצֵא הַשָּׂדֶה וְצוּדָה לִּי צידה צָיִד: 4 וַעֲשֵׂה־לִי מַטְעַמִּים כַּאֲשֶׁר אָהַבְתִּי וְהָבִיאָה לִּי וְאֹכֵלָה בַּעֲבוּר תְּבָרֶכְךָ נַפְשִׁי בְּטֶרֶם אָמוּת:

5 וְרִבְקָה שֹׁמַעַת בְּדַבֵּר יִצְחָק אֶל־עֵשָׂו בְּנוֹ וַיֵּלֶךְ עֵשָׂו הַשָּׂדֶה לָצוּד צַיִד לְהָבִיא: 6 וְרִבְקָה אָמְרָה אֶל־יַעֲקֹב בְּנָהּ לֵאמֹר הִנֵּה שָׁמַעְתִּי אֶת־אָבִיךָ מְדַבֵּר אֶל־עֵשָׂו אָחִיךָ לֵאמֹר: 7 הָבִיאָה לִּי צַיִד וַעֲשֵׂה־ לִי מַטְעַמִּים וְאֹכֵלָה וַאֲבָרֶכְכָה לִפְנֵי יְהֹוָה לִפְנֵי מוֹתִי:

8 וְעַתָּה בְנִי שְׁמַע בְּקֹלִי לַאֲשֶׁר אֲנִי מְצַוָּה אֹתָךְ: 9 לֶךְ־נָא אֶל־הַצֹּאן וְקַח־לִי מִשָּׁם שְׁנֵי גְּדָיֵי עִזִּים טֹבִים וְאֶעֱשֶׂה אֹתָם מַטְעַמִּים לְאָבִיךָ כַּאֲשֶׁר אָהֵב: 10 וְהֵבֵאתָ לְאָבִיךָ וְאָכָל בַּעֲבֻר אֲשֶׁר יְבָרֶכְךָ לִפְנֵי מוֹתוֹ: 11 וַיֹּאמֶר יַעֲקֹב אֶל־

brother Esau is a hairy man and I am a smooth-skinned man; 12] should my father feel me I will seem to him like a cheat, and I will bring a curse on myself, not a blessing!"

13] His mother then said to him, "Any curse that you get will be on me, son—just listen to me and go get [them] for me!" 14] So he went and got them and brought [them] to his mother, and his mother made tasty dishes, such as his father liked.

15] Rebekah now took the finest of her elder son Esau's garments that she had in the house, and dressed up her younger son Jacob. 16] The skins of the kids she wrapped on his hands and over the smooth part of his neck, 17] and she put the tasty food and the bread that she had made into her son Jacob's hand.

18] Going then to his father, he said, "Father!" and he replied: "Here I am; which son of mine are you?"

19] Jacob said to his father, "I am Esau your first-born; I have done as you told me; pray get up and sit and eat of my game so that you can give me your heartfelt blessing." 20] Isaac then said to his son: "How is it that you were able to find [game] so quickly, my son?" And he replied, "The Eternal your God made it happen for me." 21] "Pray come near me," said Isaac to Jacob, "so that I can feel you, son. Are you really my son Esau, or are you not?"

רִבְקָה אִמּוֹ הֵן עֵשָׂו אָחִי אִישׁ שָׂעִר וְאָנֹכִי אִישׁ חָלָק: 12 אוּלַי יְמֻשֵּׁנִי אָבִי וְהָיִיתִי בְעֵינָיו כִּמְתַעְתֵּעַ וְהֵבֵאתִי עָלַי קְלָלָה וְלֹא בְרָכָה:

13 וַתֹּאמֶר לוֹ אִמּוֹ עָלַי קִלְלָתְךָ בְּנִי אַךְ שְׁמַע בְּקֹלִי וְלֵךְ קַח־לִי: 14 וַיֵּלֶךְ וַיִּקַּח וַיָּבֵא לְאִמּוֹ וַתַּעַשׂ אִמּוֹ מַטְעַמִּים כַּאֲשֶׁר אָהֵב אָבִיו:

15 וַתִּקַּח רִבְקָה אֶת־בִּגְדֵי עֵשָׂו בְּנָהּ הַגָּדֹל הַחֲמֻדֹת אֲשֶׁר אִתָּהּ בַּבָּיִת וַתַּלְבֵּשׁ אֶת־יַעֲקֹב בְּנָהּ הַקָּטָן: 16 וְאֵת עֹרֹת גְּדָיֵי הָעִזִּים הִלְבִּישָׁה עַל־יָדָיו וְעַל חֶלְקַת צַוָּארָיו: 17 וַתִּתֵּן אֶת־הַמַּטְעַמִּים וְאֶת־הַלֶּחֶם אֲשֶׁר עָשָׂתָה בְּיַד יַעֲקֹב בְּנָהּ:

18 וַיָּבֹא אֶל־אָבִיו וַיֹּאמֶר אָבִי וַיֹּאמֶר הִנֶּנִּי מִי אַתָּה בְּנִי:

19 וַיֹּאמֶר יַעֲקֹב אֶל־אָבִיו אָנֹכִי עֵשָׂו בְּכֹרֶךָ עָשִׂיתִי כַּאֲשֶׁר דִּבַּרְתָּ אֵלָי קוּם־נָא שְׁבָה וְאָכְלָה מִצֵּידִי בַּעֲבוּר תְּבָרְכַנִּי נַפְשֶׁךָ: 20 וַיֹּאמֶר יִצְחָק אֶל־בְּנוֹ מַה־זֶּה מִהַרְתָּ לִמְצֹא בְּנִי וַיֹּאמֶר כִּי הִקְרָה יְהֹוָה אֱלֹהֶיךָ לְפָנָי: 21 וַיֹּאמֶר יִצְחָק אֶל־יַעֲקֹב גְּשָׁה־נָּא וַאֲמֻשְׁךָ בְּנִי הַאַתָּה זֶה בְּנִי עֵשָׂו אִם־לֹא:

22] Jacob approached his father Isaac, who felt him and said, "The voice is the voice of Jacob, but the hands are the hands of Esau!" 23] He did not recognize him, however, because his hands were hairy, like the hands of his brother Esau—and as he was [preparing to] bless him, 24] he said, "Are you really my son Esau?" "I am," he answered. 25] He said, "Bring [it] near me and I will eat of my son's game, so that I can give you my heartfelt blessing." He brought [it] to him and he ate; he brought him wine and he drank. 26] His father Isaac then said to him, "Pray come near and kiss me, son."

27] As he came near and kissed him, [Isaac] smelled the scent of his clothes and blessed him, saying:

"See, my son's scent is like the scent of
a field
blessed by the Eternal.
28] God give you of heaven's dew,
of earth's bounty;
abundant grain and new wine.
29] Let peoples serve you,
nations bow down to you.
Be a ruler to your brothers,
and let your mother's sons bow down
to you.
May those who curse you be cursed;
may those who bless you be blessed."

30] Just as Isaac finished blessing Jacob, at the very moment that Jacob was in the act of leaving his father Isaac's presence, his brother Esau came in from his hunt.

22 וַיִּגַּשׁ יַעֲקֹב אֶל־יִצְחָק אָבִיו וַיְמֻשֵּׁהוּ וַיֹּאמֶר הַקֹּל קוֹל יַעֲקֹב וְהַיָּדַיִם יְדֵי עֵשָׂו: 23 וְלֹא הִכִּירוֹ כִּי־הָיוּ יָדָיו כִּידֵי עֵשָׂו אָחִיו שְׂעִרֹת וַיְבָרְכֵהוּ: 24 וַיֹּאמֶר אַתָּה זֶה בְּנִי עֵשָׂו וַיֹּאמֶר אָנִי: 25 וַיֹּאמֶר הַגִּשָׁה לִּי וְאֹכְלָה מִצֵּיד בְּנִי לְמַעַן תְּבָרֶכְךָ נַפְשִׁי וַיַּגֶּשׁ־לוֹ וַיֹּאכַל וַיָּבֵא לוֹ יַיִן וַיֵּשְׁתְּ: 26 וַיֹּאמֶר אֵלָיו יִצְחָק אָבִיו גְּשָׁה־נָּא וּשְׁקָה־לִּי בְּנִי:

27 וַיִּגַּשׁ וַיִּשַּׁק־לוֹ וַיָּרַח אֶת־רֵיחַ בְּגָדָיו וַיְבָרְכֵהוּ וַיֹּאמֶר
רְאֵה רֵיחַ בְּנִי כְּרֵיחַ שָׂדֶה אֲשֶׁר בֵּרְכוֹ יְהוָה:
28 וְיִתֶּן־לְךָ הָאֱלֹהִים מִטַּל הַשָּׁמַיִם וּמִשְׁמַנֵּי הָאָרֶץ
וְרֹב דָּגָן וְתִירֹשׁ:
29 יַעַבְדוּךָ עַמִּים
וישתחו וְיִשְׁתַּחֲווּ לְךָ לְאֻמִּים
הֱוֵה גְבִיר לְאַחֶיךָ
וְיִשְׁתַּחֲווּ לְךָ בְּנֵי אִמֶּךָ
אֹרְרֶיךָ אָרוּר
וּמְבָרְכֶיךָ בָּרוּךְ:

30 וַיְהִי כַּאֲשֶׁר כִּלָּה יִצְחָק לְבָרֵךְ אֶת־יַעֲקֹב וַיְהִי אַךְ יָצֹא יָצָא יַעֲקֹב מֵאֵת פְּנֵי יִצְחָק אָבִיו וְעֵשָׂו אָחִיו בָּא מִצֵּידוֹ:

31] He too made tasty dishes that he brought to his father and he said to his father, "Let my father get ready to eat of his son's game, so that you can give me your heartfelt blessing." 32] But his father Isaac said to him, "Who are you?" So he replied, "I am your son, your first-born, Esau!" 33] Isaac now began to shudder—a shuddering exceedingly great—and he said, "Who then hunted game and brought [it] to me and I ate of it all before you came? I blessed him—and blessed he will remain!"

34] When Esau heard his father's words, he broke into an exceedingly loud and bitter howl and said to his father, "Bless me! Me too, father!" 35] But he said, "Your brother came with deceit and took away your blessing!"

36] He replied, "Is he not named Jacob? Twice now he has cheated me—he took my birthright and now, look, he has taken my blessing!" And he added, "Did you not reserve a blessing for me?" 37] Isaac responded by saying to Esau, "Look—I have appointed him your master, and given him all his kin to be his servants, and have supported him with grain and new wine; come, now, what am I to do, my son?"

38] "Do you have but one blessing, father?" said Esau to his father. "Bless me! Me too, father!" And Esau cried out and wept. 39] His father Isaac then responded and said to him:

31 וַיַּ֤עַשׂ גַּם־הוּא֙ מַטְעַמִּ֔ים וַיָּבֵ֖א לְאָבִ֑יו וַיֹּ֣אמֶר לְאָבִ֗יו יָקֻ֤ם אָבִי֙ וְיֹאכַל֙ מִצֵּ֣יד בְּנ֔וֹ בַּעֲבֻ֖ר תְּבָרֲכַ֥נִּי נַפְשֶֽׁךָ׃ 32 וַיֹּ֧אמֶר ל֛וֹ יִצְחָ֥ק אָבִ֖יו מִי־אָ֑תָּה וַיֹּ֕אמֶר אֲנִ֛י בִּנְךָ֥ בְכֹֽרְךָ֖ עֵשָֽׂו׃ 33 וַיֶּחֱרַ֨ד יִצְחָ֣ק חֲרָדָה֮ גְּדֹלָ֣ה עַד־מְאֹד֒ וַיֹּ֡אמֶר מִֽי־אֵפ֡וֹא ה֣וּא הַצָּֽד־צַ֩יִד֩ וַיָּ֨בֵא לִ֜י וָאֹכַ֥ל מִכֹּ֛ל בְּטֶ֥רֶם תָּב֖וֹא וָאֲבָרֲכֵ֑הוּ גַּם־בָּר֖וּךְ יִהְיֶֽה׃

34 כִּשְׁמֹ֤עַ עֵשָׂו֙ אֶת־דִּבְרֵ֣י אָבִ֔יו וַיִּצְעַ֣ק צְעָקָ֔ה גְּדֹלָ֥ה וּמָרָ֖ה עַד־מְאֹ֑ד וַיֹּ֣אמֶר לְאָבִ֔יו בָּרֲכֵ֥נִי גַם־אָ֖נִי אָבִֽי׃ 35 וַיֹּ֕אמֶר בָּ֥א אָחִ֖יךָ בְּמִרְמָ֑ה וַיִּקַּ֖ח בִּרְכָתֶֽךָ׃

36 וַיֹּ֡אמֶר הֲכִי֩ קָרָ֨א שְׁמ֜וֹ יַעֲקֹ֗ב וַֽיַּעְקְבֵ֨נִי֙ זֶ֣ה פַעֲמַ֔יִם אֶת־בְּכֹרָתִ֣י לָקָ֔ח וְהִנֵּ֥ה עַתָּ֖ה לָקַ֣ח בִּרְכָתִ֑י וַיֹּאמַ֕ר הֲלֹא־אָצַ֥לְתָּ לִּ֖י בְּרָכָֽה׃ 37 וַיַּ֨עַן יִצְחָ֜ק וַיֹּ֣אמֶר לְעֵשָׂ֗ו הֵ֣ן גְּבִ֞יר שַׂמְתִּ֥יו לָךְ֙ וְאֶת־כָּל־אֶחָ֗יו נָתַ֤תִּי לוֹ֙ לַעֲבָדִ֔ים וְדָגָ֥ן וְתִירֹ֖שׁ סְמַכְתִּ֑יו וּלְכָ֣ה אֵפ֔וֹא מָ֥ה אֶֽעֱשֶׂ֖ה בְּנִֽי׃

38 וַיֹּ֨אמֶר עֵשָׂ֜ו אֶל־אָבִ֗יו הַֽבְרָכָ֨ה אַחַ֤ת הִֽוא־לְךָ֙ אָבִ֔י בָּרֲכֵ֥נִי גַם־אָ֖נִי אָבִ֑י וַיִּשָּׂ֥א עֵשָׂ֛ו קֹל֖וֹ וַיֵּֽבְךְּ׃ 39 וַיַּ֛עַן יִצְחָ֥ק אָבִ֖יו וַיֹּ֥אמֶר אֵלָ֑יו

"Lo, among the fat places of the earth
    shall your dwelling be,
and with heaven's dew from above.
40] By your sword shall you live,
your brother shall you serve.
But when you move away,
You shall break his yoke off your neck."

הִנֵּה מִשְׁמַנֵּי הָאָרֶץ יִהְיֶה מוֹשָׁבֶךָ
וּמִטַּל הַשָּׁמַיִם מֵעָל:
40 וְעַל־חַרְבְּךָ תִחְיֶה
וְאֶת־אָחִיךָ תַּעֲבֹד
וְהָיָה כַּאֲשֶׁר תָּרִיד
וּפָרַקְתָּ עֻלּוֹ מֵעַל צַוָּארֶךָ:

Understanding the Story

For a short time after their marriage, Rebekah has difficulty conceiving. When she finally does become pregnant, she is told by none other than God that she is carrying twins and that from them battling nations will emerge. When the boys are born, the eldest twin is named Esau (meaning "hairy"), and the younger twin is named Jacob (meaning "heel"), because at birth his hand was holding onto Esau's heel. As they grow, Esau becomes a skilled hunter, while Jacob quietly remains within the camp. Isaac continually favors Esau, enjoying the fact that Esau always brings him his favorite food, while mother Rebekah is said to favor Jacob.

In this story, Esau, who one day finds himself extremely hungry, sells his birthright to Jacob in exchange for some stew. Later, near the time of father Isaac's death, Isaac asks Esau to go out hunting and to bring him a tasty dish, promising that in exchange he will reward Esau with a special blessing. Rebekah overhears their conversation and persuades Jacob to disguise himself in Esau's clothing and put on hairy skins so that he will fool Isaac into believing that he is Esau. His disguise appears to fool his father into believing that he is blessing Esau, and Isaac blesses Jacob, "Let peoples serve you, nations bow down to you" (Genesis 27:29). When Esau returns from the field and brings his father the tasty dish that his father had requested, Isaac informs him that he has already given away his blessing. Esau is outraged and angry, even threatening to kill his brother Jacob. The story concludes with Isaac blessing Esau, "Lo, among the fat places of the earth shall your dwelling be, and with heaven's dew from above. By your sword you shall live" (Genesis 27:39–40).

The story is bound to leave the reader with many questions. Jacob, with his mother Rebekah's help, practices outrageous deceit on his helpless father and guileless brother, and he is rewarded for his deed. Are we to understand from this biblical story that the

50

Torah condones trickery and deception? Are there times when not telling the truth and deceiving are actually permissible according to Judaism? Can the ends ever justify questionable means?

There is one additional serious problem in connection with the upbringing of Jacob and Esau. We are told in the Torah that Isaac loved Esau, whereas Rebekah loved Jacob. How is it possible that there would be favoritism in the household of two people who today are considered a patriarch and matriarch of our people?

From the Commentators

One view is that she, more than Isaac or anyone else, had a "mother's intuition" that Jacob was especially endowed with powers of wisdom to inherit the leadership of the Jewish people. Before the twins were born, God had told her: "Two nations are in your womb.... One people shall be mightier than the other, and the older shall serve the younger." She simply was following her inner voice, favoring the younger child she sensed was to be the "leader."

> Harvey J. Fields, citing *Midrash Aggadah* 27:13 in *A Torah Commentary for Our Times*, vol. 1 (New York: UAHC Press, 1998), p. 66.

The Bible is not here condoning what has been obtained by trickery. On the contrary, the way the narrative is handled makes clear that Jacob has a claim on the birthright wholly and solely by virtue of God's predetermination. In other words, the presence of the oracle in the story constitutes, in effect, a moral judgment upon Jacob's behavior.

> Nahum M. Sarna, *Understanding Genesis* (New York: Schocken Books, 1966), p. 183.

[David Kimchi] holds that Isaac was neither weak nor incapable of making clear decisions. Isaac favored Esau because he realized that Esau was weak not strong and, therefore, required more support, more help, more

Radak

Rabbi David Kimchi, or Radak (1160–1235), came from a family of Hebrew grammarians and translators originating in Spain and living in southern France. Radak's Bible commentaries were incorporated into standard editions of the Hebrew Bible, translated into Latin, and extensively used by the translators of the Bible into European languages. His comments often fuse the philological and philosophical traditions with Rabbinic midrash and the plain interpretation of Rashi. His style is lucid and simple, and his commentary makes use of the *targumim* and frequently quotes early rabbinic explanations.

direction, and care if he was to mature as a responsible adult. Isaac considered Esau the weaker son because he saw that Esau was "wild," irresponsible, undisciplined, and uncaring about others. Isaac believed that Esau would change if he gave him gifts and favored him with special attentions and blessings.

Harvey J. Fields, *A Torah Commentary for Our Times*, vol. 1, p. 65.

Don Isaac Abravanel argues that Isaac was simply blinded to Esau's faults. "Affection," Abravanel comments, "ruins judgment."

Harvey J. Fields, *A Torah Commentary for Our Times*, vol. 1, p. 65.

Isaac was an "easy victim" of duplicity; he was neither suspicious nor afraid because there was no dishonesty in his own heart. He therefore took his children at face value. The well-behaved, active son was for him also good and dutiful; Isaac did not see beyond the façade. Rebekah, however, was an expert in such matters. She knew that people could be duplicitous, and the resemblance that is common between a man and his maternal uncle she distinguished in Esau and Laban. She recognized her own family in Esau, and she knew his shortcomings and his weak points. . . .

She manipulated Isaac into blessing Jacob instead of Esau out of her love for Isaac, in an attempt to shield and protect him from the emotional shock of his own error.

Adin Steinsaltz, *Biblical Images*, trans. Yehuda Hanegbi and Yehudit Keshet (Northvale, NJ: Jason Aronson, 1994), pp. 49–51.

For when he replied "The Eternal your God made it happen," Isaac said: "I know that Esau would not mention the name of the Holy One, blessed be God; since this one does mention God, he is not Esau but Jacob."

B'reishit Rabbah 65:19.

And what of Rebecca's choice of Jacob? . . . The evidence is very thin, though the Bible does offer a clue: "Jacob was simple, dwelling among the tents" [Genesis 25:27]. Did he farm? Stay home among the women? Was he a mama's boy? Or was he versed in the gossip and politics of the tents, a bureaucrat who understood the intrigue of an enclosed society?

Burton L. Visotzky, *The Genesis of Ethics* (New York: Crown Publishers, 1996), p. 137.

Questions for Discussion

1. Why does the Bible tell us, "Thus did Esau disdain his birthright" (Genesis 25:34)?

2. Why does the Bible mention that Esau sells his birthright to Jacob but fails to mention anything about Jacob "buying" the birthright from him?

3. What do you think the Bible might mean when it says of Isaac, "his eyesight had dimmed" (Genesis 27:1)?

4. Does Isaac know who Jacob is when Jacob dresses up to look like Esau? How can this be proved from the text?

5. In your opinion, is Jacob's behavior unethical? Does the text seem to view his behavior as unethical? Why or why not?

6. The Rabbis occasionally permit white lies, especially those intended to promote peace and harmony. Can you think of an occasion in your life when you altered the truth for the sake of peace?

7. Jacob is the last of the three patriarchs. How does it make you feel to know that he engaged in deception?

8. A perplexing aspect of the Bible story is Isaac's insistence that he cannot withdraw the blessing from Jacob and restore it to Esau. The Torah never explains why a blessing given under false pretenses cannot be reassigned to its proper recipient. Can you explain Isaac's actions?

9. Later in the Torah, when Jacob falls in love with his cousin Rachel and arranges to marry her, his uncle Laban deceives him by substituting his older daughter Leah, under a heavy veil. Many commentators have noted the parallel: just as Jacob deceived his father, so is he deceived. Still later in the Book of Genesis, Jacob is deceived by ten of his sons, who trick him into thinking that another one of his sons, Joseph, has been killed by a savage beast. What do you think is the role that deception plays in the Bible? Is the Bible trying to teach us something? Are there circumstances when deception ought to be permitted? If so, what are they?

10. The Talmudic tractate *Bava M'tzia* 23b–24a observes that a scholar will never tell a lie except in three instances: tractate, bed, and hospitality. The commentators explain the first to mean that scholars, out of modesty, are permitted to declare they are unfamiliar with a tractate of the Mishnah in order not to flaunt their learning. The second is understood to mean that if persons are asked intimate questions regarding their marital life, they need not answer truthfully. The third is understood to mean that persons who have been generously treated by a host may decide not to tell the truth about their reception if they fear that as a result the host will be embarrassed by unwelcome guests. Do you agree with the Talmudic Sages? Why or why not?

7. How to Make Peace with Your Estranged Brother

The Bible Story: Genesis 32:4–33:17

Genesis 32:4] Jacob now sent messengers ahead of him to his brother Esau in the land of Seir, in the countryside of Edom. 5] He instructed them as follows: "Say this to my lord Esau: 'Thus says your servant Jacob: With Laban have I stayed and have lingered until just now.   6] I came to own cattle, donkeys, sheep, and male and female slaves, and I am sending my lord this message [in the hope] of pleasing you.'" 7] When the messengers came back to Jacob, they said, "We went to your brother Esau, and he, too—accompanied by four hundred men—is marching to meet you."

8] Jacob was terrified. So anxious was he, that he divided the people who were with him—and the flocks, the herds, and the camels—into two camps.   9] He thought: "If Esau advances on the first camp and strikes it, the remaining camp will be able to escape."   10] Then Jacob said, "God of my father Abraham and God of my father Isaac, Eternal [God] who says to me, 'Return to your native land and I will make things go well with you'!   11] I am unworthy of all the proofs of mercy and all the faithfulness that You have shown Your servant. For I crossed this Jordan with

לב ‏4 וַיִּשְׁלַ֨ח יַעֲקֹ֤ב מַלְאָכִים֙ לְפָנָ֔יו אֶל־עֵשָׂ֖ו אָחִ֑יו אַ֥רְצָה שֵׂעִ֖יר שְׂדֵ֥ה אֱדֽוֹם: 5 וַיְצַ֤ו אֹתָם֙ לֵאמֹ֔ר כֹּ֣ה תֹֽאמְר֔וּן לַֽאדֹנִ֖י לְעֵשָׂ֑ו כֹּ֤ה אָמַר֙ עַבְדְּךָ֣ יַעֲקֹ֔ב עִם־לָבָ֣ן גַּ֔רְתִּי וָאֵחַ֖ר עַד־עָֽתָּה: 6 וַֽיְהִי־לִי֙ שׁ֣וֹר וַחֲמ֔וֹר צֹ֥אן וְעֶ֖בֶד וְשִׁפְחָ֑ה וָֽאֶשְׁלְחָה֙ לְהַגִּ֣יד לַֽאדֹנִ֔י לִמְצֹא־חֵ֖ן בְּעֵינֶֽיךָ: 7 וַיָּשֻׁ֙בוּ֙ הַמַּלְאָכִ֔ים אֶֽל־יַעֲקֹ֖ב לֵאמֹ֑ר בָּ֤אנוּ אֶל־אָחִ֙יךָ֙ אֶל־עֵשָׂ֔ו וְגַם֙ הֹלֵ֣ךְ לִקְרָֽאתְךָ֔ וְאַרְבַּע־מֵא֥וֹת אִ֖ישׁ עִמּֽוֹ:

8 וַיִּירָ֧א יַעֲקֹ֛ב מְאֹ֖ד וַיֵּ֣צֶר ל֑וֹ וַיַּ֣חַץ אֶת־הָעָ֣ם אֲשֶׁר־אִתּ֗וֹ וְאֶת־הַצֹּ֛אן וְאֶת־הַבָּקָ֥ר וְהַגְּמַלִּ֖ים לִשְׁנֵ֥י מַחֲנֽוֹת: 9 וַיֹּ֕אמֶר אִם־יָב֥וֹא עֵשָׂ֛ו אֶל־הַמַּחֲנֶ֥ה הָֽאַחַ֖ת וְהִכָּ֑הוּ וְהָיָ֛ה הַמַּחֲנֶ֥ה הַנִּשְׁאָ֖ר לִפְלֵיטָֽה: 10 וַיֹּאמֶר֮ יַעֲקֹב֒ אֱלֹהֵי֙ אָבִ֣י אַבְרָהָ֔ם וֵֽאלֹהֵ֖י אָבִ֣י יִצְחָ֑ק יְהֹוָ֞ה הָאֹמֵ֣ר אֵלַ֗י שׁ֧וּב לְאַרְצְךָ֛ וּלְמֽוֹלַדְתְּךָ֖ וְאֵיטִ֥יבָה עִמָּֽךְ: 11 קָטֹ֜נְתִּי מִכֹּ֤ל הַחֲסָדִים֙ וּמִכָּל־הָ֣אֱמֶ֔ת אֲשֶׁ֥ר עָשִׂ֖יתָ אֶת־עַבְדֶּ֑ךָ כִּ֣י בְמַקְלִ֗י

[nothing but] my walking stick, and now I have become [these] two camps! 12] Save me, I pray, from my brother's hand, from Esau's hand! I am afraid of him, lest he advance on me and strike me, mother [falling] on child. 13] Yet You said, 'I will make things go well with you and make your descendants like the grains of sand along the seashore, which are too many to be counted.'"

14] After spending the night there, he chose an offering for his brother Esau from what was at hand— 15] 200 goats and 20 he-goats, 200 ewes and 20 rams, 16] 30 milch camels and their young, 40 cows and 10 bulls, 20 she-asses and 10 he-asses. 17] He put his slaves in charge of each drove separately, saying to his slaves, "Pass before me and leave some distance between one drove and the next." 18] He instructed the first as follows, "If my brother Esau meets you and asks you, 'To whom do you belong, where are you going, and whose are these ahead of you?' 19] say, 'These are your servant's, Jacob's; it is an offering sent to my lord Esau; and in fact he is following close behind us.'" 20] He instructed the second, too, and third as well, and all [the others] who were to follow the droves, saying, "This is what you shall tell Esau when you find him. 21] And say as well, 'And in fact he is [coming] behind us.'" For he reasoned, "I will win him over with an offering in advance; then, when I face him, he may pardon me." 22] And so the offering

עָבַ֫רְתִּי אֶת־הַיַּרְדֵּן֙ הַזֶּ֔ה וְעַתָּ֥ה הָיִ֖יתִי לִשְׁנֵ֥י מַחֲנֽוֹת׃ 12 הַצִּילֵ֣נִי נָ֞א מִיַּ֤ד אָחִי֙ מִיַּ֣ד עֵשָׂ֔ו כִּֽי־יָרֵ֥א אָנֹכִ֖י אֹת֑וֹ פֶּן־יָב֣וֹא וְהִכַּ֔נִי אֵ֖ם עַל־בָּנִֽים׃ 13 וְאַתָּ֣ה אָמַ֔רְתָּ הֵיטֵ֥ב אֵיטִ֖יב עִמָּ֑ךְ וְשַׂמְתִּ֤י אֶֽת־זַרְעֲךָ֙ כְּח֣וֹל הַיָּ֔ם אֲשֶׁ֥ר לֹא־יִסָּפֵ֖ר מֵרֹֽב׃

14 וַיָּ֤לֶן שָׁם֙ בַּלַּ֣יְלָה הַה֔וּא וַיִּקַּ֞ח מִן־הַבָּ֧א בְיָד֛וֹ מִנְחָ֖ה לְעֵשָׂ֥ו אָחִֽיו׃ 15 עִזִּ֣ים מָאתַ֗יִם וּתְיָשִׁים֙ עֶשְׂרִ֔ים רְחֵלִ֥ים מָאתַ֖יִם וְאֵילִ֥ים עֶשְׂרִֽים׃ 16 גְּמַלִּ֧ים מֵינִיק֛וֹת וּבְנֵיהֶ֖ם שְׁלֹשִׁ֑ים פָּר֤וֹת אַרְבָּעִים֙ וּפָרִ֣ים עֲשָׂרָ֔ה אֲתֹנֹ֣ת עֶשְׂרִ֔ים וַעְיָרִ֖ם עֲשָׂרָֽה׃ 17 וַיִּתֵּן֙ בְּיַד־עֲבָדָ֔יו עֵ֥דֶר עֵ֖דֶר לְבַדּ֑וֹ וַיֹּ֤אמֶר אֶל־עֲבָדָיו֙ עִבְר֣וּ לְפָנַ֔י וְרֶ֣וַח תָּשִׂ֔ימוּ בֵּ֥ין עֵ֖דֶר וּבֵ֥ין עֵֽדֶר׃ 18 וַיְצַ֥ו אֶת־הָרִֽאשׁוֹן֙ לֵאמֹ֔ר כִּ֣י יִֽפְגָשְׁךָ֙ עֵשָׂ֣ו אָחִ֔י וּשְׁאֵֽלְךָ֙ לֵאמֹ֔ר לְמִי־אַ֔תָּה וְאָ֣נָה תֵלֵ֔ךְ וּלְמִ֖י אֵ֥לֶּה לְפָנֶֽיךָ׃ 19 וְאָֽמַרְתָּ֙ לְעַבְדְּךָ֣ לְיַעֲקֹ֔ב מִנְחָ֥ה הִוא֙ שְׁלוּחָ֔ה לַֽאדֹנִ֖י לְעֵשָׂ֑ו וְהִנֵּ֥ה גַם־ה֖וּא אַחֲרֵֽינוּ׃ 20 וַיְצַ֡ו גַּ֣ם אֶת־הַשֵּׁנִי֩ גַּ֨ם אֶת־הַשְּׁלִישִׁ֜י גַּ֣ם אֶֽת־כָּל־הַהֹ֣לְכִ֗ים אַחֲרֵי֙ הָֽעֲדָרִ֣ים לֵאמֹ֔ר כַּדָּבָ֥ר הַזֶּ֛ה תְּדַבְּר֥וּן אֶל־עֵשָׂ֖ו בְּמֹצַאֲכֶ֥ם אֹתֽוֹ׃ 21 וַאֲמַרְתֶּ֕ם גַּ֗ם הִנֵּ֛ה עַבְדְּךָ֥ יַעֲקֹ֖ב אַחֲרֵ֑ינוּ כִּֽי־אָמַ֞ר אֲכַפְּרָ֣ה פָנָ֗יו בַּמִּנְחָה֙ הַהֹלֶ֣כֶת לְפָנָ֔י וְאַחֲרֵי־כֵן֙ אֶרְאֶ֣ה פָנָ֔יו אוּלַ֖י יִשָּׂ֥א פָנָֽי׃ 22 וַתַּעֲבֹ֥ר

went on ahead, while he remained in camp that night.

23] That same night, Jacob got up, took his two wives, his two maidservants, and his eleven children, and crossed at a ford of the Jabbok [river]. 24] After taking them across the stream, he sent across all that he owned.

25] Now Jacob was left alone, and a man wrestled with him until the rise of dawn. 26] When [the man] saw that he could not overcome him, he struck Jacob's hip-socket, so that Jacob's hip-socket was wrenched as [the man] wrestled with him. 27] Then he said, "Let me go; dawn is breaking!" But [Jacob] said, "I will not let you go unless you bless me!"

28] The other said to him, "What is your name?" and he said, "Jacob." 29] "No more shall you be called Jacob, but Israel," said the other, "for you have struggled with God and with human beings, and you have prevailed." 30] Then Jacob asked, "Pray tell me now your name." But he said, "Why do you ask my name?" And then he took his leave of him.

31] Jacob therefore named that place Peni'el—"For I have seen *God face*-to-face, yet my life has been spared." 32] The sun shone on him as he was leaving Penu'el, and he was limping on account of his thigh. 33] To this day that is why the people of Israel do not eat the thigh muscle

הַמִּנְחָה עַל־פָּנָיו וְהוּא לָן בַּלַּיְלָה־הַהוּא בַּמַּחֲנֶה:

23 וַיָּקָם | בַּלַּיְלָה הוּא וַיִּקַּח אֶת־שְׁתֵּי נָשָׁיו וְאֶת־שְׁתֵּי שִׁפְחֹתָיו וְאֶת־אַחַד עָשָׂר יְלָדָיו וַיַּעֲבֹר אֵת מַעֲבַר יַבֹּק: 24 וַיִּקָּחֵם וַיַּעֲבִרֵם אֶת־הַנָּחַל וַיַּעֲבֵר אֶת־אֲשֶׁר־לוֹ:

25 וַיִּוָּתֵר יַעֲקֹב לְבַדּוֹ וַיֵּאָבֵק אִישׁ עִמּוֹ עַד עֲלוֹת הַשָּׁחַר: 26 וַיַּרְא כִּי לֹא יָכֹל לוֹ וַיִּגַּע בְּכַף־יְרֵכוֹ וַתֵּקַע כַּף־יֶרֶךְ יַעֲקֹב בְּהֵאָבְקוֹ עִמּוֹ: 27 וַיֹּאמֶר שַׁלְּחֵנִי כִּי עָלָה הַשָּׁחַר וַיֹּאמֶר לֹא אֲשַׁלֵּחֲךָ כִּי אִם־בֵּרַכְתָּנִי:

28 וַיֹּאמֶר אֵלָיו מַה־שְּׁמֶךָ וַיֹּאמֶר יַעֲקֹב: 29 וַיֹּאמֶר לֹא יַעֲקֹב יֵאָמֵר עוֹד שִׁמְךָ כִּי אִם־יִשְׂרָאֵל כִּי־שָׂרִיתָ עִם־אֱלֹהִים וְעִם־אֲנָשִׁים וַתּוּכָל: 30 וַיִּשְׁאַל יַעֲקֹב וַיֹּאמֶר הַגִּידָה־נָּא שְׁמֶךָ וַיֹּאמֶר לָמָּה זֶּה תִּשְׁאַל לִשְׁמִי וַיְבָרֶךְ אֹתוֹ שָׁם:

31 וַיִּקְרָא יַעֲקֹב שֵׁם הַמָּקוֹם פְּנִיאֵל כִּי־רָאִיתִי אֱלֹהִים פָּנִים אֶל־פָּנִים וַתִּנָּצֵל נַפְשִׁי: 32 וַיִּזְרַח־לוֹ הַשֶּׁמֶשׁ כַּאֲשֶׁר עָבַר אֶת־פְּנוּאֵל וְהוּא צֹלֵעַ עַל־יְרֵכוֹ: 33 עַל־כֵּן לֹא־יֹאכְלוּ בְנֵי־יִשְׂרָאֵל אֶת־גִּיד

that is in the socket of the hip, because he struck Jacob's hip-socket at the thigh muscle.

33:1] When Jacob was looking into the distance, he beheld Esau coming with his four hundred men, so he divided the children among Leah, Rachel, and the two maids. **2]** He placed the maids and their children in front, Leah and her children next, with Rachel and Joseph last. **3]** He himself went on ahead of them and bowed down to the ground seven times as he approached his brother.

4] Esau, though, ran to meet him, and embraced him, and fell on his neck and kissed him. And they burst into tears.

5] When Esau looked around and saw the women and the children, he said, "Who are these? Yours?" [Jacob] answered, "The children with whom God has favored your servant." **6]** Then the lesser wives with their children approached and bowed down; **7]** Leah, too, approached with her children and bowed down; afterward, Joseph and Rachel approached and bowed down.

8] Esau said, "What, is all this camp that I came across *yours*?" And Jacob replied, "Yes, [it is all meant] to find favor in the sight of my lord." **9]** Esau said, "I have an abundance, my brother; let what is yours be yours." **10]** Jacob said, "No, please, if I have truly found favor in your sight, take

הַנָּשֶׁה אֲשֶׁר עַל־כַּף הַיָּרֵךְ עַד הַיּוֹם הַזֶּה כִּי נָגַע בְּכַף־יֶרֶךְ יַעֲקֹב בְּגִיד הַנָּשֶׁה:

לג ¹ וַיִּשָּׂא יַעֲקֹב עֵינָיו וַיַּרְא וְהִנֵּה עֵשָׂו בָּא וְעִמּוֹ אַרְבַּע מֵאוֹת אִישׁ וַיַּחַץ אֶת־הַיְלָדִים עַל־לֵאָה וְעַל־רָחֵל וְעַל שְׁתֵּי הַשְּׁפָחוֹת: ² וַיָּשֶׂם אֶת־הַשְּׁפָחוֹת וְאֶת־יַלְדֵיהֶן רִאשֹׁנָה וְאֶת־לֵאָה וִילָדֶיהָ אַחֲרֹנִים וְאֶת־רָחֵל וְאֶת־יוֹסֵף אַחֲרֹנִים: ³ וְהוּא עָבַר לִפְנֵיהֶם וַיִּשְׁתַּחוּ אַרְצָה שֶׁבַע פְּעָמִים עַד־גִּשְׁתּוֹ עַד־אָחִיו:

⁴ וַיָּרָץ עֵשָׂו לִקְרָאתוֹ וַיְחַבְּקֵהוּ וַיִּפֹּל עַל־ צַוָּארָו וַיִּשָּׁקֵהוּ וַיִּבְכּוּ:

⁵ וַיִּשָּׂא אֶת־עֵינָיו וַיַּרְא אֶת־הַנָּשִׁים וְאֶת־הַיְלָדִים וַיֹּאמֶר מִי־אֵלֶּה לָּךְ וַיֹּאמַר הַיְלָדִים אֲשֶׁר־חָנַן אֱלֹהִים אֶת־עַבְדֶּךָ: ⁶ וַתִּגַּשְׁןָ הַשְּׁפָחוֹת הֵנָּה וְיַלְדֵיהֶן וַתִּשְׁתַּחֲוֶיןָ: ⁷ וַתִּגַּשׁ גַּם־לֵאָה וִילָדֶיהָ וַיִּשְׁתַּחֲווּ וְאַחַר נִגַּשׁ יוֹסֵף וְרָחֵל וַיִּשְׁתַּחֲווּ:

⁸ וַיֹּאמֶר מִי לְךָ כָּל־הַמַּחֲנֶה הַזֶּה אֲשֶׁר פָּגָשְׁתִּי וַיֹּאמֶר לִמְצֹא־חֵן בְּעֵינֵי אֲדֹנִי: ⁹ וַיֹּאמֶר עֵשָׂו יֶשׁ־לִי רָב אָחִי יְהִי לְךָ אֲשֶׁר־לָךְ: ¹⁰ וַיֹּאמֶר יַעֲקֹב אַל־נָא אִם־ נָא מָצָאתִי חֵן בְּעֵינֶיךָ וְלָקַחְתָּ מִנְחָתִי

the offering from my hand; for to see your face is like seeing the face of God; and you have [already] shown me favor. 11] Please accept my gift of blessing that has been presented to you; God has been gracious to me, and I have all [that I need]." [Jacob] kept on pressing him until [Esau] accepted.

12] [Esau] then said, "Let us start on our way. I will go at your side." 13] But [Jacob] answered, "My lord knows that the children are delicate, and that I have to think about the sheep and cattle that are nursing. If they drive them hard a single day, the small cattle will perish! 14] Let my lord go on ahead of his servant; as for myself, let me proceed on my way at my own pace, [following] the footsteps of the livestock in front of me and [following] the footsteps of the children, until I catch up to my lord near Seir."

15] Esau said, "Pray let me then leave behind with you a portion of the force that accompanies me." But [Jacob] said, "Why should my lord show me such favor?" 16] So that day Esau started back on his way to Seir, 17] while Jacob went on to Succoth, where he built a house for himself and shelters for his livestock; that is why the place was called Succoth.

מִיָּדִ֑י כִּ֣י עַל־כֵּ֞ן רָאִ֤יתִי פָנֶ֨יךָ֙ כִּרְאֹ֣ת פְּנֵ֣י אֱלֹהִ֔ים וַתִּרְצֵֽנִי: 11 קַח־נָ֤א אֶת־בִּרְכָתִי֙ אֲשֶׁ֣ר הֻבָ֣את לָ֔ךְ כִּֽי־חַנַּ֥נִי אֱלֹהִ֖ים וְכִ֣י יֶשׁ־לִי־כֹ֑ל וַיִּפְצַר־בּ֖וֹ וַיִּקָּֽח:

12 וַיֹּ֖אמֶר נִסְעָ֣ה וְנֵלֵ֑כָה וְאֵלְכָ֖ה לְנֶגְדֶּֽךָ: 13 וַיֹּ֣אמֶר אֵלָ֗יו אֲדֹנִ֤י יֹדֵ֨עַ֙ כִּֽי־הַיְלָדִ֣ים רַכִּ֔ים וְהַצֹּ֥אן וְהַבָּקָ֖ר עָל֣וֹת עָלָ֑י וּדְפָק֤וּם י֣וֹם אֶחָ֔ד וָמֵ֖תוּ כָּל־הַצֹּֽאן: 14 יַֽעֲבָר־נָ֥א אֲדֹנִ֖י לִפְנֵ֣י עַבְדּ֑וֹ וַֽאֲנִ֞י אֶתְנַֽהֲלָ֣ה לְאִטִּ֗י לְרֶ֨גֶל הַמְּלָאכָ֤ה אֲשֶׁר־לְפָנַי֙ וּלְרֶ֣גֶל הַיְלָדִ֔ים עַ֛ד אֲשֶׁר־אָבֹ֥א אֶל־אֲדֹנִ֖י שֵׂעִֽירָה:

15 וַיֹּ֣אמֶר עֵשָׂ֔ו אַצִּֽיגָה־נָּ֣א עִמְּךָ֔ מִן־הָעָ֖ם אֲשֶׁ֣ר אִתִּ֑י וַיֹּ֨אמֶר֙ לָ֣מָּה זֶּ֔ה אֶמְצָא־חֵ֖ן בְּעֵינֵ֥י אֲדֹנִֽי: 16 וַיָּ֩שָׁב֩ בַּיּ֨וֹם הַה֥וּא עֵשָׂ֛ו לְדַרְכּ֖וֹ שֵׂעִֽירָה: 17 וְיַֽעֲקֹב֙ נָסַ֣ע סֻכֹּ֔תָה וַיִּ֥בֶן ל֖וֹ בָּ֑יִת וּלְמִקְנֵ֨הוּ֙ עָשָׂ֣ה סֻכֹּ֔ת עַל־כֵּ֛ן קָרָ֥א שֵׁם־הַמָּק֖וֹם סֻכּֽוֹת:

Understanding the Story

Twenty years have elapsed since the frightened Jacob deceived his brother, Esau. These years have changed both men. The time has come to face the past and, in doing so, secure the future. Dreading the encounter, Jacob first sends more than five hundred animals as gifts to his brother. But what does he hope to accomplish? Does he hope to buy off Esau, paying now for what he took by deceit so many years before? Surely if Esau desired, he could order his four hundred men to kill Jacob and take everything that Jacob owned.

Then in the darkness of the night, just hours before Jacob is to confront his brother Esau, a mysterious stranger comes and wrestles with Jacob. Jacob prevails in the struggle, though he emerges with a limp from the stranger grabbing his thigh, and with a new name, Yisrael (Israel). If God has given Israel a new name, why doesn't that name replace the name Jacob ever after in the Torah? Who is this mysterious stranger? Why does the assailant beg for disengagement just as the sun is coming up? Why is it so urgent that Jacob extort a blessing from the assailant? Why does the assailant strike Jacob on the hip? And what is the significance of this encounter taking place right before the brothers' meeting?

Following this encounter, the two brothers meet, and Esau's readiness to make peace with his brother comes as a surprising climax to the carefully prepared encounter. Most readers are surprised when Esau runs to greet Jacob, embracing him and kissing him. Commentators are divided as to whether Esau's hugs, kisses, and kind words are genuine. The Masoretes, who assigned vowels to the written text (500–1000 C.E.), placed dots over the word *vayishakeihu*, "he kissed him," indicating that there is something unusual about this word.

At the conclusion of this tale, the two brothers are now apparently at peace. Jacob-Israel, who has no further need to flee from Esau's wrath, settles down and builds a house in Succoth, while Esau starts back toward Seir. Is Jacob again trying to trick Esau? The episode ends as it begins, with questions.

From the Commentators

He [Esau] quickly changed his mind due to Jacob's obeisances. This (episode) reflects our relationship with Esau in exile, who feels, *"Who shall bring me down to the ground?"* (see *Obadiah* 1:3). It teaches us that we will be saved from the sword of (Esau's) pride through submission and gifts, as our Sages tell us regarding Achiyah Hashiloni who "cursed" Israel, comparing them to a reed (*Taanis* 20a) which bends in the wind. Had the Zealots (*biryoni*) guarding the city followed this policy in the time of the Second Temple, our Holy Temple would not have been destroyed.

> Ovadiah Sforno, *Sforno: Commentary on the Torah*, trans. Raphael Pelcovitz (Brooklyn, NY: Mesorah Publications, 1987), p. 180.

The purport of this Midrash is that this entire event constitutes a hint to his generations, indicating that there will be a generation from the seed of Jacob against whom Esau [Rome] will prevail to the extent of almost uprooting his seed. This occurred in one generation during the period of the Sages of the Mishnah, which was the generation of Rabbi Yehudah ben Baba and his companions.

> Ramban (Nachmanides) on Genesis 32:6, *Commentary on the Torah: Genesis*, trans. Charles Chavel (New York: Shilo Publishing House, 1971), p. 406.

We are told that the man wrestling with Jacob injured him by touching the hollow of his thigh. By "hollow of his thigh" is meant the place of his circumcision. Here, too, we have an indication of how the enemies of the Jewish people persecuted them and sought to destroy them. They would forbid Jews from practicing the ritual of circumcision through which a Jewish boy enters the covenant of Abraham.

> *Lekach Tov* in Harvey J. Fields, *A Torah Commentary for Our Times*, vol. 1 (New York: UAHC Press, 1998), p. 85.

The Commentator Rashi suggests a very different approach. He argues that the "man" with whom Jacob wrestled was "Esau's angel." Rashi points out that Jacob was worried because Esau was coming with four hundred men to kill him and to destroy his community, still bearing a grudge against him for stealing his blessing from their father, Isaac. Rashi explains that, when Jacob discovered that he was wrestling with Esau's angel, he realized that he might be able to force Esau into forgiving him for taking the blessing. If he succeeded, Jacob thought, then his community would be saved. So Jacob fought on, refusing to give up until Esau's angel cried out, "Let me go."

Harvey J. Fields, A Torah Commentary for Our Times, vol. 1, p. 85.

The answer that we propose may be found in a statement made by the Midrash, which is based on a declaration in the Zohar that this man who wrestled with Jacob was the patron angel of Esau and represented the ideology of Esau, the man of brute force. In other words, this was an ideological confrontation between the philosophy of spirituality, compassion and mercy as represented by Jacob, and that of Esau, who epitomizes egotism, crudeness, and destruction.

Abraham Chill, The Sidrot: Insights into the Weekly Torah Reading
(Jerusalem: Gefen Publishing House, 1983), p. 36.

Jacob represents human duality. His was a double life: during the day he discussed his affairs with his entourage; at night he spoke to God of immortality. We understand why. Crushed by Abraham's and Isaac's greatness, aware of his inferiority to them, Jacob viewed his own life as uninspiring, and suffered from that realization.... Distressed at not being able to also enter into the living legend of history, frustrated at having to deal with mundane and practical matters, Jacob found refuge at night....

Says the Midrash: God created the world so that day would be day and night would be night; then came Jacob and he changed day into night. Explanation: At Peniel, for the first time, Jacob behaved in the same way at night and during the day. That night the two Jacobs came together. The heroic dreamer and the inveterate fugitive, the unassuming man and the founder of a nation clashed at Peniel in a fierce and decisive battle. To kill or be killed. It was a turning point for Jacob. He had a choice: to die before dying, or to take hold of himself and fight. And win.

Elie Wiesel, Messengers of God: Biblical Portraits and Legends,
trans. Marion Wiesel (New York: Summit Books, 1976), pp. 122, 124.

Since ancient days, crossing a river has been symbolic of overcoming hazard and going forward to new experience (note such expressions as "crossing the Rubicon"). In this sense, Jacob passing over the Jabbok to meet Esau crosses the watershed of his life.... Jacob cannot fully face his own past unless he seeks reconciliation with Esau, and this he can do only as he becomes a different person. When Jacob becomes Israel he can achieve reconciliation with his brother.

W. Gunther Plaut, ed., *The Torah: A Modern Commentary*, rev. ed. (New York: URJ Press, 2005), p. 233.

[Aviva] Zornberg sees the brothers' embrace as resembling Jacob's encounter with the angel. Their embrace is a combination of hugging in love and grappling in struggle, as each one wants to merge with the other but also to defeat him.

David L. Lieber and Jules Harlow, eds., *Etz Hayim: Torah and Commentary* (New York and Philadelphia: Rabbinical Assembly and Jewish Publication Society, 2001), p. 204.

Years before, as a young man leaving the land of Canaan, Jacob had prayed (Gen. 28:20–22). Some commentators see that youthful prayer as essentially a bargaining with God. "If God protects me and brings me home safely, then I will set up a shrine to God and set aside a tithe of all that God gives me." Now he prays a more mature prayer. In place of bargaining there is the realization that he has nothing to offer God and that God has already blessed him with more than he had any right to claim—love, family, and material wealth. Jacob asks now only for God's help and protection, on two grounds: (a) God once promised him that he would be the father of a multitude, and that will not happen if Esau kills him. He has to survive to carry out God's plan for him. (b) Because what he has to do is too hard for him to do unaided, he needs God's help.

David L. Lieber and Jules Harlow, eds., *Etz Hayim: Torah and Commentary*, pp. 199–200.

Nehama Leibowitz

Former professor of Bible at Tel Aviv University, there is scarcely a community or educational institution in Israel that has not felt the impact of the personality and method of Nehama Leibowitz (1902–1997). In 1956 she was awarded the annual Israel Prize for adult education by the Ministry of Education. Leibowitz's basic goal is to activate students to teach themselves, with the aid of the most famous students of the Bible down through the ages, from Talmudic sages to modern thinkers and scholars. Her approach has much in common with contemporary literary criticism, the keynote of which is close reading for different levels of interpretation and nuances of meaning. For Leibowitz, the guiding principle is that the Torah is filled with potential meaning and its students are invited to discover its myriad of meanings. The World Zionist Organization publishes an English edition of her studies of each of the books of the Torah.

According to the midrash of *B'reishit Rabbah* 78:12, the text at first makes Esau out to be a very compassionate man. The reason for this is that Esau not only ran to kiss Jacob, but he also cried while doing so. The Tanchuma, however, presents a second, more pessimistic, view of Esau's behavior. This view sees Esau as having bit Jacob on the neck rather than kissing him. The reason for this is as follows: The word for "bite," *noshko*, is being used, not the word *nashko*, which means "kiss." In addition, many commentators state that Esau chose to hurt Jacob by biting his neck rather than by hurting him with bows and arrows.

> Based on Nehama Leibowitz, *Studies in Bereshit (Genesis) in the Context of Ancient and Modern Jewish Bible Commentary*, trans. Aryeh Newman (Jerusalem: Haomanim Press, n.d.), pp. 373–375.

"Jacob was terrified. So anxious was he, that he divided the people who were with him—and the flocks, the herds, and the camels—into two camps" (Gen. 32:8). Jacob was terrified lest he be killed. He was anxious lest he kill others.

> Rashi on Genesis 32:8.

The river as the scene of the struggle recalls the many tales of river-spirits that fight with humans who seek to cross their abodes. Insofar as rivers frequently prove to be unexpectedly treacherous, they were believed to possess some malevolent power dangerous to human life. . . . Equally widespread is the motif of a demonic being whose power is restricted to the duration of the night and who is unable to abide the breaking of the dawn.

> Nahum M. Sarna, *The JPS Torah Commentary: Genesis* (Philadelphia: Jewish Publication Society, 1996), p. 403.

Jacob's struggle with the Adversary was a numinous confrontation with the Shadow, or the dark, selfish side of him. When the Adversary wanted to quit, Jacob said, "No, I will not let you go unless you bless me." What did Jacob mean by this? He meant, "I will not part from this experience unless I find a meaning to my suffering." Suffering of itself does not heal. Only suffering that has a meaning, and is accepted willingly, has the power to heal, to transform an individual into a whole person.

> Esther Spitzer, "A Jungian Midrash on Jacob's Dream," *Reconstructionist*, October 1976, p. 78.

Questions for Discussion

1. Rabbi Yochanan once said: "If one wants to know how to deal with powerful kings or governors, he should study closely the Torah portion of Jacob and Esau" (*B'reishit Rabbah* 78:6). Explain what he might have meant by this statement.

2. Jacob's preparation for his meeting with Esau includes gifts and prayer. Commentators have often been puzzled by this combination of activities. What do you think? If you were to prepare for reconciliation with someone you might have wronged, how would you prepare? Why?

3. Of all the commentators who made suggestions regarding the unknown adversary who fought with Jacob, is there one with whom you agree? Do you have your own opinion as to the "man" with whom Jacob fought?

4. *Avot D'Rabbi Natan* suggests that Esau's kiss was a kiss of love, and yet all of Esau's deeds were motivated by hate. Describe the kiss as you see it.

5. Genesis 32:8–9 tells us that Jacob divides the people who are with him into two camps, stating that if Esau comes to one camp and strikes it, then the camp that is left will have an opportunity to escape. Our Sages have commented that Jacob prepares to employ three means of combating Esau: gifts, prayer, and battle. Yet we do not find that he makes any preparations for battle, and when he sees Esau coming, he does not divide the people into two camps. In fact, he divides his children according to their handmaids, each mother with her children (Genesis 33:1). What do you think is the reason for his change of plan?

6. Is there special meaning to the fact that Jacob's nocturnal encounter with the "man" and the change of name to Israel should occur precisely at the moment when he crosses the boundary into the first territory of the Promised Land to be occupied in the future by the people of Israel? What is the meaning of this occurrence?

7. The biblical verse that describes Jacob's limp (Genesis 32:33) underlies a requirement regarding kosher slaughter. What is this requirement, and what is the rationale behind it?

8. What do you think is meant when the Bible says that Jacob saw "God face-to-face" (Genesis 32:31)?

9. There are many explanations given for Jacob's new name *Yisrael*. Some say it means "one who saw a divine being." Others say it means "champion of God" or one who has striven with God and emerged victorious. How do these explanations affect your understanding of what it means to be part of *B'nei Yisrael*—the Children of Israel?

10. In Genesis 32:17–22, words related to the word "face" (Hebrew, *panim*) occur six times. Do you think there is a reason for this repetition, and how might it connect to the name of the place where Jacob has his encounter?

11. Do you have more than one name that people call you? Why do most people have different names that they are called by different people? How might understanding your alternate name(s) assist you in understanding Jacob's name change?

8. A Failed Seduction

The Bible Story: Genesis 39:1–23

Genesis 39:1] Now Joseph was brought down to Egypt, and Potiphar, one of Pharaoh's officers, Captain of the Guard, an Egyptian man, purchased him from the Ishmaelites who had brought him down there. 2] But the Eternal was with Joseph: he was a man who prospered. Now that he was in the household of his Egyptian master, 3] his master saw that the Eternal was with him, and that the Eternal was prospering whatever he touched. 4] Joseph [therefore] found favor in his sight and ministered to him; he [Potiphar] gave him authority over his household, and placed all that he owned in his hand. 5] From the time he gave him authority over his household and over all that he owned, the Eternal blessed the house of the Egyptian on account of Joseph; the blessing of the Eternal was on all that he owned in the house and in the field. 6] He left all that was his in Joseph's hands and gave no thought to what he had, other than the food he ate.

Now Joseph happened to be fair of form and fair of appearance, 7] and after all this, his master's wife set her sights on Joseph and said, "Lie with me!" 8] But he refused, saying to his master's wife, "Look,

לט ¹ וְיוֹסֵף הוּרַד מִצְרָיְמָה וַיִּקְנֵהוּ פּוֹטִיפַר סְרִיס פַּרְעֹה שַׂר הַטַּבָּחִים אִישׁ מִצְרִי מִיַּד הַיִּשְׁמְעֵאלִים אֲשֶׁר הוֹרִדֻהוּ שָׁמָּה: ² וַיְהִי יְהֹוָה אֶת־יוֹסֵף וַיְהִי אִישׁ מַצְלִיחַ וַיְהִי בְּבֵית אֲדֹנָיו הַמִּצְרִי: ³ וַיַּרְא אֲדֹנָיו כִּי יְהֹוָה אִתּוֹ וְכֹל אֲשֶׁר־הוּא עֹשֶׂה יְהֹוָה מַצְלִיחַ בְּיָדוֹ: ⁴ וַיִּמְצָא יוֹסֵף חֵן בְּעֵינָיו וַיְשָׁרֶת אֹתוֹ וַיַּפְקִדֵהוּ עַל־בֵּיתוֹ וְכָל־יֶשׁ־לוֹ נָתַן בְּיָדוֹ: ⁵ וַיְהִי מֵאָז הִפְקִיד אֹתוֹ בְּבֵיתוֹ וְעַל כָּל־אֲשֶׁר יֶשׁ־לוֹ וַיְבָרֶךְ יְהֹוָה אֶת־בֵּית הַמִּצְרִי בִּגְלַל יוֹסֵף וַיְהִי בִּרְכַּת יְהֹוָה בְּכָל־אֲשֶׁר יֶשׁ־לוֹ בַּבַּיִת וּבַשָּׂדֶה: ⁶ וַיַּעֲזֹב כָּל־אֲשֶׁר־לוֹ בְּיַד־יוֹסֵף וְלֹא־יָדַע אִתּוֹ מְאוּמָה כִּי אִם־הַלֶּחֶם אֲשֶׁר־הוּא אוֹכֵל

וַיְהִי יוֹסֵף יְפֵה־תֹאַר וִיפֵה מַרְאֶה: ⁷ וַיְהִי אַחַר הַדְּבָרִים הָאֵלֶּה וַתִּשָּׂא אֵשֶׁת־אֲדֹנָיו אֶת־עֵינֶיהָ אֶל־יוֹסֵף וַתֹּאמֶר שִׁכְבָה עִמִּי: ⁸ וַיְמָאֵן | וַיֹּאמֶר אֶל־אֵשֶׁת

my master gives no thought to what is in this house; all that he owns he has put into my hands. 9] There is none greater than I in this house; he has withheld nothing from me, other than you, inasmuch as you are his wife; how then could I do this great evil, and thus sin against God?" 10] And so she would sweet-talk Joseph day after day, but he did not heed her plea to lie by her and be with her.

11] On one such day, when he came into the house to do his work—and not one of the people of the household was there in the house— 12] she took hold of him by his garment, saying, "Lie with me!" He left his garment in her hand, fled, and ran outside. 13] When she saw that he had left his garment in her hand and fled outside, 14] she summoned her household servants and spoke to them, saying, "See! He brought us a Hebrew man to toy with us. He came to me to lie with me, and I cried out in a loud voice; 15] when he heard me raise my voice and cry out, he left his garment with me and fled and ran outside!" 16] And she kept his garment with her until his master came home.

17] She spoke to him in this manner, saying, "The Hebrew slave whom you brought to us to toy with me came to me; 18] but when I raised my voice and cried out, he left his garment near me and fled and ran outside!" 19] When his master heard his wife's words, namely, "Your slave did these things to me!" he was enraged. 20] So Joseph's master took

אֲדֹנָיו הֵן אֲדֹנִי לֹא־יָדַע אִתִּי מַה־בַּבָּיִת וְכֹל אֲשֶׁר־יֶשׁ־לוֹ נָתַן בְּיָדִי: 9 אֵינֶנּוּ גָדוֹל בַּבַּיִת הַזֶּה מִמֶּנִּי וְלֹא־חָשַׂךְ מִמֶּנִּי מְאוּמָה כִּי אִם־אוֹתָךְ בַּאֲשֶׁר אַתְּ־אִשְׁתּוֹ וְאֵיךְ אֶעֱשֶׂה הָרָעָה הַגְּדֹלָה הַזֹּאת וְחָטָאתִי לֵאלֹהִים: 10 וַיְהִי כְּדַבְּרָהּ אֶל־ יוֹסֵף יוֹם | יוֹם וְלֹא־שָׁמַע אֵלֶיהָ לִשְׁכַּב אֶצְלָהּ לִהְיוֹת עִמָּהּ:

11 וַיְהִי כְּהַיּוֹם הַזֶּה וַיָּבֹא הַבַּיְתָה לַעֲשׂוֹת מְלַאכְתּוֹ וְאֵין אִישׁ מֵאַנְשֵׁי הַבַּיִת שָׁם בַּבָּיִת: 12 וַתִּתְפְּשֵׂהוּ בְּבִגְדוֹ לֵאמֹר שִׁכְבָה עִמִּי וַיַּעֲזֹב בִּגְדוֹ בְּיָדָהּ וַיָּנָס וַיֵּצֵא הַחוּצָה: 13 וַיְהִי כִּרְאוֹתָהּ כִּי־ עָזַב בִּגְדוֹ בְּיָדָהּ וַיָּנָס הַחוּצָה: 14 וַתִּקְרָא לְאַנְשֵׁי בֵיתָהּ וַתֹּאמֶר לָהֶם לֵאמֹר רְאוּ הֵבִיא לָנוּ אִישׁ עִבְרִי לְצַחֶק בָּנוּ בָּא אֵלַי לִשְׁכַּב עִמִּי וָאֶקְרָא בְּקוֹל גָּדוֹל: 15 וַיְהִי כְשָׁמְעוֹ כִּי־הֲרִימֹתִי קוֹלִי וָאֶקְרָא וַיַּעֲזֹב בִּגְדוֹ אֶצְלִי וַיָּנָס וַיֵּצֵא הַחוּצָה: 16 וַתַּנַּח בִּגְדוֹ אֶצְלָהּ עַד־בּוֹא אֲדֹנָיו אֶל־בֵּיתוֹ:

17 וַתְּדַבֵּר אֵלָיו כַּדְּבָרִים הָאֵלֶּה לֵאמֹר בָּא־אֵלַי הָעֶבֶד הָעִבְרִי אֲשֶׁר־הֵבֵאתָ לָּנוּ לְצַחֶק בִּי: 18 וַיְהִי כַּהֲרִימִי קוֹלִי וָאֶקְרָא וַיַּעֲזֹב בִּגְדוֹ אֶצְלִי וַיָּנָס הַחוּצָה: 19 וַיְהִי כִשְׁמֹעַ אֲדֹנָיו אֶת־דִּבְרֵי אִשְׁתּוֹ אֲשֶׁר דִּבְּרָה אֵלָיו לֵאמֹר כַּדְּבָרִים הָאֵלֶּה עָשָׂה לִי עַבְדֶּךָ וַיִּחַר אַפּוֹ: 20 וַיִּקַּח אֲדֹנֵי יוֹסֵף

him and gave him over to the prison, the place where the Pharaoh's prisoners are kept; and there he remained, in the prison.

אֹתוֹ וַיִּתְּנֵהוּ אֶל־בֵּית הַסֹּהַר מְקוֹם אֲשֶׁר־אסורי אֲסִירֵי הַמֶּלֶךְ אֲסוּרִים וַיְהִי־שָׁם בְּבֵית הַסֹּהַר:

21] Yet the Eternal was with Joseph, and extended kindness to him, and lent him grace in the prison warden's sight. 22] The prison warden put all the prisoners of the jail in Joseph's hands, and whatever was done there was his doing. 23] The prison warden never saw anything amiss with him, because the Eternal was with him, and because whatever he did the Eternal prospered.

21 וַיְהִי יְהֹוָה אֶת־יוֹסֵף וַיֵּט אֵלָיו חָסֶד וַיִּתֵּן חִנּוֹ בְּעֵינֵי שַׂר בֵּית־הַסֹּהַר: 22 וַיִּתֵּן שַׂר בֵּית־הַסֹּהַר בְּיַד־יוֹסֵף אֵת כָּל־הָאֲסִירִם אֲשֶׁר בְּבֵית הַסֹּהַר וְאֵת כָּל־אֲשֶׁר עֹשִׂים שָׁם הוּא הָיָה עֹשֶׂה: 23 אֵין | שַׂר בֵּית־הַסֹּהַר רֹאֶה אֶת־כָּל־מְאוּמָה בְּיָדוֹ בַּאֲשֶׁר יְהֹוָה אִתּוֹ וַאֲשֶׁר־הוּא עֹשֶׂה יְהֹוָה מַצְלִיחַ:

Understanding the Story

The Joseph biography is narrated in fascinating detail. We learn at the story's beginning that Joseph is his father's favorite child, receiving the famous tunic. His narcissism and arrogance come through in the telling of his dreams. Joseph speaks his mind even if it is ultimately self-destructive. Hatred grows in his brothers, who plot to eliminate him. Will Joseph's success corrode his moral fiber? His character is about to be put to the test.

Temptation abounds as Potiphar's wife attempts to seduce Joseph. In many other cultures in biblical times adultery was merely a proprietary misdemeanor; a wife was considered property, and injury to a man's possession drew punishment. Joseph speaks in the true accents of the Bible, which clearly regards marriage as more than a relationship of civil law. Marital trust has divine sanction and is so fundamental to human relationships that Jewish tradition considers the command against adultery to be one of the Noachide laws that every person is bound to observe.

The picture of Joseph that emerges in the narrative is far different from that of the boy back in his father's home. So skillfully is the story set forth that in our sympathy and admiration for the hero's nobility of character, we forget those displeasing traits that alienated us at the outset. What has brought about this change of heart? Why would such an ambitious young man decide against a rare opportunity to advance his personal interests? Why did he resist the flirtations of Potiphar's wife, for after all, no one was at home, and Potiphar's wife is reported to have been very beautiful? Why did Joseph risk making her hostile and losing all that he had achieved? Finally, if Potiphar believed his wife's account, it seems strange that Joseph's punishment was only imprisonment in a facility for high-ranking offenders and not something harsher. These are some of the many questions that are raised by this episode.

From the Commentators

In Jewish literature, Joseph is known as a *tzadik*, or wholly exemplary man, the prototype of a righteous saint. At the feast of Tabernacles, among the seven patriarchs and prophets who each come to the *sukkah* as invited guests, Joseph the *Tzadik* figures prominently. In the Bible, however, Joseph is a strange and unpredictable figure, in spite of all the assurance and comfort evoked by the story itself.

The basis for considering Joseph the archetypal *tzadik* is drawn from the climax of the story of the wife of Potiphar, whose temptations he firmly resists. Especially when one compares it with similar incidents involving his older brothers—Reuben (with Bilhah) and Judah (with Tamar)—Joseph's self-control stands out. What is more, he was young and alone and more severely tried than they, besides being fully aware of the penalty he would have to pay for his virtue. His behavior was, therefore, truly exemplary; and, in this respect, he may be said to be deserving of the title *tzadik*.

Adin Steinsaltz, *Biblical Images*, trans. Yehuda Hanegbi and Yehudit Kesher (Northvale, NJ: Jason Aronson, 1994), p. 69.

Why did he [Joseph] refuse her [Potiphar's wife]? R. Judah the son of R. Shalum declared: He beheld his father's image, which said to him: "Joseph, the names of your brothers will be inscribed on the stones of the ephod, do you wish yours to be the only one omitted, because of your sinful conduct?" Therefore, *he refused. And said unto his master's wife: "Behold my master"* (Gen. 39:8); that is to say, he said to her: "Behold, you have your husband, are not all men alike? *He is not greater in this house than I; neither hath he kept back anything from me but thee, because thou are his wife...shall I sin against God?* (Gen. 39:9) I swear before God that I shall not commit this great evil."

Midrash Tanhuma-Yelammedenu, trans. Samuel A. Berman (Hoboken, NJ: KTAV Publishing, 1996), p. 240.

Ramban

Rabbi Moses ben Nachman, also known as Nachmanides (1194–1270), was a Spanish scholar. Like Maimonides, he was a practicing physician, and as such his commentary on the Torah often reveals a wide knowledge of the sciences as well as other secular fields. His interpretations have served as one of the basic classical biblical commentaries of the Torah throughout the generations, and his penetrating analysis both enlightens and inspires. Ramban also expounds a wide range of ethical and philosophical problems. He is one of the earliest expounders of Jewish mystical thought, and even Rabbi Isaac Luria himself spoke fervently of the Ramban's profound understanding of Kabbalah.

Scripture relates that he [Joseph] refused to do her [Potiphar's wife] will even though she was his mistress, i.e., his master's wife, and he feared her, for he feared G-d more. This is the meaning of the expression, *unto his master's wife.*

Ramban (Nachmanides) on Genesis 39:8, *Commentary on the Torah: Genesis,* trans. Charles Chavel (New York: Shilo Publishing House, 1971), p. 481.

Another interpretation: LOOK, MY MASTER—I am afraid of my master [Joseph said]. "Then I will kill him," she [Potiphar's wife] said. "It is bad enough that I would be considered an adulterer, but am I also to be counted among murderers!" he answered. . . .

Another interpretation: I am afraid of the Holy One, blessed be God. "But God is not here," she urged. *"Great is the Eternal, and highly to be praised"* (Ps. XLVIII, 2), he answered. R. Abin said: She chased him from room to room and from chamber to chamber, until she got him to her bed. Above it was a graven idol, which she covered with a sheet. "You have covered its face [for shame]; how much more then [should you be ashamed before] God of whom it is written, *The eyes of the Eternal, that run throughout the whole earth"* (Zech. IV, 10)!

B'reishit Rabbah 87:5.

The vision of Joseph's venerable father appeared to him just as the will of the young man weakened, just as he was about to sin. Potiphar's wife believed she had at last charmed and seduced him. It was then that the sudden vision gave him the strength to control himself, to triumph over his moment of weakness, and to conquer his nature.... When a child's training and upbringing are such that even if he has long been separated from the family home and even if he is lost in the midst of licentious surroundings in a faraway country, his father's influence still guides him toward moral victory; then this training is the ideal Jewish upbringing.

Sefat Emet, in Harvey J. Fields, *A Torah Commentary for Our Times*, vol. 1 (New York: UAHC Press, 1998), p. 98.

One does not provoke a woman unless one wants to. One does not love a woman—or a man—against one's will. Every relationship is a two-way affair. Joseph knew when to desist from his flirtatious and amorous maneuvers, Madame Potiphar did not; she was determined to seduce him.

Elie Wiesel, *Messengers of God: Biblical Portraits and Legends*, trans. Marion Wiesel (New York: Summit Books, 1976), p. 148.

The Jewish Study Bible

Edited by Adele Berlin, professor of Bible at University of Maryland, and Marc Zvi Brettler, professor of Bible at Brandeis University, *The Jewish Study Bible* is a one-volume resource that reflects both contemporary biblical scholarship and the richness of Jewish tradition. The book includes a running commentary beside the biblical text that provides an in-depth theological interpretation of it from the Jewish perspective, informative essays that address a wide range of topics, and full-color Oxford Bible maps.

Good looks are often a sign of divine favor in the Tanakh (e.g., 1 Sam. 9.2; 16.12), but here they set the one who bears them up for a potentially catastrophic temptation. A midrash, finding it difficult to believe that Joseph was altogether innocent, likens him to one "who would stand in the market place, put make-up around his eyes, straighten up his hair, and swing his heels." Mrs. Potiphar's proposition was thus a punishment for his narcissism and machismo (*Gen. Rab.* 87.3).

Adele Berlin and Marc Zvi Brettler, eds., *The Jewish Study Bible* (New York: Oxford University Press, 2004), pp. 78–79.

As soon as Joseph was appointed by Potiphar to a position of importance, he began to eat and drink excessively like all the rest of the Egyptian ruling class. He curled his hair and lived lavishly.

Rashi on Genesis 39:6.

Questions for Discussion

1. In Genesis 39:2, we read, "But the Eternal was with Joseph." Wouldn't we assume that God was with Joseph all the time? Rabbi Huna in *B'reishit Rabbah* interprets this verse to mean that "Joseph whispered God's name whenever he came in and whenever he went out," in other words, that Joseph cultivated his own consciousness of God's presence. What do you think "But the Eternal was with Joseph" might mean?

2. Some commentators argue that Joseph was weak and nearly seduced by Potiphar's wife. Others say that he was perfectly righteous in his response to her. What do you think?

3. The *shalshelet* musical notation appears at the beginning of Genesis 39:8 ("but he refused"). There are two other *shalshelet*s at the beginning of verses in the Book of Genesis:

> "And he [Eliezer] prayed: 'Eternal One, God of my master Abraham, please bring luck today. . . .'" (Genesis 24:12)

> "As he [Lot] vacillated, the men, in the Eternal's pity for him, seized his hand. . . ." (Genesis 19:16)

> What do these *shalshelet* verses have in common? What is the purpose of the *shalshelet*?

4. The word "hand" or "hands" occurs six times in this chapter. Find the six places. Why do you think there is so much repetition?

5. After Joseph's flight, Potiphar's wife summons the men of her household. What is her motive in relating to them all that had happened rather than trying to cover up her shameful conduct?

6. Compare the account of the deed as it is reported by Potiphar's wife to her slaves (Genesis 39:14–15) and subsequently to her husband (Genesis 39:17–18). What might explain why the reports are different in each case? What might Potiphar's wife have been thinking here?

7. Why does Joseph say in Genesis 39:9, "how then could I do this great evil, and thus sin against God?" Why do you think he mentions God in his remarks?

8. Why was Joseph made superintendent of all the other prisoners at the end of this chapter?

9. In Rabbinic literature, Joseph is known as the tzaddik—a righteous man par excellence. From all that you know about him, does it surprise you that he was called a tzaddik? Why or why not?

10. Research the Egyptian "Tale of the Two Brothers." What are the similarities between that tale and the story of Joseph and Potiphar's wife?

9. The Call to Prophecy:
Can a Man of Excuses Be a True Leader?

The Bible Story: From Exodus 2–4

Exodus 2:11] Some time after that, when Moses had grown up, he went out to his kinsfolk and witnessed their labors. He saw an Egyptian beating a Hebrew, one of his kinsmen.   **12]** He turned this way and that and, seeing no one about, he struck down the Egyptian and hid him in the sand. **13]** When he went out the next day, he found two Hebrews fighting; so he said to the offender, "Why do you strike your fellow?"   **14]** He retorted, "Who made you chief and ruler over us? Do you mean to kill me as you killed the Egyptian?" Moses was frightened, and thought: Then the matter is known! **15]** When Pharaoh learned of the matter, he sought to kill Moses; but Moses fled from Pharaoh. He arrived in the land of Midian, and sat down beside a well.

16] Now the priest of Midian had seven daughters. They came to draw water, and filled the troughs to water their father's flock;   **17]** but shepherds came and drove them off. Moses rose to their defense, and he watered their flock....

ב 11 וַיְהִי | בַּיָּמִים הָהֵם וַיִּגְדַּל מֹשֶׁה וַיֵּצֵא אֶל־אֶחָיו וַיַּרְא בְּסִבְלֹתָם וַיַּרְא אִישׁ מִצְרִי מַכֶּה אִישׁ־עִבְרִי מֵאֶחָיו: 12 וַיִּפֶן כֹּה וָכֹה וַיַּרְא כִּי אֵין אִישׁ וַיַּךְ אֶת־הַמִּצְרִי וַיִּטְמְנֵהוּ בַּחוֹל: 13 וַיֵּצֵא בַּיּוֹם הַשֵּׁנִי וְהִנֵּה שְׁנֵי־אֲנָשִׁים עִבְרִים נִצִּים וַיֹּאמֶר לָרָשָׁע לָמָּה תַכֶּה רֵעֶךָ: 14 וַיֹּאמֶר מִי שָׂמְךָ לְאִישׁ שַׂר וְשֹׁפֵט עָלֵינוּ הַלְהָרְגֵנִי אַתָּה אֹמֵר כַּאֲשֶׁר הָרַגְתָּ אֶת־הַמִּצְרִי וַיִּירָא מֹשֶׁה וַיֹּאמַר אָכֵן נוֹדַע הַדָּבָר: 15 וַיִּשְׁמַע פַּרְעֹה אֶת־הַדָּבָר הַזֶּה וַיְבַקֵּשׁ לַהֲרֹג אֶת־מֹשֶׁה וַיִּבְרַח מֹשֶׁה מִפְּנֵי פַרְעֹה וַיֵּשֶׁב בְּאֶרֶץ־מִדְיָן וַיֵּשֶׁב עַל־הַבְּאֵר:

16 וּלְכֹהֵן מִדְיָן שֶׁבַע בָּנוֹת וַתָּבֹאנָה וַתִּדְלֶנָה וַתְּמַלֶּאנָה אֶת־הָרְהָטִים לְהַשְׁקוֹת צֹאן אֲבִיהֶן: 17 וַיָּבֹאוּ הָרֹעִים וַיְגָרְשׁוּם וַיָּקָם מֹשֶׁה וַיּוֹשִׁעָן וַיַּשְׁקְ אֶת־צֹאנָם:

3:1] Now Moses, tending the flock of his father-in-law Jethro, the priest of Midian, drove the flock into the wilderness, and came to Horeb, the mountain of God. 2] An angel of the Eternal appeared to him in a blazing fire out of a bush. He gazed, and there was a bush all aflame, yet the bush was not consumed. 3] Moses said, "I must turn aside to look at this marvelous sight; why doesn't the bush burn up?" 4] When the Eternal saw that he had turned aside to look, God called to him out of the bush: "Moses! Moses!" He answered, "Here I am." 5] And [God] said, "Do not come closer! Remove your sandals from your feet, for the place on which you stand is holy ground!" 6] and continued, "I am the God of your ancestors—the God of Abraham, the God of Isaac, and the God of Jacob." And Moses hid his face, for he was afraid to look at God.

7] And the Eternal continued, "I have marked well the plight of My people in Egypt and have heeded their outcry because of their taskmasters; yes, I am mindful of their sufferings. 8] I have come down to rescue them from the Egyptians and to bring them out of that land to a good and spacious land, a land flowing with milk and honey, the region of the Canaanites, the Hittites, the Amorites, the Perizzites, the Hivites, and the Jebusites. 9] Now the cry of the Israelites has reached Me; moreover, I have seen how the Egyptians oppress them. 10] Come, therefore, I will send you to Pharaoh, and you shall free My people, the Israelites, from Egypt."

ג 1 וּמֹשֶׁה הָיָה רֹעֶה אֶת־צֹאן יִתְרוֹ חֹתְנוֹ כֹּהֵן מִדְיָן וַיִּנְהַג אֶת־הַצֹּאן אַחַר הַמִּדְבָּר וַיָּבֹא אֶל־הַר הָאֱלֹהִים חֹרֵבָה: 2 וַיֵּרָא מַלְאַךְ יְהֹוָה אֵלָיו בְּלַבַּת־אֵשׁ מִתּוֹךְ הַסְּנֶה וַיַּרְא וְהִנֵּה הַסְּנֶה בֹּעֵר בָּאֵשׁ וְהַסְּנֶה אֵינֶנּוּ אֻכָּל: 3 וַיֹּאמֶר מֹשֶׁה אָסֻרָה־נָּא וְאֶרְאֶה אֶת־הַמַּרְאֶה הַגָּדֹל הַזֶּה מַדּוּעַ לֹא־יִבְעַר הַסְּנֶה: 4 וַיַּרְא יְהֹוָה כִּי סָר לִרְאוֹת וַיִּקְרָא אֵלָיו אֱלֹהִים מִתּוֹךְ הַסְּנֶה וַיֹּאמֶר מֹשֶׁה מֹשֶׁה וַיֹּאמֶר הִנֵּנִי: 5 וַיֹּאמֶר אַל־תִּקְרַב הֲלֹם שַׁל־נְעָלֶיךָ מֵעַל רַגְלֶיךָ כִּי הַמָּקוֹם אֲשֶׁר אַתָּה עוֹמֵד עָלָיו אַדְמַת־קֹדֶשׁ הוּא: 6 וַיֹּאמֶר אָנֹכִי אֱלֹהֵי אָבִיךָ אֱלֹהֵי אַבְרָהָם אֱלֹהֵי יִצְחָק וֵאלֹהֵי יַעֲקֹב וַיַּסְתֵּר מֹשֶׁה פָּנָיו כִּי יָרֵא מֵהַבִּיט אֶל־הָאֱלֹהִים:

7 וַיֹּאמֶר יְהֹוָה רָאֹה רָאִיתִי אֶת־עֳנִי עַמִּי אֲשֶׁר בְּמִצְרָיִם וְאֶת־צַעֲקָתָם שָׁמַעְתִּי מִפְּנֵי נֹגְשָׂיו כִּי יָדַעְתִּי אֶת־מַכְאֹבָיו: 8 וָאֵרֵד לְהַצִּילוֹ | מִיַּד מִצְרַיִם וּלְהַעֲלֹתוֹ מִן־הָאָרֶץ הַהִוא אֶל־אֶרֶץ טוֹבָה וּרְחָבָה אֶל־אֶרֶץ זָבַת חָלָב וּדְבָשׁ אֶל־מְקוֹם הַכְּנַעֲנִי וְהַחִתִּי וְהָאֱמֹרִי וְהַפְּרִזִּי וְהַחִוִּי וְהַיְבוּסִי: 9 וְעַתָּה הִנֵּה צַעֲקַת בְּנֵי־יִשְׂרָאֵל בָּאָה אֵלָי וְגַם־רָאִיתִי אֶת־הַלַּחַץ אֲשֶׁר מִצְרַיִם לֹחֲצִים אֹתָם: 10 וְעַתָּה לְכָה וְאֶשְׁלָחֲךָ אֶל־פַּרְעֹה וְהוֹצֵא אֶת־עַמִּי בְנֵי־יִשְׂרָאֵל מִמִּצְרָיִם:

11] But Moses said to God, "Who am I that I should go to Pharaoh and free the Israelites from Egypt?" 12] And [God] said, "I will be with you; that shall be your sign that it was I who sent you. And when you have freed the people from Egypt, you shall worship God at this mountain."

13] Moses said to God, "When I come to the Israelites and say to them, 'The God of your ancestors has sent me to you,' and they ask me, 'What is his name?' what shall I say to them?"... 14] And God said to Moses, "Ehyeh-Asher-Ehyeh," continuing, "Thus shall you say to the Israelites, 'Ehyeh sent me to you.'" 15] And God said further to Moses, "Thus shall you speak to the Israelites: The Eternal, the God of your ancestors—the God of Abraham, the God of Isaac, and the God of Jacob—has sent me to you:

This shall be My name forever,
This My appellation for all eternity.

4:1] But Moses spoke up and said, "What if they do not believe me and do not listen to me, but say: The Eternal did not appear to you?" 2] The Eternal One said to him, "What is that in your hand?" And he replied, "A rod." 3] [God] said, "Cast it on the ground." He cast it on the ground and it became a snake; and Moses recoiled from it. 4] Then the Eternal said to Moses, "Put out your hand and grasp it by the tail"—he put out his hand and seized it, and it became a rod in his hand— 5] "that they may believe that the Eternal,

וַיֹּאמֶר מֹשֶׁה אֶל־הָאֱלֹהִים מִי אָנֹכִי 11
כִּי אֵלֵךְ אֶל־פַּרְעֹה וְכִי אוֹצִיא אֶת־בְּנֵי
יִשְׂרָאֵל מִמִּצְרָיִם: 12 וַיֹּאמֶר כִּי־אֶהְיֶה
עִמָּךְ וְזֶה־לְּךָ הָאוֹת כִּי אָנֹכִי שְׁלַחְתִּיךָ
בְּהוֹצִיאֲךָ אֶת־הָעָם מִמִּצְרַיִם תַּעַבְדוּן
אֶת־הָאֱלֹהִים עַל הָהָר הַזֶּה:

וַיֹּאמֶר מֹשֶׁה אֶל־הָאֱלֹהִים הִנֵּה אָנֹכִי 13
בָא אֶל־בְּנֵי יִשְׂרָאֵל וְאָמַרְתִּי לָהֶם אֱלֹהֵי
אֲבוֹתֵיכֶם שְׁלָחַנִי אֲלֵיכֶם וְאָמְרוּ־לִי
מַה־שְּׁמוֹ מָה אֹמַר אֲלֵהֶם: 14 וַיֹּאמֶר
אֱלֹהִים אֶל־מֹשֶׁה אֶהְיֶה אֲשֶׁר אֶהְיֶה
וַיֹּאמֶר כֹּה תֹאמַר לִבְנֵי יִשְׂרָאֵל אֶהְיֶה
שְׁלָחַנִי אֲלֵיכֶם: 15 וַיֹּאמֶר עוֹד אֱלֹהִים
אֶל־מֹשֶׁה כֹּה־תֹאמַר אֶל־בְּנֵי יִשְׂרָאֵל
יְהֹוָה אֱלֹהֵי אֲבֹתֵיכֶם אֱלֹהֵי אַבְרָהָם
אֱלֹהֵי יִצְחָק וֵאלֹהֵי יַעֲקֹב שְׁלָחַנִי אֲלֵיכֶם
זֶה־שְּׁמִי לְעֹלָם

וְזֶה זִכְרִי לְדֹר דֹּר:

ד 1 וַיַּעַן מֹשֶׁה וַיֹּאמֶר וְהֵן לֹא־יַאֲמִינוּ
לִי וְלֹא יִשְׁמְעוּ בְּקֹלִי כִּי יֹאמְרוּ לֹא־
נִרְאָה אֵלֶיךָ יְהֹוָה: 2 וַיֹּאמֶר אֵלָיו יְהֹוָה
מזה מַה־זֶּה בְיָדֶךָ וַיֹּאמֶר מַטֶּה: 3 וַיֹּאמֶר
הַשְׁלִיכֵהוּ אַרְצָה וַיַּשְׁלִכֵהוּ אַרְצָה וַיְהִי
לְנָחָשׁ וַיָּנָס מֹשֶׁה מִפָּנָיו: 4 וַיֹּאמֶר יְהֹוָה
אֶל־מֹשֶׁה שְׁלַח יָדְךָ וֶאֱחֹז בִּזְנָבוֹ וַיִּשְׁלַח
יָדוֹ וַיַּחֲזֶק בּוֹ וַיְהִי לְמַטֶּה בְכַפּוֹ: 5 לְמַעַן
יַאֲמִינוּ כִּי־נִרְאָה אֵלֶיךָ יְהֹוָה אֱלֹהֵי

the God of their ancestors, the God of Abraham, the God of Isaac, and the God of Jacob, did appear to you."…

10] But Moses said to the Eternal, "Please, O my lord, I have never been a man of words, either in times past or now that You have spoken to Your servant; I am slow of speech and slow of tongue." 11] And the Eternal said to him, "Who gives humans speech? Who makes them dumb or deaf, seeing or blind? Is it not I, the Eternal? 12] Now go, and I will be with you as you speak and will instruct you what to say." 13] But he said, "Please O my lord, make someone else Your agent." 14] The Eternal became angry with Moses and said, "There is your brother Aaron the Levite. He, I know, speaks readily. Even now he is setting out to meet you, and he will be happy to see you. 15] You shall speak to him and put the words in his mouth—I will be with you and with him as you speak, and tell both of you what to do— 16] and he shall speak for you to the people. Thus he shall serve as your spokesman, with you playing the role of God to him, 17] and take with you this rod, with which you shall perform the signs."

אֲבֹתָ֑ם אֱלֹהֵ֧י אַבְרָהָ֛ם אֱלֹהֵ֥י יִצְחָ֖ק וֵאלֹהֵ֥י יַעֲקֹֽב:

10 וַיֹּ֨אמֶר מֹשֶׁ֣ה אֶל־יְהֹוָה֮ בִּ֣י אֲדֹנָי֒ לֹא֩ אִ֨ישׁ דְּבָרִ֜ים אָנֹ֗כִי גַּ֤ם מִתְּמוֹל֙ גַּ֣ם מִשִּׁלְשֹׁ֔ם גַּ֛ם מֵאָ֥ז דַּבֶּרְךָ֖ אֶל־עַבְדֶּ֑ךָ כִּ֧י כְבַד־פֶּ֛ה וּכְבַ֥ד לָשׁ֖וֹן אָנֹֽכִי: 11 וַיֹּ֨אמֶר יְהֹוָ֜ה אֵלָ֗יו מִ֣י שָׂ֣ם פֶּה֮ לָֽאָדָם֒ א֣וֹ מִֽי־יָשׂ֣וּם אִלֵּ֗ם א֤וֹ חֵרֵשׁ֙ א֣וֹ פִקֵּ֔חַ א֖וֹ עִוֵּ֑ר הֲלֹ֥א אָנֹכִ֖י יְהֹוָֽה: 12 וְעַתָּ֖ה לֵ֑ךְ וְאָנֹכִי֙ אֶהְיֶ֣ה עִם־פִּ֔יךָ וְהוֹרֵיתִ֖יךָ אֲשֶׁ֥ר תְּדַבֵּֽר: 13 וַיֹּ֖אמֶר בִּ֣י אֲדֹנָ֑י שְֽׁלַח־נָ֖א בְּיַד־תִּשְׁלָֽח: 14 וַיִּֽחַר־אַ֨ף יְהֹוָ֜ה בְּמֹשֶׁ֗ה וַיֹּ֨אמֶר֙ הֲלֹ֨א אַהֲרֹ֤ן אָחִ֨יךָ֙ הַלֵּוִ֔י יָדַ֕עְתִּי כִּֽי־דַבֵּ֥ר יְדַבֵּ֖ר ה֑וּא וְגַ֤ם הִנֵּה־הוּא֙ יֹצֵ֣א לִקְרָאתֶ֔ךָ וְרָאֲךָ֖ וְשָׂמַ֥ח בְּלִבּֽוֹ: 15 וְדִבַּרְתָּ֣ אֵלָ֗יו וְשַׂמְתָּ֥ אֶת־הַדְּבָרִ֖ים בְּפִ֑יו וְאָנֹכִ֗י אֶֽהְיֶ֤ה עִם־פִּ֨יךָ֙ וְעִם־פִּ֔יהוּ וְהוֹרֵיתִ֣י אֶתְכֶ֔ם אֵ֖ת אֲשֶׁ֥ר תַּעֲשֽׂוּן: 16 וְדִבֶּר־ה֥וּא לְךָ֖ אֶל־הָעָ֑ם וְהָ֤יָה הוּא֙ יִֽהְיֶה־לְּךָ֣ לְפֶ֔ה וְאַתָּ֖ה תִּֽהְיֶה־לּ֥וֹ לֵֽאלֹהִֽים: 17 וְאֶת־הַמַּטֶּ֥ה הַזֶּ֖ה תִּקַּ֣ח בְּיָדֶ֑ךָ אֲשֶׁ֥ר תַּעֲשֶׂה־בּ֖וֹ אֶת־הָאֹתֹֽת:

Understanding the Story

After his birth and adoption by Pharaoh, very little is known about the early years of Moses. His first pursuit of justice as an adult ends in tragedy, when he kills an Egyptian he sees fighting with a fellow Hebrew. The lack of details in this story has left much room for commentary to fill in the gaps. Nowhere is there an explicit evaluation that either praises or condemns Moses's actions. The text does not clarify whether Moses killed the Egyptian deliberately or whether he impulsively beat him so severely that he died. The reader is left to decide.

The turning point in the career of Moses comes when he gets a glimpse of the Divine in the region of Horeb. Moses sees a burning bush that is not consumed by the flames. Soon thereafter God chooses Moses to be the leader of the people. The reader once again is left to figure out whether there was any particular quality of leadership in Moses that convinced God to send Moses on his mission.

Before accepting his mission, Moses raises a series of objections, revealing a man who not only feels unworthy of the task, but also has doubts about the efficacy of the mission itself. Patiently God attempts to answer each objection, stating that Moses will never be left alone and offering several wondrous signs, such as the rod becoming a snake, to help convince the Israelites. Moses's hesitancy to accept his mission and his bevy of excuses might lead the reader to wonder whether Moses was up to the task and what God really saw in him.

From the Commentators

Why does Moses expend so much time and energy in refusing God's call to become the leader of the Israelites?...Moses hesitated because he was not certain that he could unify the Israelites, to say nothing of the Egyptians.

Shlomo Riskin, "Sending a Leader," *The Jewish Week*, December 27, 2002.

AND THE ETERNAL SAID TO HIM: WHO GIVES HUMANS SPEECH (4:11)? God said to him: "Do not fear even if you are not a man of words. Have I not created all the mouths in the world? I have made dumb whomever I wished, and deaf and blind, and have given others the abilities of seeing and hearing; and had I wanted you to be a man of words, you would have been so, only I wish to perform a miracle with you when you are actually speaking, that your words may be appropriate, because I will be with your mouth...."

Sh'mot Rabbah 3:15.

R. Nehorai provides another interpretation. WHO AM I? Moses said to God: "You have told me to go and bring out Israel. Where can I give them shelter in summer from the heat and in winter from the cold? Where can I find enough food and drink? How many midwives are there; how many pregnant women, how many babies! What food have you prepared for their midwives? What kind of delicacies have you prepared for the pregnant women? How many parched grains and nuts have you prepared for the children?..." God said to him: "From the cake which will go forth with them from Egypt and which will be enough to satisfy them for thirty days, you will know how I will lead them!"

Sh'mot Rabbah 3:4.

Shadal [Samuel David Luzzato] provides another excuse for Moses' hesitation. He says that by the time God called Moses to return to liberate his people, Moses was an old man. He was weak and felt infirm from many years of shepherding from early in the morning until late at night. Since he had spent most of his time in silence, he could not imagine himself standing before Pharaoh and arguing for the freedom of his people. So, argues Shadal, Moses made excuses to God and asked that someone else be sent to free the Jewish People.

Harvey J. Fields, *A Torah Commentary for Our Times,* vol. 2
(New York: UAHC Press, 1998), p. 15.

[Commenting on why Moses was so hesitant to return to Egypt to lead the Israelites, Elie Wiesel writes:] There is one plausible explanation: Moses was disappointed in his Jews, and on several levels. They had not resisted, nor had they agreed to rebel. *Hasevel shesavlu bemitzraim*—They had settled into their "tolerance of suffering": resignation. (*Lisbol*, infinitive of *shesavlu*, means both to suffer and to tolerate.) He may have resented their inability to overcome their internal differences and unite against the enemy; there was too much pettiness, too much envy, too much selfishness. And then, too, they had betrayed him, their benefactor; for that there had been betrayal, he did not doubt. But who had been the informer? Well, let us see. When Moses killed the Egyptian overseer, who else had been present? Only one man: the very Jew whom Moses had saved.

For Moses this must have been a crushing experience—with terrifying implications. Could he have come to the conclusion that the Jews were, after all, not worthy of the freedom he wanted for them? That they had fallen too low, had

80

become too used to servitude to be redeemable? Could that have been the real reason why he had fled to the country? Not because of Pharaoh, but because of the Jews? He probably could have soothed the king's anger. After all, the man he had killed was an obscure overseer and such a crime was not considered terribly serious in ancient Egypt. Surely Moses would have been forgiven. But his fear of Pharaoh was insignificant compared to his disillusionment with the Jews!

Elie Wiesel, *Messengers of God: Biblical Portraits and Legends*,
trans. Marion Wiesel (New York: Summit Books, 1976), pp. 188–189.

Moses comes to Israel with the words, "the God of your fathers hath sent me unto you." It is, therefore, hardly conceivable that he should proclaim a God quite unknown unto them, as the God of their Fathers (G. B. Gray). They must have known what He was *called*, "since nothing is more unbiblical than the idea of an 'unknown God'" (B. Jacob). But since *name* means fame, "record," and in IX, 16 is synonym of "power," *What is His Name?* means "What are the mighty deeds which thou canst recount of Him—what is His power—that we should listen to thy message from Him?"

J. H. Hertz, ed. *Pentateuch and Haftorahs*
(London: Soncino Press, 1960), p. 215.

Moses intervened on three occasions to save the victim from the aggressor. Each of these represents an archetype. First he intervenes in a clash between a Jew and non-Jew, second, between two Jews and third between two non-Jews. In all three cases Moses championed the just cause.

Any further clash must needs belong to one of these three categories. Had we been told only of the first clash we might have doubted the unselfishness of his motives. Perhaps he had been activated by the sense of solidarity with his own people, hatred for the stranger oppressing his brethren rather than pure justice. Had we been faced with the second example we might still have had our doubts. Perhaps he was revolted by the disgrace of witnessing internal strife amongst his own folk, activated by national pride rather than the objective facts. Came the third clash where both parties were outsiders—neither brothers, friends nor neighbors. His sense of justice and fair play was exclusively involved.

Nehama Leibowitz, *Studies in Shemot (Exodus)*, pt. 1, trans. Aryeh Newman
(Jerusalem: Joint Authority for Jewish Zionist Education, n.d.), pp. 40–41.

Rashbam, the grandson of Rashi, also believes that Moses hesitated to accept God's call to liberate the Jewish people because he was a realist and saw no chance for success. Seeking to understand Moses' logic, Rashbam explains that Moses must have asked himself: "Is Pharaoh such a fool as to listen to me and send his slaves away to freedom?" Filled with such doubts, Moses, says Rashbam, concluded that his mission to free the Israelites would end in failure.

Harvey J. Fields, *A Torah Commentary for Our Times,* vol. 2, p. 15.

Great leaders are not blind to the difficulties they face. They realize the difficulties of the challenges before them. At times they feel unworthy and filled with doubts about themselves and those they lead. Sometimes they want to run away and hide rather than face the hard decisions that need to be made.

Harvey J. Fields, *A Torah Commentary for Our Times,* vol. 2, p. 16.

AND HE WENT OUT UNTO HIS BRETHREN. This indicates that they told him he was a Jew, and he desired to see them because they were his brethren. Now he looked on their burdens and toils and could not bear [the sight of his people enslaved]. This was why he killed the Egyptian who was smiting the oppressed Hebrew.

Ramban (Nachmanides) on Exodus 2:11, *Commentary on the Torah: Exodus,* trans. Charles Chavel (New York: Shilo Publishing House, 1971), p. 17.

Ibn Ezra

Abraham ibn Ezra (1089–1164) was a scholar and poet who lived in Spain until 1140 but thereafter journeyed extensively, visiting Italy, France, England, and perhaps Palestine. His Bible commentary is based on linguistic and factual examinations of the text and occasionally even includes daring hints that foreshadow modern Bible criticism. Ibn Ezra was also an important Hebrew grammarian, writing several original grammatical compositions. Two of his books deal with philosophic problems that figure prominently in his Bible commentary. Ibn Ezra also often includes discussions of mathematics, linguistics, and astrology within his explanations.

AND MOSES ANSWERED. God indicated to Moses that the elders would believe in him. However, He did not mention this explicitly. *And they shall hearken to thy voice* (Ex. 3:18) relates only to behavior and not to inner belief.

Ibn Ezra on Exodus 3:18.

Questions for Discussion

1. Moses expresses doubts about his ability to lead his people out of Egyptian oppression. How do you interpret his motives? Is his "humility" a demonstration of weakness or strength, of fear or leadership?

2. List all of the objections that Moses raises to God. Have there ever been times when you found you were about to take upon yourself a mission of responsibility and found excuses for not doing so? In what way were your objections similar to those of Moses? Were you able to resolve your feelings and gain the necessary strength to carry out the task? If so, what was the turning point for you? Did someone else help convince you that you would not fail?

3. Some commentators have suggested that God may be testing Moses's attention span, an important attribute of any prophet. Perhaps it is Moses's ability to "hang around" long enough to realize that the bush is "not being consumed" that offers evidence of this. What do you think convinces God to finally call Moses directly after the first appearance of the angel? Do you think that God sees any particular quality of leadership in Moses that convinces God to send Moses on his mission?

4. What do you think Moses may mean when he asks God to be revealed to him by name?

5. Samson Raphael Hirsch has explained God's name *Ehyeh-Asher-Ehyeh* to mean "I will be what I want to be," that is, stressing God's freedom to act as God wills, in contrast to earthly creatures, who are never totally free. How else can this unusual name for God be understood?

6. One midrash has explained that the reason God appears to Moses in a bush is to teach Moses that no place is devoid of God's presence, not even a lowly bush. What is your opinion of this midrash? What explanation might you have for the burning bush?

7. Why do you think that Moses is told by God to always have the rod in his hand?

8.   A midrash (*Sh'mot Rabbah* 1:26) attempting to explain the fact that Moses was slow of speech tells a story of the young Moses playing before Pharaoh. He once took the king's crown off and placed it on his own head. Pharaoh's advisors deemed this a bad omen and counseled that Moses be killed, but one of them devised a test: Give the child a choice between a gold vessel and live coals. If he chooses the former, he is clever and dangerous, but if the latter, he is slow-witted and poses no threat to Pharaoh. The test was carried out and Moses (guided by an angel) took a hot coal and put it into his mouth, burning his tongue. Thus was his life saved and thus also did Moses become slow of speech and tongue. See if you can compose an original midrash that provides a different explanation for Moses's slowness of speech. How else can his claim (Exodus 4:10) be interpreted?

9.   What is your opinion of Moses taking the law into his own hand and killing the Egyptian who was fighting with a fellow Hebrew? What does the Bible mean when it says, "He turned this way and that and, seeing no one about, he struck down the Egyptian..." (Exodus 2:12)? Could this mean that Moses knew that taking the law into his own hands was wrong?

10. The Golden Calf: The Shattered Commandments

The Bible Story: Exodus 32:1–35

Exodus 32:1] When the people saw that Moses was so long in coming down from the mountain, the people gathered against Aaron and said to him, "Come, make us a god who shall go before us, for that man Moses, who brought us from the land of Egypt—we do not know what has happened to him." **2]** Aaron said to them, "[You men,] take off the gold rings that are on the ears of your wives, your sons, and your daughters, and bring them to me." **3]** And all the people took off the gold rings that were in their ears and brought them to Aaron. **4]** This he took from them and cast in a mold, and made it into a molten calf. And they exclaimed, "This is your god, O Israel, who brought you out of the land of Egypt!" **5]** When Aaron saw this, he built an altar before it; and Aaron announced: "Tomorrow shall be a festival of the Eternal!" **6]** Early next day, the people offered up burnt offerings and brought sacrifices of well-being; they sat down to eat and drink, and then rose to dance.

7] The Eternal One spoke to Moses, "Hurry down, for your people, whom you brought out of the land of Egypt, have acted basely. **8]** They have been quick to turn aside from the way that

לב ¹ וַיַּרְא הָעָם כִּי־בֹשֵׁשׁ מֹשֶׁה לָרֶדֶת מִן־הָהָר וַיִּקָּהֵל הָעָם עַל־אַהֲרֹן וַיֹּאמְרוּ אֵלָיו קוּם ׀ עֲשֵׂה־לָנוּ אֱלֹהִים אֲשֶׁר יֵלְכוּ לְפָנֵינוּ כִּי־זֶה ׀ מֹשֶׁה הָאִישׁ אֲשֶׁר הֶעֱלָנוּ מֵאֶרֶץ מִצְרַיִם לֹא יָדַעְנוּ מֶה־הָיָה לוֹ: ² וַיֹּאמֶר אֲלֵהֶם אַהֲרֹן פָּרְקוּ נִזְמֵי הַזָּהָב אֲשֶׁר בְּאָזְנֵי נְשֵׁיכֶם בְּנֵיכֶם וּבְנֹתֵיכֶם וְהָבִיאוּ אֵלָי: ³ וַיִּתְפָּרְקוּ כָּל־הָעָם אֶת־נִזְמֵי הַזָּהָב אֲשֶׁר בְּאָזְנֵיהֶם וַיָּבִיאוּ אֶל־אַהֲרֹן: ⁴ וַיִּקַּח מִיָּדָם וַיָּצַר אֹתוֹ בַּחֶרֶט וַיַּעֲשֵׂהוּ עֵגֶל מַסֵּכָה וַיֹּאמְרוּ אֵלֶּה אֱלֹהֶיךָ יִשְׂרָאֵל אֲשֶׁר הֶעֱלוּךָ מֵאֶרֶץ מִצְרָיִם: ⁵ וַיַּרְא אַהֲרֹן וַיִּבֶן מִזְבֵּחַ לְפָנָיו וַיִּקְרָא אַהֲרֹן וַיֹּאמַר חַג לַיהֹוָה מָחָר: ⁶ וַיַּשְׁכִּימוּ מִמָּחֳרָת וַיַּעֲלוּ עֹלֹת וַיַּגִּשׁוּ שְׁלָמִים וַיֵּשֶׁב הָעָם לֶאֱכֹל וְשָׁתוֹ וַיָּקֻמוּ לְצַחֵק:

⁷ וַיְדַבֵּר יְהֹוָה אֶל־מֹשֶׁה לֶךְ־רֵד כִּי שִׁחֵת עַמְּךָ אֲשֶׁר הֶעֱלֵיתָ מֵאֶרֶץ מִצְרָיִם: ⁸ סָרוּ מַהֵר מִן־הַדֶּרֶךְ אֲשֶׁר צִוִּיתִם עָשׂוּ לָהֶם

I enjoined upon them. They have made themselves a molten calf and bowed low to it and sacrificed to it, saying: 'This is your god, O Israel, who brought you out of the land of Egypt!'"

9] The Eternal further said to Moses, "I see that this is a stiffnecked people. 10] Now, let Me be, that My anger may blaze forth against them and that I may destroy them, and make of you a great nation." 11] But Moses implored the Eternal his God, saying, "Let not Your anger, Eternal One, blaze forth against Your people, whom You delivered from the land of Egypt with great power and with a mighty hand. 12] Let not the Egyptians say, 'It was with evil intent that he delivered them, only to kill them off in the mountains and annihilate them from the face of the earth.' Turn from Your blazing anger, and renounce the plan to punish Your people. 13] Remember Your servants, Abraham, Isaac, and Israel, how You swore to them by Your Self and said to them: I will make your offspring as numerous as the stars of heaven, and I will give to your offspring this whole land of which I spoke, to possess forever." 14] And the Eternal renounced the punishment planned for God's people.

15] Thereupon Moses turned and went down from the mountain bearing the two tablets of the Pact, tablets inscribed on both their surfaces: they were inscribed on the one side and on the other. 16] The tablets were God's work, and the writing was God's writing, incised upon the tablets.

עֵ֤גֶל מַסֵּכָה֙ וַיִּֽשְׁתַּחֲווּ־ל֔וֹ וַיִּזְבְּחוּ־ל֑וֹ וַיֹּ֣אמְר֔וּ אֵ֤לֶּה אֱלֹהֶ֨יךָ֙ יִשְׂרָאֵ֔ל אֲשֶׁ֥ר הֶעֱל֖וּךָ מֵאֶ֥רֶץ מִצְרָֽיִם:

9 וַיֹּ֥אמֶר יְהֹוָ֖ה אֶל־מֹשֶׁ֑ה רָאִ֨יתִי֙ אֶת־הָעָ֣ם הַזֶּ֔ה וְהִנֵּ֥ה עַם־קְשֵׁה־עֹ֖רֶף הֽוּא: 10 וְעַתָּה֙ הַנִּ֣יחָה לִּ֔י וְיִֽחַר־אַפִּ֥י בָהֶ֖ם וַאֲכַלֵּ֑ם וְאֶֽעֱשֶׂ֥ה אֽוֹתְךָ֖ לְג֥וֹי גָּדֽוֹל: 11 וַיְחַ֣ל מֹשֶׁ֔ה אֶת־פְּנֵ֖י יְהֹוָ֣ה אֱלֹהָ֑יו וַיֹּ֗אמֶר לָמָ֤ה יְהֹוָה֙ יֶחֱרֶ֤ה אַפְּךָ֙ בְּעַמֶּ֔ךָ אֲשֶׁ֤ר הוֹצֵ֨אתָ֙ מֵאֶ֣רֶץ מִצְרַ֔יִם בְּכֹ֥חַ גָּד֖וֹל וּבְיָ֥ד חֲזָקָֽה: 12 לָ֣מָּה יֹֽאמְר֪וּ מִצְרַ֟יִם לֵאמֹ֗ר בְּרָעָ֤ה הֽוֹצִיאָם֙ לַֽהֲרֹ֣ג אֹתָ֔ם בֶּֽהָרִ֔ים וּ֨לְכַלֹּתָ֔ם מֵעַ֖ל פְּנֵ֣י הָֽאֲדָמָ֑ה שׁ֚וּב מֵֽחֲר֣וֹן אַפֶּ֔ךָ וְהִנָּחֵ֥ם עַל־הָֽרָעָ֖ה לְעַמֶּֽךָ: 13 זְכֹ֡ר לְאַבְרָהָם֩ לְיִצְחָ֨ק וּלְיִשְׂרָאֵ֜ל עֲבָדֶ֗יךָ אֲשֶׁ֨ר נִשְׁבַּ֤עְתָּ לָהֶם֙ בָּ֔ךְ וַתְּדַבֵּ֣ר אֲלֵהֶ֔ם אַרְבֶּה֙ אֶֽת־זַרְעֲכֶ֔ם כְּכֽוֹכְבֵ֖י הַשָּׁמָ֑יִם וְכָל־הָאָ֨רֶץ הַזֹּ֜את אֲשֶׁ֣ר אָמַ֗רְתִּי אֶתֵּן֙ לְזַרְעֲכֶ֔ם וְנָֽחֲל֖וּ לְעֹלָֽם: 14 וַיִּנָּ֖חֶם יְהֹוָ֑ה עַל־הָ֣רָעָ֔ה אֲשֶׁ֥ר דִּבֶּ֖ר לַֽעֲשׂ֥וֹת לְעַמּֽוֹ:

15 וַיִּ֜פֶן וַיֵּ֤רֶד מֹשֶׁה֙ מִן־הָהָ֔ר וּשְׁנֵ֛י לֻחֹ֥ת הָֽעֵדֻ֖ת בְּיָד֑וֹ לֻחֹ֗ת כְּתֻבִים֙ מִשְּׁנֵ֣י עֶבְרֵיהֶ֔ם מִזֶּ֥ה וּמִזֶּ֖ה הֵ֥ם כְּתֻבִֽים: 16 וְהַ֨לֻּחֹ֔ת מַֽעֲשֵׂ֥ה אֱלֹהִ֖ים הֵ֑מָּה וְהַמִּכְתָּ֗ב מִכְתַּ֤ב אֱלֹהִים֙ ה֔וּא חָר֖וּת

17] When Joshua heard the sound of the people in its boisterousness, he said to Moses, "There is a cry of war in the camp." 18] But he answered,

"It is not the sound of the tune of triumph,
Or the sound of the tune of defeat;
It is the sound of song that I hear!"

19] As soon as Moses came near the camp and saw the calf and the dancing, he became enraged; and he hurled the tablets from his hands and shattered them at the foot of the mountain.   20] He took the calf that they had made and burned it; he ground it to powder and strewed it upon the water and so made the Israelites drink it.

21] Moses said to Aaron, "What did this people do to you that you have brought such great sin upon them?"   22] Aaron said, "Let not my lord be enraged. You know that this people is bent on evil. 23] They said to me, 'Make us a god to lead us; for that man Moses, who brought us from the land of Egypt—we do not know what has happened to him.'   24] So I said to them, 'Whoever has gold, take it off!' They gave it to me and I hurled it into the fire and out came this calf!"

25] Moses saw that the people were out of control—since Aaron had let them get out of control—so that they were a menace to

עַל־הַלֻּחֹת: 17 וַיִּשְׁמַע יְהוֹשֻׁעַ אֶת־קוֹל הָעָם בְּרֵעֹה וַיֹּאמֶר אֶל־מֹשֶׁה קוֹל מִלְחָמָה בַּמַּחֲנֶה: 18 וַיֹּאמֶר
אֵין קוֹל עֲנוֹת גְּבוּרָה
וְאֵין קוֹל עֲנוֹת חֲלוּשָׁה
קוֹל עַנּוֹת אָנֹכִי שֹׁמֵעַ:

19 וַיְהִי כַּאֲשֶׁר קָרַב אֶל־הַמַּחֲנֶה וַיַּרְא אֶת־הָעֵגֶל וּמְחֹלֹת וַיִּחַר־אַף מֹשֶׁה וַיַּשְׁלֵךְ מִיָּדָו מידו אֶת־הַלֻּחֹת וַיְשַׁבֵּר אֹתָם תַּחַת הָהָר: 20 וַיִּקַּח אֶת־הָעֵגֶל אֲשֶׁר עָשׂוּ וַיִּשְׂרֹף בָּאֵשׁ וַיִּטְחַן עַד אֲשֶׁר־דָּק וַיִּזֶר עַל־פְּנֵי הַמַּיִם וַיַּשְׁקְ אֶת־בְּנֵי יִשְׂרָאֵל:

21 וַיֹּאמֶר מֹשֶׁה אֶל־אַהֲרֹן מֶה־עָשָׂה לְךָ הָעָם הַזֶּה כִּי־הֵבֵאתָ עָלָיו חֲטָאָה גְדֹלָה: 22 וַיֹּאמֶר אַהֲרֹן אַל־יִחַר אַף אֲדֹנִי אַתָּה יָדַעְתָּ אֶת־הָעָם כִּי בְרָע הוּא: 23 וַיֹּאמְרוּ לִי עֲשֵׂה־לָנוּ אֱלֹהִים אֲשֶׁר יֵלְכוּ לְפָנֵינוּ כִּי־זֶה ׀ מֹשֶׁה הָאִישׁ אֲשֶׁר הֶעֱלָנוּ מֵאֶרֶץ מִצְרַיִם לֹא יָדַעְנוּ מֶה־הָיָה לוֹ: 24 וָאֹמַר לָהֶם לְמִי זָהָב הִתְפָּרָקוּ וַיִּתְּנוּ־לִי וָאַשְׁלִכֵהוּ בָאֵשׁ וַיֵּצֵא הָעֵגֶל הַזֶּה:

25 וַיַּרְא מֹשֶׁה אֶת־הָעָם כִּי פָרֻעַ הוּא כִּי־פְרָעֹה אַהֲרֹן לְשִׁמְצָה בְּקָמֵיהֶם:

any who might oppose them.   26] Moses stood up in the gate of the camp and said, "Whoever is for the Eternal, come here!" And all the men of Levi rallied to him. 27] He said to them, "Thus says the Eternal, the God of Israel: Each of you put sword on thigh, go back and forth from gate to gate throughout the camp, and slay sibling, neighbor, and kin."   28] The men of Levi did as Moses had bidden; and some three thousand of the people fell that day. 29] And Moses said, "Dedicate yourselves to the Eternal this day—for each of you has been against blood relations—that [God] may bestow a blessing upon you today."

30] The next day Moses said to the people, "You have been guilty of a great sin. Yet I will now go up to the Eternal; perhaps I may win forgiveness for your sin." 31] Moses went back to the Eternal and said, "Alas, this people is guilty of a great sin in making for themselves a god of gold. 32] Now, if You will forgive their sin [well and good]; but if not, erase me from the record which You have written!"   33] But the Eternal said to Moses, "Only one who has sinned against Me will I erase from My record.   34] Go now, lead the people where I told you. See, My angel shall go before you. But when I make an accounting, I will bring them to account for their sins."

35] Then the Eternal sent a plague upon the people, for what they did with the calf that Aaron made.

26 וַיַּעֲמֹד מֹשֶׁה בְּשַׁעַר הַמַּחֲנֶה וַיֹּאמֶר מִי לַיהֹוָה אֵלָי וַיֵּאָסְפוּ אֵלָיו כָּל־בְּנֵי לֵוִי: 27 וַיֹּאמֶר לָהֶם כֹּה־אָמַר יְהֹוָה אֱלֹהֵי יִשְׂרָאֵל שִׂימוּ אִישׁ־חַרְבּוֹ עַל־יְרֵכוֹ עִבְרוּ וָשׁוּבוּ מִשַּׁעַר לָשַׁעַר בַּמַּחֲנֶה וְהִרְגוּ אִישׁ־אֶת־אָחִיו וְאִישׁ אֶת־רֵעֵהוּ וְאִישׁ אֶת־קְרֹבוֹ: 28 וַיַּעֲשׂוּ בְנֵי־לֵוִי כִּדְבַר מֹשֶׁה וַיִּפֹּל מִן־הָעָם בַּיּוֹם הַהוּא כִּשְׁלֹשֶׁת אַלְפֵי אִישׁ: 29 וַיֹּאמֶר מֹשֶׁה מִלְאוּ יֶדְכֶם הַיּוֹם לַיהֹוָה כִּי אִישׁ בִּבְנוֹ וּבְאָחִיו וְלָתֵת עֲלֵיכֶם הַיּוֹם בְּרָכָה:

30 וַיְהִי מִמָּחֳרָת וַיֹּאמֶר מֹשֶׁה אֶל־הָעָם אַתֶּם חֲטָאתֶם חֲטָאָה גְדֹלָה וְעַתָּה אֶעֱלֶה אֶל־יְהֹוָה אוּלַי אֲכַפְּרָה בְּעַד חַטַּאתְכֶם: 31 וַיָּשָׁב מֹשֶׁה אֶל־יְהֹוָה וַיֹּאמַר אָנָּא חָטָא הָעָם הַזֶּה חֲטָאָה גְדֹלָה וַיַּעֲשׂוּ לָהֶם אֱלֹהֵי זָהָב: 32 וְעַתָּה אִם־תִּשָּׂא חַטָּאתָם וְאִם־אַיִן מְחֵנִי נָא מִסִּפְרְךָ אֲשֶׁר כָּתָבְתָּ: 33 וַיֹּאמֶר יְהֹוָה אֶל־מֹשֶׁה מִי אֲשֶׁר חָטָא־לִי אֶמְחֶנּוּ מִסִּפְרִי: 34 וְעַתָּה לֵךְ | נְחֵה אֶת־הָעָם אֶל אֲשֶׁר־דִּבַּרְתִּי לָךְ הִנֵּה מַלְאָכִי יֵלֵךְ לְפָנֶיךָ וּבְיוֹם פָּקְדִי וּפָקַדְתִּי עֲלֵהֶם חַטָּאתָם:

35 וַיִּגֹּף יְהֹוָה אֶת־הָעָם עַל אֲשֶׁר עָשׂוּ אֶת־הָעֵגֶל אֲשֶׁר עָשָׂה אַהֲרֹן:

Understanding the Story

The incident of the Golden Calf left deep scars in the collective memory of Israel. A midrash (*Sh'mot Rabbah* 43:2) teaches that all the ills that have befallen the people since that time are in part traceable to the sin of the Golden Calf.

While Moses remains on Mount Sinai, the Israelites protest to Aaron and, in their need to have something to worship, ask him to make them a god. Surprisingly, Aaron follows through, and the Israelites offer sacrifices before the Golden Calf, sitting down to drink and making merry in service to their new idol. God tells Moses what the people have done and threatens to destroy them. Moses intercedes and argues with God, asking for compassion toward the people. His argument convinces God not to punish the Israelites.

Holding the tablets, Moses comes down the mountain. When he sees the Israelites dancing before the Golden Calf, he angrily shatters the tablets on the ground and burns the Golden Calf. He grinds the idol to powder, mixes it with water, and forces the Israelites to drink. Aaron immediately blames the people, explaining that they had requested the idol. He also explains to Moses that he told them to give him their gold, which he "hurled into the fire and out came this calf" (Exodus 32:24)!

Judging that the people are out of control, Moses calls upon all who are loyal to God to join him. All of the Levites come forward and, following his direction, kill those who have demonstrated disloyalty to God. In addition, a plague is sent among the people as punishment for the sin of creating the Golden Calf.

Many questions and problems are raised by this complicated story in the Torah. How could the Israelites, so soon after receiving the Ten Commandments, revert to idolatry? Why does Aaron acquiesce to the people's demands? Why does Moses ask God not to punish the people? And why, since God had already forewarned him what the people had done, would Moses hurl the holy tablets to the ground? Were his actions appropriate for a leader? Can he be a fitting role model? There are questions about the tablets themselves as well. In Exodus 34:1, Moses receives another set of tablets. What, if anything, are the differences between the two sets?

From the Commentators

Midrash Rabbah

Midrash Rabbah is the collective title of a ten-part set of fifth- and sixth-century midrashic collections of homiletical and narrative material, covering the Torah and the Five *M'gillot* (Ruth, Song of Songs, Ecclesiastes, Lamentations, and Esther). These books come from different periods and present new meanings in addition to the literal one found in the Scriptures. The attempt of the midrashim is to "fill in" one's understanding of a Torah verse, which is often bare bones, with Rabbinic interpretation that uses much imagination and imagery. *Midrash Rabbah* is a popular resource for rabbinic sermons and *divrei Torah*.

What lies did they [Israel] speak against God? R. Akiva taught: They argued, "Was God occupied with *us*? Of course not, but only with God. God redeemed only God and not us, for it says, *nations and gods before Your people, whom You redeemed for Yourself from Egypt.*" (II Sam. 7:23).

Sh'mot Rabbah 42:3.

This is what Moses did; when Israel perpetrated that act, he took the Tables and shattered them, as if to imply that had Israel foreseen the punishment awaiting them, they would not have thus sinned. Moses moreover said: "Far better that they be judged as having done it unintentionally, than as if they had willfully committed the act"; because in the Decalogue it says, *I am the Lord thy God*, and the punishment for breaking this command is: "*He that sacrifices unto the gods, save unto the Lord only, shall be utterly destroyed.*" Therefore did he break the Tables.

Sh'mot Rabbah 43:1, in *Midrash Rabbah: Exodus*, p. 495.

Philosopher Yehudah Halevi...claims that only 3,000 of the 600,000 people liberated actually requested that Aaron build the golden calf. These people were not really idolaters, Halevi explains. In the absence of Moses, they were simply desperate to have "a tangible object of worship like the other nations without repudiating God who had brought them out of Egypt." Having waited so long for Moses to return, they were overcome with frustration, confusion, and dissension. As a result, they divided into angry parties, differing with one another over what they should do. No longer able to control their fears, a vocal minority pressured Aaron into taking their gold and casting it into a golden calf.

Furthermore, argues Halevi, the creation of the golden calf was not such a serious sin. After all, he explains, making images or using them for worship was accepted religious practice during ancient times. God had commanded the people to create the cherubim and place them above the ark. If the people made a mistake, Halevi says, it was not in refusing to worship God, but in their impatience. Instead of waiting for the return of Moses or for a message from God, they took matters into their own hands and acted as if they had been commanded to replace their leader with a golden idol. It was for their impatience, not for creating an idol, that they were punished.

Harvey J. Fields, *A Torah Commentary for Our Times,* vol. 2
(New York: UAHC Press, 1998), pp. 80–81.

While Aaron wants to express the idea of God by an understandable image, Moses demands unconditional surrender to an almighty invisible deity. Aaron is convinced that the people will not believe in a god they cannot see. It is the clash between the ideal that the crowd needs to worship and the pure idea of deity—the collision between corporeality and spirituality. When Moses rebukes Aaron because he has sullied the purity of the faith, Aaron points out that the tablets Moses is carrying are also corporeal corruptions of total purity. In sudden despair Moses smashes the tablets, whereupon Aaron rebukes him because the tablets could have helped Israel's faith.

A. Schönberg, in *The Torah: A Modern Commentary,* rev. ed.,
ed. W. Gunther Plaut (New York: URJ Press, 2005), p. 603.

[Commenting on the verse "Come, make us a god who shall go before us, for that man Moses, who brought us from the land Egypt—we do not know what has happened to him" (Exodus 32:1), Buber asserts that the Israelites were in a state of panic and said to one another:] The man [Moses], has vanished completely. . . . It must be supposed that that God of his made away with him. . . . What are we to do now? We must take matters into our own hands. An image has to be made, and then the power of the God will enter the image and there will be proper guidance.

Martin Buber, *Moses: The Revelation and the Covenant*
(New York: Harper and Row, 1958), p. 151.

How was it conceivable that forty days after the Sinai Revelation, with the commandments "I am the Lord" "Thou shall have no other gods but Me" still ringing in their ears, they could seek other gods? Evidently the Torah wished to impress on us for all time that such a thing was conceivable. The assumption that people who have scaled the loftiest heights of Divine communion are not capable of descending into the depths of depravity is without foundation. ... One single religious experience, however profound, was not capable of changing the people from idol worshippers into monotheists. Only a prolonged disciplining in the precepts of the Torah directing every moment of their existence could accomplish that.

Nehama Leibowitz, *Studies in Shemot (Exodus)*, pt. 2, trans. Aryeh Newman
(Jerusalem: Joint Authority for Jewish Zionist Education, n.d.), pp. 554–556.

Even the Tablets—"the writing of God"—were not intrinsically holy, but only so on account of you. The moment Israel sinned and transgressed what was written thereon, they became mere bric a brac devoid of sanctity.

To sum up, there is nothing intrinsically holy in the world save the Lord Blessed be He, to whom alone reverence, praise and homage is due. The holy comes into being in response to specific Divine commandments, as for example those calling on us to build Him a house of worship or sacrifice offerings to Him. Now we may understand why Moses on perceiving the physical and mental state of the people promptly broke the Tablets. He feared they would deify them as they had done the calf. Had he brought them the Tablets intact, they would have substituted them for the calf and not reformed their ways. But now that he had broken the Tablets, they realized how far they had fallen short of true faith.

For this reason God approved of Moses' action and said "More power to thee for having broken them." By this he had demonstrated that the Tablets themselves possessed no intrinsic holiness.

Rabbi Meier Simchah HaKohen of Dvinsk, in Nehama Leibowitz,
Studies in Shemot (Exodus), pt. 2, p. 613.

[Commenting on the line "As soon as Moses came near the camp and saw the calf and the dancing, he became enraged; and he hurled the tablets from his hands and shattered them at the foot of the mountain" (Exodus 32:19), Rashi states:] If the Passover sacrifice, which is but one of the 613 mitzvot, cannot be partaken by a stranger, since the Torah said no stranger shall eat of it, how much more is it true that the whole Torah may not be partaken of by the Israelites when the Israelites are apostates (strangers to it). Strangers to the Torah do not need, or want, the tablets, so Moses breaks them.

Rashi on Exodus 32:19.

When he [Moses] beheld the calf, all his vitality ebbed away from him and he just managed to push the Tablets far enough away so as not to fall on his feet, like a person for whom the burden becomes too much. So have I seen in Pirkei Derabbi Eliezer ("Moses could not carry himself nor the tablets and cast them from his hands and they broke"). That is its plain sense.

Rashbam, in Nehama Leibowitz, *Studies in Shemot (Exodus)*, pt. 2, p. 605–606.

[Commenting on the verse "...perhaps I may win forgiveness for your sin" (Exodus 32:30), the midrash states:] R. Huna said in the name of R. Johanan:... Moses said: "Lord of the Universe! You ignored the entire world and caused your children to be enslaved only in Egypt, where all worshipped lambs, and from whom your children have learned [to do corruptly]. It is for this reason that they also have made a Calf," and for this reason does it say, THAT YOU HAVE BROUGHT FORTH OUT OF THE LAND OF EGYPT, as if to say: "Bear in mind whence you have brought them forth."

Sh'mot Rabbah 43:7.

Jewish tradition says that Rosh Chodesh was a holiday given to women as a reward for their refusal to give their earrings to be used to make the golden calf....

But where does this notion that women did not participate in the building of the calf come from? "Aaron said to them, 'Take off the rings of gold that are on the ears of your wives, your sons, and your daughters, and bring them to me.' And all the people took off the rings of gold that were in their ears and brought them to Aaron." It does not say that the women refused. For a woman, reading these few lines with a feminist awareness not present in the Torah, the truth hits hard. For when Aaron speaks to "the people," he is speaking to the men, telling them to "take off the rings of gold that are on the ears of your wives, your sons, and your daughters." And therefore, when "all the people took off the rings of gold that were in their ears," "all the people" can refer only to the men.

In Elyse Goldstein, ed., *The Women's Torah Commentary: New Insights from Women Rabbis on the 54 Weekly Torah Portions* (Woodstock, VT: Jewish Lights Publishing, 2000), pp. 164–165.

Questions for Discussion

1. Why do you think Moses hurls the tablets to the ground? How do you see his action in light of the fact that God already told him what to expect? Is he serving as a good role model for the people?

2. How would you assess Aaron's leadership in the story? Explain.

3. What are Moses's compelling arguments to God that help convince God not to harm the Israelites? Are his arguments typical of a good leader? Why? If not, how should a good leader have acted?

4. Why are the Israelites impatient with Moses? Why do you think they wish to revert so quickly to producing their own god?

5. How do you interpret Aaron's decision to immediately begin to work for the people by asking for a collection of jewelry? Explain.

6. How could an argument be made that society today still worships idols? What are our modern-day golden calves?

7. How can fear and frustration cause a people to abandon democracy or freedom? What examples can you think of?

8. Of all the explanations provided by the commentators regarding the reason the Israelites needed the Golden Calf, which is most similar to your own?

9. Some of the commentators seem to be trying to find ways to make the Israelites' actions seem forgivable or at least understandable. Why do you think they would do this?

10. The *Zohar* suggests that idolatry occurring so soon after the Exodus and Sinai reveals to Moses a flaw in his leadership. If the people could sink this low, part of the blame must fall on his own shoulders, as every leader is responsible for training and elevating someone to take his place when he is absent. Moses neglected to do this, and his breaking of the tablets is perhaps his way of sharing in the Israelites' sin, and therefore punishment. What do you think of the *Zohar*'s suggestion? Do you think Moses bears some of the blame for this tragic story? Why or why not? Do you think God bears some of the blame? Why or why not?

11. Grumblings in the Desert: "We Want Meat!"

The Bible Story: Numbers 11:1–23

Numbers 11:1] The people took to complaining bitterly before the Eternal. The Eternal heard and was incensed: a fire of the Eternal broke out against them, ravaging the outskirts of the camp. **2]** The people cried out to Moses. Moses prayed to the Eternal, and the fire died down. **3]** That place was named Taberah, because a fire of the Eternal had broken out against them.

4] The riffraff in their midst felt a gluttonous craving; and then the Israelites wept and said, "If only we had meat to eat! **5]** We remember the fish that we used to eat free in Egypt, the cucumbers, the melons, the leeks, the onions, and the garlic. **6]** Now our gullets are shriveled. There is nothing at all! Nothing but this manna to look to!"

7] Now the manna was like coriander seed, and in color it was like bdellium. **8]** The people would go about and gather it, grind it between millstones or pound it in a mortar, boil it in a pot, and make it into cakes. It tasted like rich cream. **9]** When the dew fell on the camp at night, the manna would fall upon it.

יא ¹ וַיְהִי הָעָם כְּמִתְאֹנְנִים רַע בְּאָזְנֵי יְהֹוָה וַיִּשְׁמַע יְהֹוָה וַיִּחַר אַפּוֹ וַתִּבְעַר־בָּם אֵשׁ יְהֹוָה וַתֹּאכַל בִּקְצֵה הַמַּחֲנֶה: ² וַיִּצְעַק הָעָם אֶל־מֹשֶׁה וַיִּתְפַּלֵּל מֹשֶׁה אֶל־יְהֹוָה וַתִּשְׁקַע הָאֵשׁ: ³ וַיִּקְרָא שֵׁם־הַמָּקוֹם הַהוּא תַּבְעֵרָה כִּי־בָעֲרָה בָם אֵשׁ יְהֹוָה:

⁴ וְהָאסַפְסֻף אֲשֶׁר בְּקִרְבּוֹ הִתְאַוּוּ תַּאֲוָה וַיָּשֻׁבוּ וַיִּבְכּוּ גַּם בְּנֵי יִשְׂרָאֵל וַיֹּאמְרוּ מִי יַאֲכִלֵנוּ בָּשָׂר: ⁵ זָכַרְנוּ אֶת־הַדָּגָה אֲשֶׁר־נֹאכַל בְּמִצְרַיִם חִנָּם אֵת הַקִּשֻּׁאִים וְאֵת הָאֲבַטִּחִים וְאֶת־הֶחָצִיר וְאֶת־הַבְּצָלִים וְאֶת־הַשּׁוּמִים: ⁶ וְעַתָּה נַפְשֵׁנוּ יְבֵשָׁה אֵין כֹּל בִּלְתִּי אֶל־הַמָּן עֵינֵינוּ:

⁷ וְהַמָּן כִּזְרַע־גַּד הוּא וְעֵינוֹ כְּעֵין הַבְּדֹלַח: ⁸ שָׁטוּ הָעָם וְלָקְטוּ וְטָחֲנוּ בָרֵחַיִם אוֹ דָכוּ בַּמְּדֹכָה וּבִשְּׁלוּ בַּפָּרוּר וְעָשׂוּ אֹתוֹ עֻגוֹת וְהָיָה טַעְמוֹ כְּטַעַם לְשַׁד הַשָּׁמֶן: ⁹ וּבְרֶדֶת הַטַּל עַל־הַמַּחֲנֶה לָיְלָה יֵרֵד הַמָּן עָלָיו:

10] Moses heard the people weeping, every clan apart, at the entrance of each tent. The Eternal was very angry, and Moses was distressed. 11] And Moses said to the Eternal, "Why have You dealt ill with Your servant, and why have I not enjoyed Your favor, that You have laid the burden of all this people upon me? 12] Did I conceive all this people, did I bear them, that You should say to me, 'Carry them in your bosom as a nurse carries an infant,' to the land that You have promised on oath to their ancestors? 13] Where am I to get meat to give to all this people, when they whine before me and say, 'Give us meat to eat!' 14] I cannot carry all this people by myself, for it is too much for me. 15] If You would deal thus with me, kill me rather, I beg You, and let me see no more of my wretchedness!"

16] Then the Eternal One said to Moses, "Gather for me seventy of Israel's elders of whom you have experience as elders and officers of the people, and bring them to the Tent of Meeting and let them take their place there with you. 17] I will come down and speak with you there, and I will draw upon the spirit that is on you and put it upon them; they shall share the burden of the people with you, and you shall not bear it alone. 18] And say to the people: Purify yourselves for tomorrow and you shall eat meat, for you have kept whining before the Eternal and saying, 'If only we

10 וַיִּשְׁמַ֨ע מֹשֶׁ֜ה אֶת־הָעָ֗ם בֹּכֶה֙ לְמִשְׁפְּחֹתָ֔יו אִ֖ישׁ לְפֶ֣תַח אׇהֳל֑וֹ וַיִּֽחַר־ אַ֤ף יְהֹוָה֙ מְאֹ֔ד וּבְעֵינֵ֥י מֹשֶׁ֖ה רָֽע: 11 וַיֹּ֨אמֶר מֹשֶׁ֜ה אֶל־יְהֹוָ֗ה לָמָ֤ה הֲרֵעֹ֙תָ֙ לְעַבְדֶּ֔ךָ וְלָ֛מָּה לֹא־מָצָ֥תִי חֵ֖ן בְּעֵינֶ֑יךָ לָשׂ֗וּם אֶת־מַשָּׂ֛א כׇּל־הָעָ֥ם הַזֶּ֖ה עָלָֽי: 12 הֶאָנֹכִ֣י הָרִ֗יתִי אֵ֚ת כׇּל־הָעָ֣ם הַזֶּ֔ה אִם־ אָנֹכִ֖י יְלִדְתִּ֑יהוּ כִּֽי־תֹאמַ֣ר אֵלַ֗י שָׂאֵ֤הוּ בְחֵיקֶ֙ךָ֙ כַּאֲשֶׁ֨ר יִשָּׂ֤א הָֽאֹמֵן֙ אֶת־הַיֹּנֵ֔ק עַ֚ל הָֽאֲדָמָ֔ה אֲשֶׁ֥ר נִשְׁבַּ֖עְתָּ לַאֲבֹתָֽיו: 13 מֵאַ֤יִן לִי֙ בָּשָׂ֔ר לָתֵ֖ת לְכׇל־הָעָ֣ם הַזֶּ֑ה כִּֽי־יִבְכּ֤וּ עָלַי֙ לֵאמֹ֔ר תְּנָה־לָּ֥נוּ בָשָׂ֖ר וְנֹאכֵֽלָה: 14 לֹֽא־אוּכַ֤ל אָנֹכִי֙ לְבַדִּ֔י לָשֵׂ֖את אֶת־כׇּל־הָעָ֣ם הַזֶּ֑ה כִּ֥י כָבֵ֖ד מִמֶּֽנִּי: 15 וְאִם־כָּ֣כָה ׀ אַתְּ־עֹ֣שֶׂה לִּ֗י הׇרְגֵ֤נִי נָא֙ הָרֹ֔ג אִם־מָצָ֥אתִי חֵ֖ן בְּעֵינֶ֑יךָ וְאַל־ אֶרְאֶ֖ה בְּרָעָתִֽי:

16 וַיֹּ֨אמֶר יְהֹוָ֜ה אֶל־מֹשֶׁ֗ה אֶסְפָה־לִּ֞י שִׁבְעִ֣ים אִישׁ֮ מִזִּקְנֵ֣י יִשְׂרָאֵל֒ אֲשֶׁ֣ר יָדַ֔עְתָּ כִּי־הֵ֛ם זִקְנֵ֥י הָעָ֖ם וְשֹׁטְרָ֑יו וְלָקַחְתָּ֤ אֹתָם֙ אֶל־אֹ֣הֶל מוֹעֵ֔ד וְהִֽתְיַצְּב֥וּ שָׁ֖ם עִמָּֽךְ: 17 וְיָרַדְתִּ֗י וְדִבַּרְתִּ֣י עִמְּךָ֮ שָׁם֒ וְאָצַלְתִּ֗י מִן־הָר֛וּחַ אֲשֶׁ֥ר עָלֶ֖יךָ וְשַׂמְתִּ֣י עֲלֵיהֶ֑ם וְנָשְׂא֤וּ אִתְּךָ֙ בְּמַשָּׂ֣א הָעָ֔ם וְלֹא־ תִשָּׂ֥א אַתָּ֖ה לְבַדֶּֽךָ: 18 וְאֶל־הָעָ֣ם תֹּאמַ֡ר הִתְקַדְּשׁ֨וּ לְמָחָר֮ וַאֲכַלְתֶּ֣ם בָּשָׂר֒ כִּ֣י בְּכִיתֶ֗ם בְּאׇזְנֵ֤י יְהֹוָה֙ לֵאמֹ֔ר מִ֥י יַאֲכִלֵ֙נוּ֙

had meat to eat! Indeed, we were better off in Egypt!' The Eternal will give you meat and you shall eat.   19] You shall eat not one day, not two, not even five days or ten or twenty,   20] but a whole month, until it comes out of your nostrils and becomes loathsome to you. For you have rejected the Eternal who is among you, by whining before [God] and saying, 'Oh, why did we ever leave Egypt!'"

21] But Moses said, "The people who are with me number six hundred thousand foot soldiers; yet You say, 'I will give them enough meat to eat for a whole month.' 22] Could enough flocks and herds be slaughtered to suffice them? Or could all the fish of the sea be gathered for them to suffice them?"   23] And the Eternal answered Moses, "Is there a limit to the Eternal's power? You shall soon see whether what I have said happens to you or not!"

בָּשָׂר כִּי־טוֹב לָנוּ בְּמִצְרָיִם וְנָתַן יְהֹוָה לָכֶם בָּשָׂר וַאֲכַלְתֶּם: 19 לֹא יוֹם אֶחָד תֹּאכְלוּן וְלֹא יוֹמָיִם וְלֹא | חֲמִשָּׁה יָמִים וְלֹא עֲשָׂרָה יָמִים וְלֹא עֶשְׂרִים יוֹם: 20 עַד | חֹדֶשׁ יָמִים עַד אֲשֶׁר־יֵצֵא מֵאַפְּכֶם וְהָיָה לָכֶם לְזָרָא יַעַן כִּי־ מְאַסְתֶּם אֶת־יְהֹוָה אֲשֶׁר בְּקִרְבְּכֶם וַתִּבְכּוּ לְפָנָיו לֵאמֹר לָמָּה זֶּה יָצָאנוּ מִמִּצְרָיִם:

21 וַיֹּאמֶר מֹשֶׁה שֵׁשׁ־מֵאוֹת אֶלֶף רַגְלִי הָעָם אֲשֶׁר אָנֹכִי בְּקִרְבּוֹ וְאַתָּה אָמַרְתָּ בָּשָׂר אֶתֵּן לָהֶם וְאָכְלוּ חֹדֶשׁ יָמִים: 22 הֲצֹאן וּבָקָר יִשָּׁחֵט לָהֶם וּמָצָא לָהֶם אִם אֶת־כָּל־דְּגֵי הַיָּם יֵאָסֵף לָהֶם וּמָצָא לָהֶם: 23 וַיֹּאמֶר יְהֹוָה אֶל־מֹשֶׁה הֲיַד יְהֹוָה תִּקְצָר עַתָּה תִרְאֶה הֲיִקְרְךָ דְבָרִי אִם־לֹא:

Understanding the Story

Shortly after the Israelites are freed from Egyptian bondage, they approach Moses with complaints about their conditions in the desert. Moses responds by requesting that God provide them with food and water. They are given manna each day, and fresh water too. Now, two years later, after receiving the Ten Commandments and building their Tabernacle, the Israelites once again raise their voices with bitter complaints. For protesting their living conditions in the desert, God punishes them with fire throughout the camp. Seeing this, Moses intervenes, and the fire ceases. The complaints, however, are only beginning. The Israelites wax nostalgic, deceiving themselves about the conditions under which they had lived in Egypt: "If only we had meat to eat!...There is nothing...but this manna to look to" (Numbers 11:4, 6).

The Torah commentators have asked many questions about these grievances and grumblings. Are the complaints justifiable? With both food (manna) and enough water supplied, what seems to be the real problem? Are they suffering from boredom? Are they lacking in faith?

Moses is totally overwhelmed by their criticism. He cannot handle their complaints by himself without any support. And so God instructs Moses, as Jethro had counseled him earlier, to appoint elders and officers with whom to share the responsibility of leadership. God then places the spirit of prophecy upon the seventy appointed leaders. Two of these, Eldad and Medad, continue to speak in the spirit of prophecy, seeking to challenge the authority of Moses and Aaron. Joshua, Moses's trusted attendant, reports the matter to Moses, who refuses to restrain them. He tells Joshua, "Would that all of God's people were prophets!"

It is not clear why Eldad and Medad did not join in the mass ecstasy at the tent or why they separated themselves. Evidently Moses's chief aid, Joshua, considered them a source of danger. Yet Moses took the opposite view and welcomed their unique status. What was the reason for Moses's acceptance of Eldad and Medad? Were Eldad and Medad heroes of humility, people to be emulated, or did they cautiously wait to see what effect the ecstatic seizures would have on the others before opening themselves up to the experience?

From the Commentators

[Sifrei] connects "*katzeh*" (outskirts) with *katzin* (leader), commenting that it was the leaders' attitude that caused the people's sullen mood.

David L. Lieber and Jules Harlow, eds., *Etz Hayim: Torah and Commentary* (New York and Philadelphia: Rabbinical Assembly and Jewish Publication Society, 2001), p. 827.

Maimonides claims that the phrase "the LORD was very angry" occurs only as a divine response to instances of idolatry. This grumbling is perceived not as a comment about the food but as a rebellion against God's providence.

Etz Hayim: Torah and Commentary, p. 828.

Why did the people complain about the manna, when the Torah makes a point of telling us how delicious it was? To feel prosperous, it is not enough for a person to have everything that is needed. One must have more than one's neighbors have. The manna was psychologically unsatisfying because everyone had it in abundance.

Etz Hayim: Torah and Commentary, p. 828.

The term *k'mitonenim*, "like complainers," means the Israelites acted out of pretext, "*mitonenim*." The Israelites sought a method to separate themselves from the word of the Lord.... "Before the Eternal" means that they intended their evil acts to reach the ear of the Lord. They stated, "Woe unto us, we are exhausted from three days of journeying without rest." And the Eternal's anger glowed. He said, "It was My plan, for your benefit, to bring you to the land quickly."

Rashi on Numbers 11:1.

Thus when scripture states that they felt anxious and upset, it has thereby already mentioned and told [the nature of] their sin. It states that they were *k'mithon'nim* ("as" murmurers), meaning that they spoke in the bitterness of their soul as do people who suffer pain, and this was evil in the sight of the Eternal, since they should have followed him *with joyfulness, and with gladness of heart by reason of the abundance of all good things* (Deuteronomy 28:47) which He gave them, but they behaved like people acting under duress and compulsion, murmuring and complaining about their condition. It is for this reason that He states with regard to the second [sin, or punishment], *and the children of Israel also wept "again"* (Numbers 11:4), meaning that their first sin consisted of complaining about their lack of comforts in the wilderness, and now they again did a similar thing, and *they did not receive correction* (Jeremiah 7:28) from the fire of God which devoured them.

Ramban (Nachmanides) on Numbers 11:1, Commentary on the Torah: Numbers,
trans. Charles Chavel (New York: Shilo Publishing House, 1971), p. 96.

Rabbi Samson Raphael Hirsch offers a different viewpoint. The Israelites, he argues, suffer not from nostalgia but from boredom. All their needs are met. They enjoy a near perfect situation in the wilderness. Each day they are given manna and plenty of fresh water. Nothing is lacking. Nonetheless, comments Hirsch, they "felt themselves buried alive."

"The people," he continues, "were as if in mourning over themselves. They look on themselves as already dead." With all their needs met, their Torah given, their sanctuary complete, their lives "offer them no compensation, remain worthless and without meaning in their eyes." Frustrated at having no new goal, challenge, or mission, they begin murmuring against Moses and God.

Harvey J. Fields, A Torah Commentary for Our
Times, vol. 3 (New York: UAHC Press, 1998), p. 29.

A Torah Commentary for Our Times

Written by Rabbi Harvey J. Fields, a noted lecturer, historian, and writer, and Reform rabbi. In this commentary, Rabbi Fields has devised an interesting and informative strategy for teaching and reading the Torah. Each Torah portion is presented with a brief overview of the text, the themes of the Torah portion, and the author's commentary, which includes commentaries from a variety of sources and questions for study and discussion to stimulate the reader's understanding. Throughout the book are the views, interpretations, and comments of both ancient and modern commentators. A bibliography and glossary of commentaries and interpreters are provided as well.

Rabbi Meir Simcha Ha-Cohen (1845–1926), author of the commentary *Meshekh Hochmah,* suggests that not only the moral laws of Torah cause the early Israelites to rebel. They also object to other restrictions, especially those that regulate what they may or may not eat. The laws of *kashrut* forbid the eating of pork and certain other meat products and define how animals are to be slaughtered. Ha-Cohen claims that the Israelites protest because they want to eat meat without restrictions as they did in Egypt. "Stop making matters difficult for us," they gripe to Moses. "Let us eat whatever we desire."

Harvey J. Fields, A Torah Commentary for Our Times, vol. 3, p. 31.

They [the Israelites] did not remember the lashes. They did not remember the brutal hand of the oppressor coming down upon them with all of its weight. And now in the wilderness they recalled those days in Egypt, and their memories became an accusation against Moses. . . . And so we see that memory can be a dangerous thing.

> Morris Adler, *The Voice Still Speaks*
> (New York: Bloch Publishing, 1969), p. 297.

Fear of the future even diluted their recollection of past suffering; the perceived security of slavery was preferable to the risks of freedom.

> Ismar Schorsch, "Beha'alotekha 5756," *Learn @JTS: Parashat HaShavua*,
> http://learn.jtsa.edu/topics/parashah/5756/behaalotekha.shtml

[Commenting on the line, "But Moses said to him, 'Are you wrought up on my account? Would that all the Eternal's people were prophets, that the Eternal put [the divine] spirit upon them!'" (Numbers 11:29), Samson Raphael Hirsch states:] Moreover, we see that endowment with the Divine spirit is not dependent on any special "office" or "vocation." The humblest in the nation may be deemed just as worthy of a portion of the Divine as the foremost holder of the most exalted office.

> Samson Raphael Hirsch, *The Pentateuch*, ed. Ephraim Oratz,
> trans. Getrude Hirschler, (New York: Judaica Press, 1997), p. 557.

Significantly Moses himself took the opposite view and welcomed their novel status. "Would that all the Eternal's people were prophets," he says in gentle rebuke to his zealous servant. For Moses is secure in his own relationship with God and convinced that only as more and more people experience the blessing of the divine Presence can the dream of a holy people be realized. The ability to share is a sign of greatness; lesser leaders feel impelled to protect their status at all times.

> W. Gunther Plaut, ed., *The Torah: A Modern Commentary*, rev. ed., p. 969.

[The story of Eldad and Medad] may reflect an ancient debate concerning whether there is only one legitimate prophet at a time, . . . or if there may be many prophets in a single era.

> Adele Berlin and Marc Zvi Brettler, eds., *The Jewish Study Bible*
> (New York: Oxford University Press, 2004), p. 307.

[Commenting on the verse, "We remember the fish that we used to eat free in Egypt, the cucumbers, the melons, the leeks, the onions, and the garlic" (Numbers 11:5), Hillel E. Silverman writes:] Memory plays strange tricks. Was their "security" while in bondage as pleasurable as they now remembered it?

In times of hardship and distress, we are inclined to look backward to some imagined "happiness." When we suffer loneliness, despair, failure, or bereavement, we begin to romanticize the past. We recall only the happier aspects of our childhood and schooling, camping, early jobs, friends, family, and business associates.

Hillel E. Silverman, *From Week to Week: Reflections on the Sabbath Torah Readings* (Bridgeport, CT: Hartmore House, 1975), p. 134.

Questions for Discussion

1. According to Rashi, Joshua was so modest that he was offended by the prophecy predicting his replacement of Moses. Sforno says that Joshua wanted Eldad and Medad jailed because he was jealous of their prophetic ability and was afraid that they would replace him. Which of these two interpretations do you think is a more accurate reflection of Joshua's character as described in the Torah? Which do you think is more likely in the real world?

2. Why do you think Moses refers to himself (Numbers 11:12) as a nursing father who carries the suckling child? Do you think this is a helpful metaphor? Why or why not?

3. This Torah story is one about complaints. When are you allowed or even encouraged to complain, and when do your complaints become an ugly form of rebellion? Can you think of situations at home, school, or work when complaining would be appropriate and, conversely, when it would be inappropriate?

4. Why is it important for leaders to share the protests of their constituents, as Moses did, rather than bear the burden alone?

5. A modern rabbinic teacher was once quoted as saying, "The challenge facing the rabbi today is to become dispensable." How does this quote dovetail with the quote of Moses when he says: "Would that all the Eternal's people were prophets" (Numbers 11:29)? What is the relationship between these two quotations?

6. The term "burnout" refers to a growing inability to feel, care, or work effectively. In this story Moses is faced with unlimited demands. He receives only negative feedback and feels that he has failed. Do you think that Moses is suffering from what would today be called burnout? What does the story suggest was helpful to him as leader of the people?

7. In Numbers 11:25 God speaks to Moses, and "the Eternal drew upon the spirit that was on him and put it upon the seventy elders." What does it mean when the spirit of God is placed on a person? Have you ever felt the spirit of God enter within you? Is your life somehow changed by such an experience, or do you revert to being the same person you were before? Explain.

8. Chapter 11 of the Book of Numbers begins with the people complaining bitterly before God. The basis for their complaint is not stated. According to Rashbam, they complained about their living conditions. What do you think that they might have been complaining about?

9. How would you characterize Moses's leadership skills in this chapter? What are the positives of his leadership style? Where is he lacking?

10. *B'reishit Rabbah* 54:3 contains the following quote: "Love unaccompanied by criticism is not love." What does this mean, and how might this quote relate to the story told in Numbers 11?

12. The Ten Scouts: Demoralizing a People

The Bible Story: From Numbers 13–14

Numbers 13:1] The Eternal One spoke to Moses, saying,   **2]** "Send notables to scout the land of Canaan, which I am giving to the Israelite people; send one man from each of their ancestral tribes, each one a chieftain among them."...

17] When Moses sent them to scout the land of Canaan, he said to them, "Go up there into the Negeb and on into the hill country,   **18]** and see what kind of country it is. Are the people who dwell in it strong or weak, few or many?   **19]** Is the country in which they dwell good or bad? Are the towns they live in open or fortified?   **20]** Is the soil rich or poor? Is it wooded or not? And take pains to bring back some of the fruit of the land."—Now it happened to be the season of the first ripe grapes....

25] At the end of forty days they returned from scouting the land.   **26]** They went straight to Moses and Aaron and the whole

יג 1 וַיְדַבֵּ֥ר יְהֹוָ֖ה אֶל־מֹשֶׁ֥ה לֵּאמֹֽר:
2 שְׁלַח־לְךָ֣ אֲנָשִׁ֗ים וְיָתֻ֙רוּ֙ אֶת־אֶ֣רֶץ כְּנַ֔עַן אֲשֶׁר־אֲנִ֥י נֹתֵ֖ן לִבְנֵ֣י יִשְׂרָאֵ֑ל אִ֣ישׁ אֶחָד֩ אִ֨ישׁ אֶחָ֜ד לְמַטֵּ֤ה אֲבֹתָיו֙ תִּשְׁלָ֔חוּ כֹּ֖ל נָשִׂ֥יא בָהֶֽם:

17 וַיִּשְׁלַ֤ח אֹתָם֙ מֹשֶׁ֔ה לָת֖וּר אֶת־אֶ֣רֶץ כְּנָ֑עַן וַיֹּ֣אמֶר אֲלֵהֶ֗ם עֲל֥וּ זֶה֙ בַּנֶּ֔גֶב וַעֲלִיתֶ֖ם אֶת־הָהָֽר: 18 וּרְאִיתֶ֥ם אֶת־הָאָ֖רֶץ מַה־הִ֑וא וְאֶת־הָעָם֙ הַיֹּשֵׁ֣ב עָלֶ֔יהָ הֶחָזָ֥ק הוּא֙ הֲרָפֶ֔ה הַמְעַ֥ט ה֖וּא אִם־רָֽב: 19 וּמָ֣ה הָאָ֗רֶץ אֲשֶׁר־הוּא֙ יֹשֵׁ֣ב בָּ֔הּ הֲטוֹבָ֥ה הִ֖וא אִם־רָעָ֑ה וּמָ֣ה הֶעָרִ֗ים אֲשֶׁר־הוּא֙ יוֹשֵׁ֣ב בָּהֵ֔נָּה הַבְּמַֽחֲנִ֖ים אִ֥ם בְּמִבְצָרִֽים: 20 וּמָ֣ה הָ֠אָ֠רֶץ הַשְּׁמֵנָ֨ה הִ֜וא אִם־רָזָ֗ה הֲיֵֽשׁ־בָּ֥הּ עֵץ֙ אִם־אַ֔יִן וְהִ֨תְחַזַּקְתֶּ֔ם וּלְקַחְתֶּ֖ם מִפְּרִ֣י הָאָ֑רֶץ וְהַ֨יָּמִ֔ים יְמֵ֖י בִּכּוּרֵ֥י עֲנָבִֽים:

25 וַיָּשֻׁ֕בוּ מִתּ֖וּר הָאָ֑רֶץ מִקֵּ֖ץ אַרְבָּעִ֥ים י֑וֹם: 26 וַיֵּלְכ֡וּ וַיָּבֹ֩אוּ֩ אֶל־מֹשֶׁ֨ה וְאֶל־

Israelite community at Kadesh in the wilderness of Paran, and they made their report to them and to the whole community, as they showed them the fruit of the land. 27] This is what they told him: "We came to the land you sent us to; it does indeed flow with milk and honey, and this is its fruit. 28] However, the people who inhabit the country are powerful, and the cities are fortified and very large; moreover, we saw the Anakites there. 29] Amalekites dwell in the Negeb region; Hittites, Jebusites, and Amorites inhabit the hill country; and Canaanites dwell by the Sea and along the Jordan."

30] Caleb hushed the people before Moses and said, "Let us by all means go up, and we shall gain possession of it, for we shall surely overcome it." 31] But the notables who had gone up with him said, "We cannot attack that people, for it is stronger than we." 32] Thus they spread calumnies among the Israelites about the land they had scouted, saying, "The country that we traversed and scouted is one that devours its settlers. All the people that we saw in it are of great size; 33] we saw the Nephilim there—the Anakites are part of the Nephilim—and we looked like grasshoppers to ourselves, and so we must have looked to them."

14:1] The whole community broke into loud cries, and the people wept that night. 2] All the Israelites railed against Moses and Aaron. "If only we had died in the land of Egypt," the whole community

אַהֲרֹן וְאֶל־כָּל־עֲדַת בְּנֵי־יִשְׂרָאֵל אֶל־מִדְבַּר פָּארָן קָדֵשָׁה וַיָּשִׁיבוּ אֹתָם דָּבָר וְאֶת־כָּל־הָעֵדָה וַיַּרְאוּם אֶת־פְּרִי הָאָרֶץ: 27 וַיְסַפְּרוּ־לוֹ וַיֹּאמְרוּ בָּאנוּ אֶל־הָאָרֶץ אֲשֶׁר שְׁלַחְתָּנוּ וְגַם זָבַת חָלָב וּדְבַשׁ הִוא וְזֶה־פִּרְיָהּ: 28 אֶפֶס כִּי־עַז הָעָם הַיֹּשֵׁב בָּאָרֶץ וְהֶעָרִים בְּצֻרוֹת גְּדֹלֹת מְאֹד וְגַם־יְלִדֵי הָעֲנָק רָאִינוּ שָׁם: 29 עֲמָלֵק יוֹשֵׁב בְּאֶרֶץ הַנֶּגֶב וְהַחִתִּי וְהַיְבוּסִי וְהָאֱמֹרִי יוֹשֵׁב בָּהָר וְהַכְּנַעֲנִי יוֹשֵׁב עַל־הַיָּם וְעַל יַד הַיַּרְדֵּן:

30 וַיַּהַס כָּלֵב אֶת־הָעָם אֶל־מֹשֶׁה וַיֹּאמֶר עָלֹה נַעֲלֶה וְיָרַשְׁנוּ אֹתָהּ כִּי־יָכוֹל נוּכַל לָהּ: 31 וְהָאֲנָשִׁים אֲשֶׁר־עָלוּ עִמּוֹ אָמְרוּ לֹא נוּכַל לַעֲלוֹת אֶל־הָעָם כִּי־חָזָק הוּא מִמֶּנּוּ: 32 וַיֹּצִיאוּ דִּבַּת הָאָרֶץ אֲשֶׁר תָּרוּ אֹתָהּ אֶל־בְּנֵי יִשְׂרָאֵל לֵאמֹר הָאָרֶץ אֲשֶׁר עָבַרְנוּ בָהּ לָתוּר אֹתָהּ אֶרֶץ אֹכֶלֶת יוֹשְׁבֶיהָ הִוא וְכָל־הָעָם אֲשֶׁר־רָאִינוּ בְתוֹכָהּ אַנְשֵׁי מִדּוֹת: 33 וְשָׁם רָאִינוּ אֶת־הַנְּפִילִים בְּנֵי עֲנָק מִן־הַנְּפִלִים וַנְּהִי בְעֵינֵינוּ כַּחֲגָבִים וְכֵן הָיִינוּ בְּעֵינֵיהֶם:

יד 1 וַתִּשָּׂא כָּל־הָעֵדָה וַיִּתְּנוּ אֶת־קוֹלָם וַיִּבְכּוּ הָעָם בַּלַּיְלָה הַהוּא: 2 וַיִּלֹּנוּ עַל־מֹשֶׁה וְעַל־אַהֲרֹן כֹּל בְּנֵי יִשְׂרָאֵל וַיֹּאמְרוּ אֲלֵהֶם כָּל־הָעֵדָה לוּ־מַתְנוּ בְּאֶרֶץ

shouted at them, "or if only we might die in this wilderness!"   3] "Why is the Eternal taking us to that land to fall by the sword?" "Our wives and children will be carried off! It would be better for us to go back to Egypt!"   4] And they said to one another, "Let us head back for Egypt."

5] Then Moses and Aaron fell on their faces before all the assembled congregation of Israelites.   6] And Joshua son of Nun and Caleb son of Jephunneh, of those who had scouted the land, rent their clothes   7] and exhorted the whole Israelite community: "The land that we traversed and scouted is an exceedingly good land.   8] If pleased with us, the Eternal will bring us into that land, a land that flows with milk and honey, and give it to us;   9] only you must not rebel against the Eternal. Have no fear then of the people of the country, for they are our prey: their protection has departed from them, but the Eternal is with us. Have no fear of them!"   10] As the whole community threatened to pelt them with stones, the Presence of the Eternal appeared in the Tent of Meeting to all the Israelites.

11] And the Eternal One said to Moses, "How long will this people spurn Me, and how long will they have no faith in Me despite all the signs that I have performed in their midst?   12] I will strike them with pestilence and disown them, and I will make of you a nation far more numerous than they!" . . .

מִצְרַיִם אוֹ בַּמִּדְבָּר הַזֶּה לוּ־מָתְנוּ: 3 וְלָמָה יְהֹוָה מֵבִיא אֹתָנוּ אֶל־הָאָרֶץ הַזֹּאת לִנְפֹּל בַּחֶרֶב נָשֵׁינוּ וְטַפֵּנוּ יִהְיוּ לָבַז הֲלוֹא טוֹב לָנוּ שׁוּב מִצְרָיְמָה: 4 וַיֹּאמְרוּ אִישׁ אֶל־אָחִיו נִתְּנָה רֹאשׁ וְנָשׁוּבָה מִצְרָיְמָה:

5 וַיִּפֹּל מֹשֶׁה וְאַהֲרֹן עַל־פְּנֵיהֶם לִפְנֵי כָּל־קְהַל עֲדַת בְּנֵי יִשְׂרָאֵל: 6 וִיהוֹשֻׁעַ בִּן־נוּן וְכָלֵב בֶּן־יְפֻנֶּה מִן־הַתָּרִים אֶת־הָאָרֶץ קָרְעוּ בִּגְדֵיהֶם: 7 וַיֹּאמְרוּ אֶל־כָּל־עֲדַת בְּנֵי־יִשְׂרָאֵל לֵאמֹר הָאָרֶץ אֲשֶׁר עָבַרְנוּ בָהּ לָתוּר אֹתָהּ טוֹבָה הָאָרֶץ מְאֹד מְאֹד: 8 אִם־חָפֵץ בָּנוּ יְהֹוָה וְהֵבִיא אֹתָנוּ אֶל־הָאָרֶץ הַזֹּאת וּנְתָנָהּ לָנוּ אֶרֶץ אֲשֶׁר־הִוא זָבַת חָלָב וּדְבָשׁ: 9 אַךְ בַּיהֹוָה אַל־תִּמְרֹדוּ וְאַתֶּם אַל־תִּירְאוּ אֶת־עַם הָאָרֶץ כִּי לַחְמֵנוּ הֵם סָר צִלָּם מֵעֲלֵיהֶם וַיהֹוָה אִתָּנוּ אַל־תִּירָאֻם: 10 וַיֹּאמְרוּ כָּל־הָעֵדָה לִרְגּוֹם אֹתָם בָּאֲבָנִים וּכְבוֹד יְהֹוָה נִרְאָה בְּאֹהֶל מוֹעֵד אֶל־כָּל־בְּנֵי יִשְׂרָאֵל:

11 וַיֹּאמֶר יְהֹוָה אֶל־מֹשֶׁה עַד־אָנָה יְנַאֲצֻנִי הָעָם הַזֶּה וְעַד־אָנָה לֹא־יַאֲמִינוּ בִי בְּכֹל הָאֹתוֹת אֲשֶׁר עָשִׂיתִי בְּקִרְבּוֹ: 12 אַכֶּנּוּ בַדֶּבֶר וְאוֹרִשֶׁנּוּ וְאֶעֱשֶׂה אֹתְךָ לְגוֹי־גָּדוֹל וְעָצוּם מִמֶּנּוּ:

106

26] The Eternal One spoke further to Moses and Aaron, 27] "How much longer shall that wicked community keep muttering against Me?..."

30] Not one shall enter the land in which I swore to settle you...."

36] As for the notables whom Moses sent to scout the land, those who came back and caused the whole community to mutter against him by spreading calumnies about the land— 37] those who spread such calumnies about the land died of plague, by the will of the Eternal. 38] Of those notables who had gone to scout the land, only Joshua son of Nun and Caleb son of Jephunneh survived.

26 וַיְדַבֵּ֣ר יְהֹוָ֔ה אֶל־מֹשֶׁ֥ה וְאֶֽל־אַהֲרֹ֖ן לֵאמֹֽר׃ 27 עַד־מָתַ֗י לָעֵדָ֤ה הָֽרָעָה֙ הַזֹּ֔את אֲשֶׁ֨ר הֵ֧מָּה מַלִּינִ֛ים עָלָ֖י אֶת־תְּלֻנֹּ֣ות בְּנֵ֣י יִשְׂרָאֵ֑ל אֲשֶׁ֨ר הֵ֧מָּה מַלִּינִ֛ים עָלַ֖י שָׁמָֽעְתִּי׃

30 אִם־אַתֶּם֙ תָּבֹ֣אוּ אֶל־הָאָ֔רֶץ אֲשֶׁ֤ר נָשָׂ֙אתִי֙ אֶת־יָדִ֔י לְשַׁכֵּ֥ן אֶתְכֶ֖ם בָּ֑הּ׃...

36 וְהָ֣אֲנָשִׁ֔ים אֲשֶׁר־שָׁלַ֥ח מֹשֶׁ֖ה לָת֣וּר אֶת־הָאָ֑רֶץ וַיָּשֻׁ֙בוּ֙ וילונו [וַיַּלִּ֣ינוּ] עָלָ֔יו אֶת־כׇּל־הָ֣עֵדָ֔ה לְהוֹצִ֥יא דִבָּ֖ה עַל־הָאָֽרֶץ׃ 37 וַיָּמֻ֙תוּ֙ הָֽאֲנָשִׁ֔ים מוֹצִאֵ֥י דִבַּת־הָאָ֖רֶץ רָעָ֑ה בַּמַּגֵּפָ֖ה לִפְנֵ֥י יְהֹוָֽה׃ 38 וִיהוֹשֻׁ֣עַ בִּן־נ֗וּן וְכָלֵ֣ב בֶּן־יְפֻנֶּ֔ה חָיוּ֙ מִן־הָֽאֲנָשִׁ֣ים הָהֵ֔ם הַהֹֽלְכִ֖ים לָת֥וּר אֶת־הָאָֽרֶץ׃

Understanding the Story

This story, perhaps the most famous spy story in the entire Bible, tells of twelve "notables," each of whom represented one of Israel's tribes, scouting the Land of Israel. After forty days they return. Ten of the scouts (or spies, as they are often referred to in English) report that although the land is fruitful, its cities are filled with powerful giants, making the Israelites in comparison to them look like grasshoppers. The report terrifies the community. Seeking to assure the Israelites, Caleb says that by all means the people should go up and gain possession of the land, for they will surely win any battles that will come their way.

It is then that the entire community turns on Moses and Aaron, suggesting that all return to Egypt. Joshua and Caleb try to reassure the Israelites that the land is indeed exceedingly good and that, with faith in God, they will surely defeat the enemy. Rejecting this advice, the people threaten to pelt them with stones. It is at this point that God tells Moses that none shall enter the Promised Land, except for Caleb and Joshua.

What is the actual sin of the scouts? What is it about the response to their report that so very much angers God? Do Caleb and Joshua act appropriately as leaders? Do Moses and Aaron? What is the primary lesson that can be derived from the story? There are a plethora of commentaries that attempt to answer these complicated questions.

From the Commentators

Wildavsky suggests that the sin of the scouts is more serious than the heinous sin of slander. The Israelites have left Egypt with the promise of conquering the Land of Israel. That is their goal. The scouts return and take advantage of the people's anticipation of their report to "discredit the entire enterprise." That is their sin. They conspire to convince the people that God is leading them to disaster. Thus they essentially kill the hopes of their people, and thus their generation is condemned to wander and die in the wilderness.

Based on Aaron Wildavsky, *The Nursing Father: Moses as a Political Leader* (Tuscaloosa: University of Alabama Press, 1984), pp. 114–118.

Chassidut discusses the reason why the spies did not wish to enter the Land of Israel: they did not want to become involved with the materialism of the world. For the duration of the Jewish people's stay in the desert, they were free from mundane involvements: their bread came from heaven (the manna); they had water from the well of Miriam; and even their garments were cleaned and pressed by the clouds of glory. Thus they did not wish to leave the wilderness to enter the Land of Israel. In the Land of Israel they would have to become involved with ploughing [sic], sowing, and so forth.

> Menachem M. Schneerson, *Likkutei Sichot: An Anthology of Talks Relating to the Weekly Sections of the Torah and Special Occasions in the Jewish Calendar* (North Bergen, NJ: "Kehot" Publication Society, 1992), p. 113.

The dramatic public debate brought out the subtle tendency of the spies to spread fear and panic among the people, while Caleb and Joshua combated this tendency. In their demoralizing campaign the spies keep mentioning the *anakim*, the dreadful breed of giants whose presence in the land of Canaan would make it impossible for the Israelites to conquer the land. The repeated mention of the *anakim* discourages the people, "takes out" their hearts and "melts it away."

> Pinchus Peli, *Torah Today: A Renewed Encounter with Scripture* (Washington, D.C.: B'nai Brith Books, 1987), pp. 171–172.

"The country that we traversed and scouted is one that devours its settlers" (Numbers 13:32). It is not disputed that the nation that dwells there is strong, but this is not because of the value of the land. The land is only hospitable to the strong. They are strong by nature, and the others die by the poor climate.

"and we looked like grasshoppers to ourselves, and so we must have looked to them" (Numbers 13:33). [The scouts were saying:] We looked like grasshoppers or smaller creatures. They did not rise against us. They did not think that we were important enough in their eyes to do evil to us.

> Sforno on Numbers 13:33–34.

The statement of the spies "We cannot go up" (Numbers 13:31) embodies far more than

Sforno

Obadiah ben Jacob Sforno (1475–1550) was a fifteenth-century Italian physician and Bible commentator. His Bible commentaries, like those of Rashi, rely on the plain meaning of the text and sometimes on philosophy. Unlike Rashi, his commentary does not include linguistic observations. His outlook has been called humanistic because he seldom emphasizes the difference between Jews and non-Jews, choosing to teach that all people are God's treasure.

physical fear of the people of Canaan. It expressed an unwillingness to elevate themselves spiritually. They were not willing to make the sacrifices necessary in order to merit the three gifts mentioned earlier. Their suggestion of the alternative, namely a return to Egypt, clearly shows that their orientation lay in the pursuit of physical and material pleasures, such as abounded in Egypt.

Yitzchak Arama, *Akeydat Yitzchak: Commentary of Rabbi Yitzchak Arama on the Torah*, trans. Eliyahu Munk (New York: Lambda Publishers, 2001), pp. 718–719.

Their sin, says Nachmanides, is the tone in which they deliver their information. Upon their return they begin speaking in glowing, positive terms about the wonderful fruit of the land; then, however, they turn negative. Using the world *efes*, or "but," they declare, "But the people of the land are powerful." That evaluation, concludes Nachmanides, "signifies something negative, beyond human capability, something impossible to achieve under any circumstances." It produces fear. Quite obviously it is the negative presentation by the spies that panics the people and causes them to reject conquering the Land of Israel.

Harvey J. Fields, *A Torah Commentary for Our Times*, vol. 3 (New York: UAHC Press, 1998), p. 40.

Chasidic teacher Yitzhak Meir...comments that the sin of the spies is not their plan to undermine the expectations of the people to settle the land but their actual carrying out of the plan after their scouting mission. Human beings, observes Rabbi Meir of Ger, are not held responsible for evil thoughts or for evil plans. They sin when they translate their evil plans into the reality of deeds. This is the sin of the spies. With their unfavorable report they turn the whole nation away from its goal of conquering the land.

Harvey J. Fields, *A Torah Commentary for Our Times*, vol. 3, p. 39.

[Commenting on the line "and we looked like grasshoppers to ourselves, and so we must have looked to them" (Numbers 13:33), Seymour Essrog states:] The *Midrash*—rabbinic commentary, in its usual allegorical style, depicts God as being angry with the spies and challenging them: "How do you know what you looked like to them? Perhaps you appeared to them like angels?"

The rabbis touch upon a great truth and teaching for all of us. We often tend to underestimate ourselves and demand our own importance as a people. We do not realize our importance, for example, to those whose lives we touch—our children, our spouses, our friends. We all need each other's love, understanding, appreciation, gratitude, and encouragement.

Seymour L. Essrog, "Guidelines" (sermon, Congregation Beth Israel, Owings Mills, MD, June 8, 1991).

THEY WENT STRAIGHT TO MOSES AND AARON...AND THEY MADE THEIR REPORT TO HIM...THEY TOLD HIM: WE CAME TO THE LAND YOU SENT US TO; IT DOES INDEED FLOW WITH MILK AND HONEY...HOWEVER, THE PEOPLE WHO INHABIT THE COUNTRY ARE FORTIFIED AND VERY LARGE (13:26). Such is the way of people who utter slander; they begin by speaking well of some one and conclude by speaking ill.

B'midbar Rabbah 16:17.

The oath was: *Surely none of the men that came up out of Egypt, from twenty years old and upward, shall see the land* (Numbers 32:11). A man who was twenty years old died whether he was of the same mind as the spies or not. [Note: In the latter case, because he did not openly dissociate himself from them.]

B'midbar Rabbah 16:23, in *Midrash Rabbah: Numbers*, p. 690.

The Talmud (*Sotah* 35a) and, later, Rashi suggest one possibility based on the last word in Num. 13:31. Following upon Caleb's calming words in the previous verse, "Let us indeed go up, and we will possess it, for we can prevail over it" (Num. 13:30), the faint-hearted spies speak out again, saying: "We cannot go up against that people, for it is stronger than we [*mimenu*]" (Num. 13:31). But grammatically, *mimenu* could mean either "than we" or "than he"; thus, it is possible that the ten spies are suggesting that the people in that country are stronger than He, that is, God. Such a failure of trust in God equals the insult of the golden calf, and leads God to reject this first generation as inheritors of God's land.

Lisa A. Edwards, "The Grasshoppers and the Giants," in *The Women's Torah Commentary: New Insights from Women Rabbis on the 54 Weekly Torah Portions*, ed. Elyse Goldstein (Woodstock, VT: Jewish Lights Publishing, 2000), p. 280.

Questions for Discussion

1. Why does God tell Moses to send scouts? If, in God's infinite wisdom, God knows they will bring back a false report, what is the point in sending them?

2. Moses asks the scouts to bring him clear and precise answers to these questions: (a) what kind of country it is; (b) whether the people are strong or weak, few or many; (c) whether the land is good or bad; (d) whether the towns are open or fortified; and (e) whether the soil is rich or poor, wooded or not. Are there any other questions that you would have added to this list? What are the questions that you think need to be answered when a person explores a new place in which to make his or her home?

3. There are commentators who state that the sin of the scouts is in the use of the word "however." They say, "However, the people who inhabit the country are powerful, and the cities are fortified and very large" (Numbers 13:28). Had they left out the word "however," the spies would have stayed within the limits of a factual report. When they added the word "however," it was no longer a factual account, but rather an attempt to sway public opinion. How do you react to this commentary? Do you agree or disagree?

4. According to the text, "The country...is one that devours its settlers" (Numbers 13:32). If the land consumed its inhabitants, then how could there have existed people of great size? What might this expression mean?

5. Do you think that the scouts are in any way repudiating their trust in God? Can you prove this from the text itself?

6. Do you feel that God's punishment of the Israelites is commensurate with their crime? Why or why not? What is the sin of the Israelites? In your opinion, what is the sin of the scouts?

7. The scouts are quoted as saying: "We looked like grasshoppers to ourselves, and so we must have looked to them" (Numbers 13:33). How could the spies know how they appeared in the sight of the inhabitants of the land? How might you explain their words?

8. Our Sages once enunciated this principle in a midrash: "A lie, to succeed, must contain a grain of truth." How does this principle apply to this story? To which specific verse can this principle be applied?

9. The Kotzker Rebbe asserts that the sin of the scouts was their statement "We looked like grasshoppers to ourselves, and so we must have looked to them" (Numbers 13:33). The Rebbe continued his explanation by stating that one can understand their statement "we looked like grasshoppers to ourselves," for that was the way they really saw themselves. However, what right did the scouts have to say, "and so we must have looked to them"? What difference should it make how we appeared to them? What are your thoughts on the Kotzker Rebbe's comments? Can you think of a modern-day example that would help to explain his interpretation?

10. Is it ever appropriate for a person to "fudge the truth" for some greater cause? Can you think of contemporary examples where this might be necessary?

11. What lessons can be learned from the story of the scouts? Explain.

12. How does this story relate to our relationship with the modern State of Israel today? Do you think a Jew is being disloyal if he/she spreads "an evil report" about the State of Israel?

13. The Curse of Balaam: Can a Donkey Really Talk?

The Bible Story: From Numbers 22–24

Numbers 22:4] . . . Balak son of Zippor, who was king of Moab at that time, 5] sent messengers to Balaam son of Beor in Pethor, which is by the Euphrates, in the land of his kinsfolk, to invite him, saying, "There is a people that came out of Egypt; it hides the earth from view, and it is settled next to me. 6] Come then, put a curse upon this people for me, since they are too numerous for me; perhaps I can thus defeat them and drive them out of the land. For I know that he whom you bless is blessed indeed, and he whom you curse is cursed." . . .

9] God came to Balaam and said, "What do these people want of you?" 10] Balaam said to God, "Balak son of Zippor, king of Moab, sent me this message: 11] Here is a people that came out from Egypt and hides the earth from view. Come now and curse them for me; perhaps I can engage them in battle and drive them off." 12] But God said to Balaam, "Do not go with them. You must not curse that people, for they are blessed."

כב ‏4 ‏. . . וּבָלָק בֶּן־צִפּוֹר מֶלֶךְ לְמוֹאָב בָּעֵת הַהִוא: ‏5 ‏וַיִּשְׁלַח מַלְאָכִים אֶל־בִּלְעָם בֶּן־בְּעוֹר פְּתוֹרָה אֲשֶׁר עַל־הַנָּהָר אֶרֶץ בְּנֵי־עַמּוֹ לִקְרֹא־לוֹ לֵאמֹר הִנֵּה עַם יָצָא מִמִּצְרַיִם הִנֵּה כִסָּה אֶת־עֵין הָאָרֶץ וְהוּא יֹשֵׁב מִמֻּלִי: ‏6 ‏וְעַתָּה לְכָה־נָּא אָרָה־לִּי אֶת־הָעָם הַזֶּה כִּי־עָצוּם הוּא מִמֶּנִּי אוּלַי אוּכַל נַכֶּה־בּוֹ וַאֲגָרְשֶׁנּוּ מִן־הָאָרֶץ כִּי יָדַעְתִּי אֵת אֲשֶׁר־תְּבָרֵךְ מְבֹרָךְ וַאֲשֶׁר תָּאֹר יוּאָר:

‏9 ‏וַיָּבֹא אֱלֹהִים אֶל־בִּלְעָם וַיֹּאמֶר מִי הָאֲנָשִׁים הָאֵלֶּה עִמָּךְ: ‏10 ‏וַיֹּאמֶר בִּלְעָם אֶל־הָאֱלֹהִים בָּלָק בֶּן־צִפֹּר מֶלֶךְ מוֹאָב שָׁלַח אֵלָי: ‏11 ‏הִנֵּה הָעָם הַיֹּצֵא מִמִּצְרַיִם וַיְכַס אֶת־עֵין הָאָרֶץ עַתָּה לְכָה קָבָה־לִּי אֹתוֹ אוּלַי אוּכַל לְהִלָּחֶם בּוֹ וְגֵרַשְׁתִּיו: ‏12 ‏וַיֹּאמֶר אֱלֹהִים אֶל־בִּלְעָם לֹא תֵלֵךְ עִמָּהֶם לֹא תָאֹר אֶת־הָעָם כִּי בָרוּךְ הוּא:

13] Balaam arose in the morning and said to Balak's dignitaries, "Go back to your own country, for the Eternal will not let me go with you." 14] The Moabite dignitaries left, and they came to Balak and said, "Balaam refused to come with us."

15] Then Balak sent other dignitaries, more numerous and distinguished than the first. 16] They came to Balaam and said to him, "Thus says Balak son of Zippor: Please do not refuse to come to me. 17] I will reward you richly and I will do anything you ask of me. Only come and damn this people for me." 18] Balaam replied to Balak's officials, "Though Balak were to give me his house full of silver and gold, I could not do anything, big or little, contrary to the command of the Eternal my God. 19] So you, too, stay here overnight, and let me find out what else the Eternal may say to me." 20] That night God came to Balaam and said to him, "If these personages have come to invite you, you may go with them. But whatever I command you, that you shall do."

21] When he arose in the morning, Balaam saddled his ass and departed with the Moabite dignitaries. 22] But God was incensed at his going; so an angel of the Eternal stood planted in his way as an adversary.

וַיָּ֤קָם בִּלְעָם֙ בַּבֹּ֔קֶר וַיֹּ֙אמֶר֙ אֶל־שָׂרֵ֣י 13
בָלָ֔ק לְכ֖וּ אֶל־אַרְצְכֶ֑ם כִּ֚י מֵאֵ֣ן יְהֹוָ֔ה
לְתִתִּ֖י לַהֲלֹ֥ךְ עִמָּכֶֽם: וַיָּק֙וּמוּ֙ שָׂרֵ֣י 14
מוֹאָ֔ב וַיָּבֹ֖אוּ אֶל־בָּלָ֑ק וַיֹּ֣אמְר֔וּ מֵאֵ֥ן
בִּלְעָ֖ם הֲלֹ֥ךְ עִמָּֽנוּ:

וַיֹּ֥סֶף ע֖וֹד בָּלָ֑ק שְׁלֹ֣חַ שָׂרִ֔ים רַבִּ֖ים 15
וְנִכְבַּדִּ֥ים מֵאֵֽלֶּה: וַיָּבֹ֖אוּ אֶל־בִּלְעָ֑ם 16
וַיֹּ֣אמְרוּ ל֗וֹ כֹּ֤ה אָמַר֙ בָּלָ֣ק בֶּן־צִפּ֔וֹר אַל־
נָ֥א תִמָּנַ֖ע מֵהֲלֹ֥ךְ אֵלָֽי: כִּֽי־כַבֵּ֙ד 17
אֲכַבֶּדְךָ֙ מְאֹ֔ד וְכֹ֛ל אֲשֶׁר־תֹּאמַ֥ר אֵלַ֖י
אֶֽעֱשֶׂ֑ה וּלְכָה־נָּא֙ קָֽבָה־לִּ֔י אֵ֖ת הָעָ֥ם
הַזֶּֽה: וַיַּ֣עַן בִּלְעָ֗ם וַיֹּ֙אמֶר֙ אֶל־עַבְדֵ֣י 18
בָלָ֔ק אִם־יִתֶּן־לִ֥י בָלָ֛ק מְלֹ֥א בֵית֖וֹ כֶּ֣סֶף
וְזָהָ֑ב לֹ֣א אוּכַ֗ל לַעֲבֹר֙ אֶת־פִּ֙י֙ יְהֹוָ֣ה
אֱלֹהָ֔י לַעֲשׂ֥וֹת קְטַנָּ֖ה א֥וֹ גְדוֹלָֽה:
וְעַתָּ֗ה שְׁב֙וּ נָ֥א בָזֶ֛ה גַּם־אַתֶּ֖ם הַלָּ֑יְלָה 19
וְאֵ֣דְעָ֔ה מַה־יֹּסֵ֥ף יְהֹוָ֖ה דַּבֵּ֥ר עִמִּֽי:
וַיָּבֹ֨א אֱלֹהִ֥ים | אֶל־בִּלְעָם֮ לַ֒יְלָה֒ 20
וַיֹּ֣אמֶר ל֗וֹ אִם־לִקְרֹ֤א לְךָ֙ בָּ֣אוּ הָֽאֲנָשִׁ֔ים
ק֖וּם לֵ֣ךְ אִתָּ֑ם וְאַ֗ךְ אֶת־הַדָּבָ֛ר אֲשֶׁר־
אֲדַבֵּ֥ר אֵלֶ֖יךָ אֹת֥וֹ תַעֲשֶֽׂה:

וַיָּ֤קָם בִּלְעָם֙ בַּבֹּ֔קֶר וַֽיַּחֲבֹ֖שׁ אֶת־אֲתֹנ֑וֹ 21
וַיֵּ֖לֶךְ עִם־שָׂרֵ֥י מוֹאָֽב: וַיִּֽחַר־אַ֣ף 22
אֱלֹהִים֮ כִּֽי־הוֹלֵ֣ךְ הוּא֒ וַיִּתְיַצֵּ֞ב מַלְאַ֧ךְ
יְהֹוָ֛ה בַּדֶּ֖רֶךְ לְשָׂטָ֣ן לֽוֹ

He was riding on his she-ass, with his two servants alongside, 23] when the ass caught sight of the angel of the Eternal standing in the way, with his drawn sword in his hand. The ass swerved from the road and went into the fields; and Balaam beat the ass to turn her back onto the road. 24] The angel of the Eternal then stationed himself in a lane between the vineyards, with a fence on either side. 25] The ass, seeing the angel of the Eternal, pressed herself against the wall and squeezed Balaam's foot against the wall; so he beat her again. 26] Once more the angel of the Eternal moved forward and stationed himself on a spot so narrow that there was no room to swerve right or left. 27] When the ass now saw the angel of the Eternal, she lay down under Balaam; and Balaam was furious and beat the ass with his stick.

28] Then the Eternal opened the ass's mouth, and she said to Balaam, "What have I done to you that you have beaten me these three times?" 29] Balaam said to the ass, "You have made a mockery of me! If I had a sword with me, I'd kill you." 30] The ass said to Balaam, "Look, I am the ass that you have been riding all along until this day! Have I been in the habit of doing thus to you?" And he answered, "No."

31] Then the Eternal uncovered Balaam's eyes, and he saw the angel of the Eternal standing in the way, his drawn sword in his hand; thereupon he bowed right down to the ground. 32] The angel of the Eternal

וְה֥וּא רֹכֵ֣ב עַל־אֲתֹנ֔וֹ וּשְׁנֵ֥י נְעָרָ֖יו עִמּֽוֹ: 23 וַתֵּ֣רֶא הָאָתוֹן֩ אֶת־מַלְאַ֨ךְ יְהֹוָ֜ה נִצָּ֣ב בַּדֶּ֗רֶךְ וְחַרְבּ֤וֹ שְׁלוּפָה֙ בְּיָד֔וֹ וַתֵּ֤ט הָאָתוֹן֙ מִן־הַדֶּ֔רֶךְ וַתֵּ֖לֶךְ בַּשָּׂדֶ֑ה וַיַּ֤ךְ בִּלְעָם֙ אֶת־הָ֣אָת֔וֹן לְהַטֹּתָ֖הּ הַדָּֽרֶךְ: 24 וַֽיַּעֲמֹד֙ מַלְאַ֣ךְ יְהֹוָ֔ה בְּמִשְׁע֖וֹל הַכְּרָמִ֑ים גָּדֵ֥ר מִזֶּ֖ה וְגָדֵ֥ר מִזֶּֽה: 25 וַתֵּ֨רֶא הָאָת֜וֹן אֶת־מַלְאַ֣ךְ יְהֹוָ֗ה וַתִּלָּחֵץ֙ אֶל־הַקִּ֔יר וַתִּלְחַ֛ץ אֶת־רֶ֥גֶל בִּלְעָ֖ם אֶל־הַקִּ֑יר וַיֹּ֖סֶף לְהַכֹּתָֽהּ: 26 וַיּ֥וֹסֶף מַלְאַךְ־יְהֹוָ֖ה עֲב֑וֹר וַיַּֽעֲמֹד֙ בְּמָק֣וֹם צָ֔ר אֲשֶׁ֛ר אֵֽין־דֶּ֥רֶךְ לִנְט֖וֹת יָמִ֥ין וּשְׂמֹֽאול: 27 וַתֵּ֤רֶא הָֽאָתוֹן֙ אֶת־מַלְאַ֣ךְ יְהֹוָ֔ה וַתִּרְבַּ֖ץ תַּ֣חַת בִּלְעָ֑ם וַיִּֽחַר־אַ֣ף בִּלְעָ֔ם וַיַּ֥ךְ אֶת־הָאָת֖וֹן בַּמַּקֵּֽל:

28 וַיִּפְתַּ֥ח יְהֹוָ֖ה אֶת־פִּ֣י הָאָת֑וֹן וַתֹּ֤אמֶר לְבִלְעָם֙ מֶה־עָשִׂ֣יתִי לְךָ֔ כִּ֣י הִכִּיתַ֔נִי זֶ֖ה שָׁלֹ֥שׁ רְגָלִֽים: 29 וַיֹּ֤אמֶר בִּלְעָם֙ לָֽאָת֔וֹן כִּ֥י הִתְעַלַּ֖לְתְּ בִּ֑י ל֤וּ יֶשׁ־חֶ֙רֶב֙ בְּיָדִ֔י כִּ֥י עַתָּ֖ה הֲרַגְתִּֽיךְ: 30 וַתֹּ֨אמֶר הָאָת֜וֹן אֶל־בִּלְעָ֗ם הֲלוֹא֩ אָֽנֹכִ֨י אֲתֹֽנְךָ֜ אֲשֶׁר־רָכַ֣בְתָּ עָלַ֗י מֵעֽוֹדְךָ֙ עַד־הַיּ֣וֹם הַזֶּ֔ה הַֽהַסְכֵּ֣ן הִסְכַּ֔נְתִּי לַעֲשׂ֥וֹת לְךָ֖ כֹּ֑ה וַיֹּ֖אמֶר לֹֽא: 31 וַיְגַ֣ל יְהֹוָה֮ אֶת־עֵינֵ֣י בִלְעָם֒ וַיַּ֞רְא אֶת־מַלְאַ֤ךְ יְהֹוָה֙ נִצָּ֣ב בַּדֶּ֔רֶךְ וְחַרְבּ֥וֹ שְׁלֻפָ֖ה בְּיָד֑וֹ וַיִּקֹּ֥ד וַיִּשְׁתַּ֖חוּ לְאַפָּֽיו: 32 וַיֹּ֤אמֶר אֵלָיו֙ מַלְאַ֣ךְ יְהֹוָ֔ה עַל־מָ֗ה הִכִּ֙יתָ֙ אֶת־

said to him, "Why have you beaten your ass these three times? It is I who came out as an adversary, for the errand is obnoxious to me. 33] And when the ass saw me, she shied away because of me those three times. If she had not shied away from me, you are the one I should have killed, while sparing her." 34] Balaam said to the angel of the Eternal, "I erred because I did not know that you were standing in my way. If you still disapprove, I will turn back." 35] But the angel of the Eternal said to Balaam, "Go with those mortals. But you must say nothing except what I tell you." So Balaam went on with Balak's dignitaries....

23:4] God became manifest to Balaam, who stated, "I have set up the seven altars and offered up a bull and a ram on each altar." 5] And the Eternal put a word in Balaam's mouth and said, "Return to Balak and speak thus." 6] So he returned to him and found him standing beside his offerings, and all the Moabite dignitaries with him....

17]...Balak asked him, "What did the Eternal say?" 18] And he took up his theme, and said:

Up, Balak, attend,

Give ear unto me, son of Zippor!

19] God is not human to be capricious,

Or mortal to have a change of heart.

Would [God] speak and not act,

Promise and not fulfill?

אֲתֹנְךָ זֶה שָׁלֹשׁ רְגָלִים הִנֵּה אָנֹכִי יָצָאתִי לְשָׂטָן כִּי־יָרַט הַדֶּרֶךְ לְנֶגְדִּי: 33 וַתִּרְאַנִי הָאָתוֹן וַתֵּט לְפָנַי זֶה שָׁלֹשׁ רְגָלִים אוּלַי נָטְתָה מִפָּנַי כִּי עַתָּה גַּם־אֹתְכָה הָרַגְתִּי וְאוֹתָהּ הֶחֱיֵיתִי: 34 וַיֹּאמֶר בִּלְעָם אֶל־מַלְאַךְ יְהֹוָה חָטָאתִי כִּי לֹא יָדַעְתִּי כִּי אַתָּה נִצָּב לִקְרָאתִי בַּדָּרֶךְ וְעַתָּה אִם־רַע בְּעֵינֶיךָ אָשׁוּבָה לִּי: 35 וַיֹּאמֶר מַלְאַךְ יְהֹוָה אֶל־בִּלְעָם לֵךְ עִם־הָאֲנָשִׁים וְאֶפֶס אֶת־הַדָּבָר אֲשֶׁר־אֲדַבֵּר אֵלֶיךָ אֹתוֹ תְדַבֵּר וַיֵּלֶךְ בִּלְעָם עִם־שָׂרֵי בָלָק:

כג 4 וַיִּקָּר אֱלֹהִים אֶל־בִּלְעָם וַיֹּאמֶר אֵלָיו אֶת־שִׁבְעַת הַמִּזְבְּחֹת עָרַכְתִּי וָאַעַל פָּר וָאַיִל בַּמִּזְבֵּחַ: 5 וַיָּשֶׂם יְהֹוָה דָּבָר בְּפִי בִלְעָם וַיֹּאמֶר שׁוּב אֶל־בָּלָק וְכֹה תְדַבֵּר: 6 וַיָּשָׁב אֵלָיו וְהִנֵּה נִצָּב עַל־עֹלָתוֹ הוּא וְכָל־שָׂרֵי מוֹאָב:

17 ...וַיֹּאמֶר לוֹ בָּלָק מַה־דִּבֶּר יְהֹוָה: 18 וַיִּשָּׂא מְשָׁלוֹ וַיֹּאמַר

קוּם בָּלָק וּשְׁמָע

הַאֲזִינָה עָדַי בְּנוֹ צִפֹּר: 19 לֹא אִישׁ אֵל וִיכַזֵּב

וּבֶן־אָדָם וְיִתְנֶחָם

הַהוּא אָמַר וְלֹא יַעֲשֶׂה

וְדִבֶּר וְלֹא יְקִימֶנָּה:

20] My message was to bless:
When [God] blesses, I cannot reverse
  it. . . .

25] Thereupon Balak said to Balaam,
"Don't curse them and don't bless them!"
26] In reply, Balaam said to Balak, "But
I told you: Whatever the Eternal says, that
I must do." . . .

24:1] Now Balaam, seeing that it pleased
the Eternal to bless Israel, did not, as on
previous occasions, go in search of omens,
but turned his face toward the wilderness.
2] As Balaam looked up and saw Israel
encamped tribe by tribe, the spirit of God
came upon him. 3] Taking up his theme,
he said:

Word of Balaam son of Beor,

Word of the man whose eye is true,

4] Word of him who hears God's speech,

Who beholds visions from the Almighty,

Prostrate, but with eyes unveiled:

5] How fair are your tents, O Jacob,

Your dwellings, O Israel! . . .

10] Enraged at Balaam, Balak struck his
hands together. "I called you," Balak said
to Balaam, "to damn my enemies, and
instead you have blessed them these three
times! 11] Back with you at once to your
own place! I was going to reward you

20 הִנֵּה בָרֵךְ לָקָחְתִּי
וּבֵרֵךְ וְלֹא אֲשִׁיבֶנָּה:

25 וַיֹּאמֶר בָּלָק אֶל־בִּלְעָם גַּם־קֹב לֹא
תִקֳּבֶנּוּ גַּם־בָּרֵךְ לֹא תְבָרֲכֶנּוּ: 26 וַיַּעַן
בִּלְעָם וַיֹּאמֶר אֶל־בָּלָק הֲלֹא דִּבַּרְתִּי
אֵלֶיךָ לֵאמֹר כֹּל אֲשֶׁר־יְדַבֵּר יְהוָה אֹתוֹ
אֶעֱשֶׂה:

כד 1 וַיַּרְא בִּלְעָם כִּי טוֹב בְּעֵינֵי יְהוָה
לְבָרֵךְ אֶת־יִשְׂרָאֵל וְלֹא־הָלַךְ כְּפַעַם־
בְּפַעַם לִקְרַאת נְחָשִׁים וַיָּשֶׁת אֶל־
הַמִּדְבָּר פָּנָיו: 2 וַיִּשָּׂא בִלְעָם אֶת־עֵינָיו
וַיַּרְא אֶת־יִשְׂרָאֵל שֹׁכֵן לִשְׁבָטָיו וַתְּהִי
עָלָיו רוּחַ אֱלֹהִים: 3 וַיִּשָּׂא מְשָׁלוֹ וַיֹּאמַר
נְאֻם בִּלְעָם בְּנוֹ בְעֹר
וּנְאֻם הַגֶּבֶר שְׁתֻם הָעָיִן:
4 נְאֻם שֹׁמֵעַ אִמְרֵי־אֵל
אֲשֶׁר מַחֲזֵה שַׁדַּי יֶחֱזֶה
נֹפֵל וּגְלוּי עֵינָיִם:
5 מַה־טֹּבוּ אֹהָלֶיךָ יַעֲקֹב
מִשְׁכְּנֹתֶיךָ יִשְׂרָאֵל:

10 וַיִּחַר־אַף בָּלָק אֶל־בִּלְעָם וַיִּסְפֹּק אֶת־
כַּפָּיו וַיֹּאמֶר בָּלָק אֶל־בִּלְעָם לָקֹב אֹיְבַי
קְרָאתִיךָ וְהִנֵּה בֵּרַכְתָּ בָרֵךְ זֶה שָׁלֹשׁ
פְּעָמִים: 11 וְעַתָּה בְּרַח־לְךָ אֶל־מְקוֹמֶךָ
אָמַרְתִּי כַּבֵּד אֲכַבֶּדְךָ וְהִנֵּה מְנָעֲךָ יְהוָה

richly, but the Eternal has denied you the reward." 12] Balaam replied to Balak, "But I even told the messengers you sent to me, 13] 'Though Balak were to give me his house full of silver and gold, I could not of my own accord do anything good or bad contrary to the Eternal's command....' 14] And now, as I go back to my people, let me inform you of what this people will do to your people in days to come."...

מִכָּבְוֹד: 12 וַיֹּאמֶר בִּלְעָם אֶל־בָּלָק הֲלֹא גַּם אֶל־מַלְאָכֶיךָ אֲשֶׁר־שָׁלַחְתָּ אֵלַי דִּבַּרְתִּי לֵאמֹר: 13 אִם־יִתֶּן־לִי בָלָק מְלֹא בֵיתוֹ כֶּסֶף וְזָהָב לֹא אוּכַל לַעֲבֹר אֶת־פִּי יְהֹוָה לַעֲשׂוֹת טוֹבָה אוֹ רָעָה מִלִּבִּי אֲשֶׁר־יְדַבֵּר יְהֹוָה אֹתוֹ אֲדַבֵּר: 14 וְעַתָּה הִנְנִי הוֹלֵךְ לְעַמִּי לְכָה אִיעָצְךָ אֲשֶׁר יַעֲשֶׂה הָעָם הַזֶּה לְעַמְּךָ בְּאַחֲרִית הַיָּמִים:

25] Then Balaam set out on his journey back home; and Balak also went his way.

25 וַיָּקָם בִּלְעָם וַיֵּלֶךְ וַיָּשָׁב לִמְקֹמוֹ וְגַם־בָּלָק הָלַךְ לְדַרְכּוֹ:

Understanding the Story

Mr. Ed, the talking horse of the popular 1960s television show, was not the first of his kind. Long before the advent of television, the Torah had its own talking animal: Balaam's donkey. The story of Balak, Balaam, and his talking donkey is one of the most fascinating and intriguing in all of the Torah. Balak, king of Moab, fears that the Israelites will attack his country. Balak thus decides to send for Balaam, a pagan prophet known for his special powers to bless and curse. Balak promises to richly reward Balaam for cursing Israel, and Balaam takes some time to consider the offer. During the night God tells Balaam that he must not curse the Israelites, for they are a people who are blessed. Later on in the Bible story, God tells Balaam to go with the messengers, but to say only what God commands.

Balaam sets out for Moab on his donkey. At this point, a macabre dialogue in the Torah ensues. God opens the mouth of the donkey, and she says to Balaam, "What have I done to you that you have beaten me these three times?" Finally, God opens Balaam's eyes, and he sees the angel of God standing in front of him with a drawn sword. The angel scolds Balaam for striking his donkey, and Balaam, realizing how God opposes his mission to curse the Israelites, tries to pacify him. Finally, the angel permits Balaam to resume his journey on the one condition that he say only what God tells him. Instead of damning the Israelites, Balaam blesses them, promising that the Israelites will triumph over all of their enemies, including the Moabites.

The story raises numerous questions and problems. Interestingly, the Talmud (*Bava Batra* 15a) calls this biblical story "The Book of Balaam." Who is Balaam? What are his powers? Is he an enemy or a friend of the Jewish people? Does God really speak to Balaam and appear to his donkey? How significant are these events in which the main characters are non-Israelites? Is Balaam a prophet? Why spend three whole chapters of the Bible with Moabite and Mesopotamian potentates? Why should we care if a pagan prophet listens or does not listen to his employer's instructions? Why has the text left Israel in the middle of her journeys in the wilderness? Why does the Talmud consider this one story to be a whole book of its own? And where is Moses? Since the birth of Moses at the beginning of Exodus, the Torah has not left him alone for a moment. And now, for three chapters, he is not mentioned even once.

From the Commentators

On the basis of his [W. F. Albright] reading of the text (with some vocalizations changed), he comes to the conclusion that "Balaam was really a North-Syrian diviner from the Euphrates Valley, that he became a convert to Yahwism [Israel's faith], and that he later abandoned Israel and joined the Midianites in fighting against the Yahwists." In this reading, Balaam's oracles are those not of an unwilling adversary but of a convert, and so they speak with all the fervor of a person who has discovered a new faith.

> W. Gunther Plaut, ed., *The Torah: A Modern Commentary*, rev. ed.
> (New York: URJ Press, 2005), p. 1,063.

Bala'am, [Martin] Buber explains, is not "commissioned," not "sent" by God. He fails to make decisions on his own. Rather, "God makes use of him." Bala'am may have the potential to be a prophet and take initiative, but he never fulfills that potential. He remains detached and aloof from others. He never engages others. Instead, he announces God's words, exercising no will of his own. He speaks about tomorrow but does not participate in making the choices and decisions that will shape the future. Consequently, he remains a common magician.

> Harvey J. Fields, *A Torah Commentary for Our Times,* vol. 3 (New York: UAHC Press, 1998), pp. 69–70.

Martin Buber

Together with Franz Rosenzweig, Martin Buber (1876–1965) published a German translation of the Bible. From 1924 to 1933 he was professor of philosophy of Jewish religion and ethics at Frankfort-on-Main, and in 1938 he settled in Jerusalem as professor of the sociology of religion at Hebrew University. Buber conceives religious faith as a dialogue between man and God. This conception, known as "I-Thou," permeates the Bible, which for Buber is the record of experience in which Israel knows itself to be addressed by the Divine and tries to respond by listening and obeying.

Why does God go to the trouble of directing his [Balaam's] speech?...[Anselm] Astruc suggests that God did this lest others interpret any disaster that might befall Israel as resulting from Balaam's curse, strengthening their belief in wizardry.

> David L. Lieber and Jules Harlow, eds., *Etz Hayim: Torah and Commentary* (New York and Philadelphia: Rabbinical Assembly and Jewish Publication Society, 2001), p. 899.

Maimonides himself in his *Guide for the Perplexed* finds no difficulty, since he assumes that the whole encounter between Balaam and the ass, till it opened its mouth, took place in a prophetic vision as in similar instances of visions recorded in Scriptures.

> Nehama Leibowitz, *Studies in Bamidbar (Numbers)*, trans. Aryeh Newman (Jerusalem: Joint Authority for Jewish Zionist Education, n.d.), p. 298.

Following early rabbinic tradition, Ibn Ezra claims that Bala'am is a deceptive schemer, a dangerous man. He substantiates his accusation by pointing out that Bala'am never tells Balak's messengers that God will not permit him to curse the Israelites. He allows them to believe that he is willing to damn the king's enemies. Moreover, Bala'am orders Balak to build altars and make sacrifices without telling Balak that God will permit him only to bless the Israelites. Bala'am withholds information and distorts the truth. He seeks to take advantage of the king's fears for his own financial gain.

> Harvey J. Fields, *A Torah Commentary for Our Times,* vol. 3, p. 68.

Why does God go to the trouble of directing his [Balaam's] speech?...Abravanel says that it is to avoid Israel's enemies' gaining confidence from Balaam's words.

Etz Hayim: Torah and Commentary, p. 899.

[Ibn] Kaspi notes, "A true friend will spare his friend mental anguish and concern, even if he knows there is not basis for it." The Israelites, having grown up in Egypt, a land of superstition and sorcery, might tend to take Balaam's curses seriously and thus be demoralized. By the same token, they might be strengthened by his blessings. Praise from a prominent gentile might heighten their devotion to achieving their goals.

Etz Hayim: Torah and Commentary, p. 899.

When Balaam says, "Though Balak were to give me his house full of silver and gold, I could not do anything, big or little, contrary to the command of the Eternal my God" (Numbers 22:18), we learn that he is forced to admit that he is under the influence of other individuals. He inadvertently states here that he is unable to annul blessings given to the Patriarchs from the mouth of God.

Rashi on Numbers 22:18.

What I have always found astonishing is the absence of concern about Bil'am's treatment of his animal.... Bil'am's behavior and the donkey's response translate in our modern day to an issue of empowerment.... What we learn from the donkey is clear: if we are on the receiving end of any kind of abuse, we have an obligation to speak out against our abuser.... The story of Bil'am and his donkey provides an important model of an abuser, reacting by venting misdirected anger in verbal abuse or physical violence, and the recipient of his abuse, finally deciding that she has had enough.

Diane Aronson Cohen, "The End of Abuse," in *The Women's Torah Commentary: New Insights from Women Rabbis on the 54 Weekly Torah Portions*, ed. Elyse Goldstein (Woodstock, VT: Jewish Lights Publishing, 2000), pp. 303–306.

Questions for Discussion

1. The biblical commentator Nehama Leibowitz writes that Balaam may have begun with sinister intentions toward Israel, but evolves into a person whose faith in God increases with experience. He ascends from a common sorcerer to a prophet who hears the word of God. What do you think of Leibowitz's assertion? Do you think Balaam is a true prophet? Why or why not?

2. The Talmud (*Bava Batra* 60a) provides a reason for Balaam's inability to curse Israel. Balaam looked up and saw Israel encamped "tribe by tribe" (Numbers 24:2). He saw that the tribes were set apart from each other and that the tent openings did not face each other. No one could see into the tent of anyone else. This became the source for the ruling that one may not build a door directly opposite a door of a neighbor or make a window in line with a neighbor's window. This ensures privacy and respect of personal dignity and is in keeping with the value of modesty in behavior. Why might this Israelite practice deter Balaam from cursing the Israelites? How is privacy ensured for each person in your house?

3. The last blessing that Balaam offers is, "How fair are your tents, O Jacob, your dwellings, O Israel" (in Hebrew, *mah tovu ohalecha Yaakov mishk'notecha Yisrael*) (Numbers 24:5). In what prayer do you find these words? Why do you think that they were chosen for inclusion in the siddur? How do you feel about the words of a pagan being chosen for a Jewish prayer?

4. Some rabbinic commentators have placed Balaam in the same category as Haman or an Amalek. Others call him a prophet on par with Moses. How do you explain these two different views? What evidence is there of both evil and good in Balaam?

5. Rabbi Daniel Shevitz writes that the more we are drawn into the story of Balaam, the more questions confront us. Why spend three whole chapters of the Bible with the Moabites? What do we care if a pagan prophet listens or does not listen to his employer's instructions? Why have we left Israel in the middle of her journeys? Where is Moses in the Balaam story? Rabbi Shevitz also notes that Moses and Balaam are never seen together. When Moses leaves, Balaam arrives. When Balaam departs for Mesopotamia at the end of his mission, Moses reappears. In short, Rabbi Shevitz hypothesizes that Moses and Balaam are the same person! What evidence in the text might support this theory? Can you find any traces of a resemblance in the Bible story between Moses and Balaam?

6. Why do you think that God needs to prevent Balaam from cursing the Israelites? Why should they care about the curse of a pagan prophet?

7. According to the *Sifrei*, "There has never arisen a prophet in Israel like Moses, but in the gentile world there has arisen. And who? Balaam, the son of Beor." What do you think of the *Sifrei*'s commentary? Why is Balaam so very special? Explain.

8. The name of the Torah portion in which this story occurs is *Balak*, and yet the story is really much more about Balaam. Why do you think that the Rabbis chose to name the story *Balak*, and not *Balaam*?

9. There is no question in the story that Balaam's donkey is more sensitive to the presence of God than is Balaam. Why do you think that the text might want to make this particular point?

10. God gives Balaam permission to go with Balak's men (Numbers 22:20), but later (Numbers 22:22) God gets angry and sends an angel to stop him. According to the commentator Saadyah Gaon, God could read Balaam's thoughts and knew that Balaam was going to Balak with the intent to curse Israel and make a profit. That is why God got angry with him. Why do you think God might have given Balaam permission and then sent the angel to stop him?

11. Rabbi Jacob Chinitz once asked, "Is it true that the ultimate blessing is the one that comes from the enemy? Is there something valid in the desire to be complimented by one's opponent?" How would you answer these questions?

12. Rabbi Howard Addison once said that the lesson to be derived from this Bible story is that Balaam, a great visionary of the heathen world, was a living testimony to the seduction of profit and self-aggrandizing glory. Thus the story is a morality tale. Obsessed with the hope of personal gain, Balaam, the greatest of seers, cannot see what is apparent to even the donkey—the dumbest of creatures itself. What is your opinion of Rabbi Addison's comments? What are the lessons that you derive from the story?

13. The Talmud (*B'rachot* 12b) relates that the Sages wanted to include the section of Balak attempting to get Balaam to curse the Israelites in the *Sh'ma*. They wished to do this because they thought that Balaam's blessings would project the positive feelings of an outsider toward the Jewish community. What is your opinion of this idea? Would it have been a good one? Why or why not?

14. In *Pirkei Avot* 5:6 we are told that Balaam's donkey was one of ten miraculous things that God created at twilight just before the first Shabbat. Other miracles included the *shamir* (rock-eating worm), the rainbow, manna, the mouth of the earth, the mouth of the well, Moses's rod, the script, the writing instrument, and the tablets. Why do you think that Balaam's donkey was included among these miracles?

Who's Who of Commentators

Classical Commentators and Commentaries

Abravanel, Don Isaac (1437–1508). Spanish commentator.

Arama, Isaac (1420–1494). Spanish commentator and author of the Torah commentary *Akedat Yitzchak*.

Astruc, Anselm. Fourteenth-century author of Torah commentary *Midrashei Torah*. Murdered in an attack on the Jewish community of Barcelona in 1391.

Be'er Mayim Chayim. A supercommentary on Rashi's Torah commentary, written by Chayim ben Bezalel (1520–1588), a Talmudic scholar and elder brother of the famous Judah Loew ben Bezalel of Prague.

Bunem, Simcha (1765–1827). Polish Chasidic rabbi.

Chafetz Chayim (Israel Meir HaKohen, 1838–1933). Rabbi, ethical writer, and Talmudist who became universally known as Chafetz Chayim after the title of his first work.

Chatam Sofer (Moses Sofer, 1762–1839). Rabbi and leader of Orthodox Jewry.

Eybeschuetz, Jonathan (1690–1764). German rabbi and commentator.

Gerondi, Nissim ben Reuben (1320–1380). Spanish commentator. Also known as HaRan.

HaLevi, Y'hudah: Eleventh-century Spanish philosopher.

Hirsch, Samson Raphael (1808–1888). German commentator.

Hizzkuni (Hezekiah ben Manoach). Thirteenth-century French commentator. Tradition relates that in memory of his father, who lost his right hand because of his loyalty to his ancestral faith, he wrote a commentary called *Hizzkuni* ("Strengthen Me").

Ibn Ezra, Abraham (1089–1164). Spanish commentator.

Ibn Kaspi, Joseph (1279–1340). Philosopher and biblical commentator. Composed more than thirty books in his lifetime, while living successively in Arles, Tarascon, Aragon, and Catalonia.

Ibn Pakuda, Bachya. Eleventh-century Spanish poet and author of the classic study of Jewish ethics *Chovot HaLevavot*, "Duties of the Heart."

Jonathan ben Uzziel. In the second half of the first century C.E., wrote *Targum Yonatan*, a paraphrase of the Bible in Aramaic. A pupil of Hillel.

Kimchi, David (1160–1235). French-Spanish commentator. Also known as Radak.

K'li Yakar. Torah commentary written by Solomon Ephraim ben Chaim Lunchitz, a Polish scholar (1550–1619).

Lekach Tov. A collection of midrashim on the Torah and the Five *M'gillot*, by Tobias ben Eliezer (eleventh century C.E.).

Luzzato, Samuel David (1800–1865). Italian commentator.

Maimonides, Moses (1135–1204). Spanish Jewish philosopher.

Malbim, M. L. (1809–1879). Russian rabbi and commentator.

Meir Simchah HaKohen of Dvinsk (1843–1926). Talmudic scholar and commentator from western Russia. Author of *Meshech Chochmah*, a commentary on the Torah.

Menachem Mendel of Kotzk (1787–1859). Polish Chasidic scholar and commentator.

Midrash HaGadol. A collection of Rabbinic interpretations dating to the first and second centuries, by David ben Amram Adani, a thirteenth-century Yemenite scholar.

Midrash Rabbah. Collection of aggadic midrashim to the Torah (fifth and sixth century C.E.).

Nachmanides (Moses ben Nachman, 1194–1268). Spanish biblical commentator. Also known as Ramban.

Pirkei Avot. A tractate of the Mishnah in *N'zikin*; contains pithy sayings and ethical teachings of the third-century Rabbinic Sages.

Pirkei D'Rabbi Eliezer. Eighth-century midrashic narrative.

Rashbam (Samuel ben Meir, 1085–1174). French commentator.

Rashi (Solomon ben Isaac, 1040–1105). French commentator.

S'fat Emet (Y'hudah Aryeh Leib Alter of Ger, 1847–1905). Polish Chasidic leader and commentator who became known by the title of his Torah commentary, *S'fat Emet*.

Sforno, Obadiah (1475–1550). Italian commentator.

Shneur Zalman of Lyady (1745–1813). Lithuanian founder of Chabad Chasidism.

Sifrei*.* Midrash on Numbers and Deuteronomy, ca. third century C.E.

Symmachus. Hellenistic Jew of the second century C.E. who wrote a literal Greek version of the Torah.

Tanchuma*.* Ninth-century midrashic compilation on the Torah.

Targum Yonatan*.* An early translation and commentary on the Torah.

Tosefta*.* A supplement to the Mishnah (300 C.E.).

Vilna Gaon (Elijah ben Solomon Zalman, 1720–1797). Talmudist famed for his scholarship, who wrote many commentaries on the Bible. Founded the academy in Vilna.

Contemporary Commentators

Adler, Morris (1906–1966). Conservative rabbinic thinker.

Albright. W. F. (1891–1971). American biblical archaeologist and Middle East scholar.

Artson, Brad. Conservative rabbi and dean of the Ziegler School of Rabbinics at the University of Judaism.

Berlin, Adele. Professor of Hebrew Bible at the University of Maryland.

Brettler, Marc Zvi. Professor of biblical studies and chair of the Department of Near Eastern and Judaic Studies at Brandeis University.

Buber, Martin (1878–1965). Philosopher whose *Moses* is a commentary on the Book of Exodus.

Cassuto, Umberto (1883–1951). Italian commentator.

Chill, Abraham. Twentieth-century commentator.

Cohen, Diane Aronson. Ordained by the Jewish Theological Seminary of America in 1993; rabbi of Temple Ohev Shalom in Colonia, New Jersey.

Cohen, Norman J. Dean of the New York School of Hebrew Union College–Jewish Institute of Religion and professor of midrash.

Dershowitz, Alan. Professor of law at Harvard University.

Edwards, Lisa A. Ordained by Hebrew Union College–Jewish Institute of Religion in 1994; she is rabbi of Beth Chayim Chadashim in Los Angeles.

Essrog, Seymour. Twentieth-century Conservative rabbi who served Beth Israel Congregation in Owings Mills, Maryland, for several decades.

Fields, Harvey J. Rabbi emeritus of Wilshire Boulevard Temple in Los Angeles; a popular lecturer, historian, and writer whose articles have appeared in numerous newspapers and magazines.

Forman, Lori. Conservative rabbi ordained by the Jewish Theological Seminary in 1988; she is currently the director of Jewish resources for UJA-Federation of New York.

Hertz, Joseph (1872–1946). Rabbi and commentator, known for editing *Pentateuch and Haftorahs*, still used in many Conservative synagogues today. Also the Chief Rabbi of the British Empire.

Horwitz, Joshua. Writer and publisher; has produced award-winning documentaries for PBS. A student of Naomi H. Rosenblatt.

Karff, Samuel E. Rabbi emeritus of the Reform Congregation Beth Israel in Houston, Texas. Lectures widely throughout the country.

Kushner, Harold. Conservative rabbi who wrote of a limited God in his 1981 best seller *When Bad Things Happen to Good People*.

Laufer, Nathan. Modern Orthodox rabbi who teaches and lectures across the country.

Leibowitz, Nehama (1902–1997). Professor of Bible at Tel Aviv University in Israel, known for her weekly "teach yourself" Torah study guides.

Levenson, Jon. Professor at the Harvard Divinity School.

Lippman, Ellen. Ordained by Hebrew Union College–Jewish Institute of Religion in 1991, rabbi of Kolot Chayeinu/Voices of Our Lives, a progressive Jewish community in Brooklyn.

Maslow, Abraham (1908–1970). Professor of psychology at Brandeis University.

Peli, Pinchas H. Twentieth-century scholar whose "Torah Today" column appeared weekly in the *Jerusalem Post*.

Pitzele, Peter. Director of psychodrama services at Four Winds Hospital in New York. Also teaches at Hebrew Union College and Union Theological Seminary.

Plaut, W. Gunther. Reform rabbi, scholar, and editor of *The Torah: A Modern Commentary*, used in the Reform Movement. Senior scholar of Holy Blossom Temple, Toronto, Canada.

Riskin, Shlomo. Orthodox commentator, whose Bible commentaries appear in Jewish newspapers nationwide.

Rosenblatt, Naomi H. Psychotherapist, lecturer, and adult Bible class teacher, who teaches several popular Bible classes in New York and Washington.

Sarna, Nahum (1923–2005). Was Professor of Bible at Brandeis University.

Schneerson, Menachem (1902–1994). Son-in-law and successor to Joseph Isaac Schneerson who continued to build the Chabad Chasidic community.

Schorch, Ismar. Former chancellor of the Jewish Theological Seminary of America and professor of Jewish history.

Silver, Daniel. Graduate of Harvard College (1948) and ordained at Hebrew Union College (1952). Served as rabbi of The Temple in Cleveland, Ohio, from 1956 until his death in 1989.

Silverman, Hillel E. Commentator and rabbi of Sinai Temple of Los Angeles.

Steinsaltz, Adin. Israeli Talmudist and commentator.

Tigay, Jeffrey. Bible commentator and professor at the University of Pennsylvania.

Visotzky, Burton L. Chair of midrash and interreligious studies at the Jewish Theological Seminary of America.

Wiesel, Elie. Novelist, outspoken Holocaust survivor and human rights activist, Nobel Peace Prize winner, and professor at Boston University.

Yanow, Dvora. Professor of public affairs and administration at California State University.

Zangwill, Israel (1864–1926). English author and founder of the Jewish Territorial Organization.

Zornberg, Aviva. Gifted Bible lecturer in Israel, known for her psychological interpretations of the Bible.

Zweig, Arnold (1887–1968). German novelist.

Books for Further Study

Torah Commentaries

Berlin, Adele, and Marc Zvi Brettler, eds. *The Jewish Study Bible*. New York: Oxford University Press, 2004.

Cassuto, Umberto. *A Commentary on the Book of Exodus*. Translated by Israel Abrahams. Jerusalem: Magnes Press, 1961.

————. *A Commentary on the Book of Genesis*. Translated by Israel Abrahams. Jerusalem: Magnes Press, 1961.

Dershowitz, Alan M. *The Genesis of Justice*. New York: Time Warner Books, 2000.

Fox, Everett. *The Five Books of Moses: The Schocken Bible, Volume 1*. New York: Schocken Books, 1995.

Friedman, Richard Elliot, ed. *Commentary on the Torah*. New York: Harper Collins, 2001.

Hertz, J. H., ed. *Pentateuch and Haftorahs*. London: Soncino Press, 1960.

Leibowitz, Nehama. *Studies in Chumash*. Jerusalem: Chemed Books, 1995.

Lieber, David L., and Jules Harlow, eds. *Etz Hayim: Torah and Commentary*. New York and Philadelphia: Rabbinical Assembly and Jewish Publication Society, 2001.

Pitzele, Peter. *Our Fathers' Wells: A Personal Encounter with the Myths of Genesis*. San Francisco: HarperSanFrancisco, 1995.

Plaut, W. Gunther, ed. *The Torah: A Modern Commentary*, rev. ed.. New York: URJ Press, 2005.

Sarna, Nahum M. *Understanding Genesis*. New York: Schocken Books, 1966.

————. *Exploring Exodus: The Origins of Biblical Israel*. New York: Schocken Books, reprinted 1996.

Sarna, Nahum M., and Chaim Potok, eds. *The JPS Torah Commentary Series: The Complete Five-Volume Set*. Philadelphia: Jewish Publication Society, 1996.

Scherman, Nosson, and Meir Zlotowitz, eds. *The Chumash: The Stone Edition*. Brooklyn, NY: Mesorah Publications, 1999.

Torah Commentaries for Families

Fields, Harvey J. *A Torah Commentary for Our Times*. New York: UAHC Press, 1998.

Grishaver, Joel Lurie. *Being Torah: A First Book of Torah Texts*. Los Angeles: Torah Aura Productions, 1986.

Loeb, Sorel Goldberg, and Barbara Binder Kadden. *Teaching Torah*. Denver: A.R.E. Publishing House, 1997.

Simon, Solomon, and Morrison David Bial. *The Rabbi's Bible*, vol. 1. New York: Behrman House, 1966.

Haftarah Commentaries

Fishbane, Michael, ed. *The JPS Bible Commentary: Haftarot*. Philadelphia: Jewish Publication Society, 2002.

Lieber, Laura Suzanne. *Study Guide to JPS Bible Commentary: Haftarot*. Philadelphia: Jewish Publication Society, 2002.

Plaut, W. Gunther, ed. *The Haftarah Commentary*. New York: UAHC Press, 1998.

Medieval Commentaries in Translation

Chavel, Charles, ed. *Ramban (Nachmanides): Commentary on the Torah*. New York: Shilo Publishing House, 1971.

Pelcovitz, Raphael, ed. *Sforno: Commentary on the Torah*. Brooklyn, NY: Mesorah Publications, 1987.

Silberman, A. M., ed. *Chumash with Rashi*. New York: Philipp Feldheim, reprinted 1985.

Rabbinic Literature in Translation

Friedlander, Gerald, ed. and trans. *Pirke de Rabbi Eliezer*. New York: Hermon Press, 1970.

Ginzberg, Louis, ed. *Legends of the Jews*. Translated by Henrietta Szold. Baltimore, MD: Johns Hopkins University Press, reprinted 1988. Also available on CD-ROM, www.davka.com.

Psychological and Spiritual Commentaries

Cohen, Norman J. *Self, Struggle and Change: Family Conflict Stories in Genesis and Their Healing Insights for Our Lives*. Woodstock, VT: Jewish Lights Publishing, 1996.

Kushner, Lawrence S., and Kerry M. Olitzky. *Sparks Beneath the Surface: A Spiritual Commentary on the Torah*. Northvale, NJ: Jason Aronson, 1993.

Rosenblatt, Naomi H., with Joshua Horwitz. *Wrestling with Angels: What Genesis Teaches Us About Our Spiritual Identity, Sexuality and Personal Relationships*. New York: Dell Publishing, 1996.

Zornberg, Aviva. *The Beginning of Desire: Reflections on Genesis*. New York: Image Books, 1996.

———. *The Particulars of Rapture: Reflections on Exodus*. New York: Image Books, 2002.

Women's Perspectives

Antonelli, Judith S. *In the Image of God: A Feminist Commentary on the Torah*. Northvale, NJ: Jason Aronson, 1997.

Buchmann, Christina, and Celina Spiegel. *Out of the Garden: Women Writers on the Bible*. New York: Ballantine Books, reprinted 1995.

Elper, Ora Wiskind, and Susan Handelman, eds. *Torah of the Mothers: Contemporary Jewish Women Read Classical Jewish Text*. New York: Urim Publications, 2000.

Frankel, Ellen. *The Five Books of Miriam: A Women's Commentary on the Torah*. San Francisco: HarperSanFrancisco, reprinted 1998.

Frymer-Kensky, Tikva. *Reading the Women of the Bible: A New Interpretation of Their Stories*. New York: Schocken Books, 2002.

Goldstein, Elyse, ed. *The Women's Haftarah Commentary: New Insights from Women Rabbis on the 54 Weekly Haftarah Portions, the Five Megillot and Special Shabbatot*. Woodstock, VT: Jewish Lights Publishing, 2004.

———. *The Women's Torah Commentary: New Insights from Women Rabbis on the 54 Weekly Torah Portions*. Woodstock, VT: Jewish Lights Publishing, 2000.

Goldstein, Elyse, and Irving Greenberg. *ReVisions: Seeing Torah Through a Feminist Lens*. Woodstock, VT: Jewish Lights Publishing, 2001.

Computer Software and Audio Cassettes

Bible Scholar, from Jewish Software. Available in both Mac and Windows versions, www.jewishsoftware.com.

Engaging Torah: Contemporary Insights on Tape, prepared by the Union of American Hebrew Congregations in cooperation with Hebrew Union College–Jewish Institute of Religion.

Judaic Scholar Digital Reference Library, from Varda Books. www.publishersrow.com.

Navigating the Bible II, developed by ORT International for Davka. Available in Windows only, www.davka.com.